PREFACE

Swimming and water safety instruction continue to be the most fundamental parts of the American Red Cross total water safety program. Each year, over 40,000 individuals are trained as Red Cross instructors, more than 160,000 instructors are authorized to conduct Red Cross courses of instruction, and more than two million course completion certificates are issued to the participants of these courses.

This publication is intended primarily for use by Red Cross volunteer water safety instructors and basic swimming instructors. They will find it a valuable resource, since it contains comprehensive information about swimming strokes, entries into the water, and other related aquatics skills, as well as suggestions for teaching, analyzing, and evaluating these skills.

All persons who swim reasonably well and, in addition, possess a sufficient number of safety skills, should be able to take care of themselves in most water emergencies. Without skilled swimmers, there could be no lifesaving training program because individuals should be capable swimmers before they can acquire the skills necessary for making a swimming rescue. Furthermore, the ability to swim should be a prerequisite for active participation in such aquatic activities as sailing, boating, canoeing, water skiing, surfing, and skin and scuba diving.

When Commodore Wilbert E. Longfellow started the Life Saving Service of the American Red Cross in 1914, he recognized the need for providing swimming instruction as part of the water safety program. In an attempt to meet this need, nonswimmers were taught simple skills through the employment of a mass instruction approach. By 1934, it had become evident that too many beginners did not have an opportunity to progress beyond this level and, in fact, had probably learned to swim just enough to get into trouble.

In 1938, the American Red Cross published *Swimming and Diving* as the resource that would enable water safety instructors to teach a program of swimming courses that started at the beginner level and progressed through the advanced swimmer level. For 30 years, this text was used as the technical reference for all Red Cross swimming instruction in this country and it filled a great need.

The level, scope, and knowledge of aquatics increased rapidly from 1938, and in an attempt to keep pace with the rising interest and activity, the American Red Cross published the *Swimming and Water Safety* textbook in 1968. The American Red Cross has published *Swimming and Aquatics Safety* to provide its trained instructors with even more comprehensive information than did *Swimming and Diving* and *Swimming and Water Safety* about teaching and evaluating the skills that are included in the Red Cross swimming and water safety courses.

The task of "waterproofing" America is still a major challenge. Each year, it is estimated that more than 100 million Americans actively engage in some form of aquatic recreation, and many millions still cannot swim or swim so poorly that they are frequently in danger of drowning. In fact, everyone should know how to swim because yearly drowning statistics prove that over 60 percent of all drowning fatalities involve people who accidentally find themselves in the water.

This book, developed by Orin Myers, national director of the American Red Cross Water Safety Program, is dedicated to the great task of teaching and learning the art of swimming and water safety. It is the textbook and instructor's manual for Red Cross swimming instruction courses. At the same time, it is an authoritative resource for all swimming instructors and provides information useful to all persons interested in furthering safety in, on, or around the water.

ACKNOWLEDGMENTS

The American Red Cross wishes to acknowledge with appreciation the contributions made by Carroll L. Bryant, Richard L. Brown, and Edmond J. Mongeon, former national directors of its Water Safety Program, upon whose writings much of the material in this publication is based.

Special acknowledgment and thanks are extended to the following Red Cross volunteers who contributed significantly to the development of this publication: John Bruce, Men's Physical Education Department and former men's varsity swimming coach, The Ohio State University; Dr. Milton A. Orphan, Physical Education Department, Highline College, Washington; Kathryn Scott, Department of Physical Education, University of California, Berkeley; Dr. Donald Van Rossen, Department of Physical Education and former men's varsity swimming coach, University of Oregon; Mrs. Virginia Van Rossen, Department of Physical Education and women's varsity swimming coach, University of Oregon; and Mrs. Audrey Whiteman, director, Albany Swimming Pool, Albany, California.

Considerable credit goes to Dr. Ruth Harris, Department of Physical Education, University of Michigan; Dr. John Hunsucker, University of Houston, Texas; and John Waterhouse, Round Lake Park, Illinois, for their assistance in developing the chapter on physical laws applied to movements in the water.

Special gratitude and acknowledgment are extended to the following American Red Cross Safety Services professional staff members from chapters and divisions for their considerable contributions: Mrs. Mollie Hench, Harrisburg, Pennsylvania; John Howell, Houston, Texas; Larry Lovington, Tennessee Division; John Malatak, Knoxville, Tennessee; Bill Miller, Columbus, Ohio; Mary Rafalovich, San Diego, California; Mrs. Rita Swank, Rochester, New York; and Ector Thyfault, Grand Rapids, Michigan.

Suggestions and reactions from many other dedicated Red Cross volunteers and career staff have contributed significantly to the development of this publication. Very special thanks are extended to Safety Services staff at national headquarters and to a group of excellent volunteers from the Harrisburg Area Chapter, Pennsylvania.

Last, but certainly not least, is the deep appreciation extended by the author to Richard Guy for his patience and talent in developing the illustrations.

CONTENTS

Commodore Wilbert E. Longfellow

CHAPTER 1

AMERICAN RED CROSS
WATER SAFETY PROGRAM

*"In The Water 'Save Face' And
It May Save Your Life!"*

The Commodore

More than to any other one man, the aquatics-minded people of this aquatics-minded land owe a debt of gratitude to Commodore Wilbert E. Longfellow. The Commodore was among the first to see, at the turn of the century, that the rapidly mounting toll of death from drowning, unless soon curbed, would assume the proportions of a national tragedy. He saw the need for a nationwide program of swimming and lifesaving instruction. His vision, plus his aquatics skills, teaching abilities, showmanship, and enthusiasm, made him the natural leader for the enterprise.

Keenly interested and anxious to do what he could to prevent needless loss of life, Longfellow carefully studied available literature on aquatics trends, activities, and safety procedures; wrote features on water safety; and reported waterfront rescues and steps taken to safeguard swimmers. He became highly proficient in the various swimming styles and lifesaving skills. He also offered his spare-time services to the U.S. Volunteer Life Saving Corps, a young organization with headquarters in New York City, and began sharing his aquatics knowledge and skills with other swimmers. Soon he was organizing his more outstanding pupils into volunteer crews for safeguarding the lives of bathers. The work gradually spread, under his direction, to nearby towns and cities.

In 1905, in recognition of his already noteworthy achievements, Longfellow was awarded the title of "Commodore" by the U.S. Volunteer Life Saving Corps. In 1910, the U.S. Volunteer Life Saving Corps appointed Longfellow to the salaried post of Commodore in Chief and designated him as general superintendent of the organization in further recognition of his abilities and achievements.

THE WATERPROOFING OF AMERICA

Proceeding with a large-scale program of water safety and lifesaving education in and around New York City, where the Corps' activities, chiefly financed by the city of New York, were centered, the Commodore began planning his most ambitious program, "the waterproofing of America." However, the Life Saving Corps decided against a nationwide expansion of its activities because it would require the raising of a large amount of additional funds.

Looking for a way to accomplish his great purpose, Longfellow presented his plan to the American Red Cross in 1912. A committee representing a number of national organizations was established to prepare and to submit a definite program for consideration by the Red Cross.

The committee's plan for a nationwide program was adopted by the Red Cross in January 1914, and the following month the Red Cross Life Saving Corps, forerunner of the present-day Red Cross Water Safety Program, came into being. Longfellow was appointed to organize the lifesaving program, and, at the same time, was awarded Red Cross Lifesaving Certificate Number One and the lifesaving emblem that has since been earned and proudly worn by millions.

In the succeeding months of 1914, at beaches and swimming pools all over the country, the big fellow with the Red Cross emblem on his swimsuit began to appear. Everywhere he was recognized as a man experienced and well-versed in aquatic arts and lifesaving skills.

The Commodore's first step in putting the lifesaving plan into operation was simplicity itself. In each community, he gathered a group of good swimmers, trained them in the methods of lifesaving and resuscitation, organized them into a volunteer corps, and asked them to accept responsibility for supervision of bathing activities in the community.

He then persuaded owners and operators of swimming facilities to man their beaches and pools with trained lifeguards.

The next step — more difficult and perhaps more important — was to provide sound, large-scale instruction in swimming. Longfellow accomplished this by selecting outstanding swimmers from each corps that he organized, by giving them additional training, and, in each community, by authorizing these individuals to teach swimming on a voluntary basis. In this way, sound swimming instruction was multiplied many times over.

Finally there came the business of consolidating public interest and support. This the Commodore did with amazing success. He gave talks and demonstrations, wrote for newspapers and periodicals, created and produced water pageants, and, with the advent of radio in the twenties, put his message on the air. The water pageants perhaps best illustrate the Commodore's philosophy of teaching, which was to "entertain the public hugely while educating them gently." Under Longfellow's guidance, a pleasurable activity for participants and spectators alike became a solid educational experience.

He was always the cheerful crusader, the self-styled "amiable whale," the man whose terrestrial mission was to lure Americans to the water in order to teach them how to be at home in it, how to have fun in it, and how **not** to drown.

"Water is a good friend or a deadly enemy," the Commodore was wont to tell his pupils. "After you have been properly introduced to it, keep on good terms with it. Don't slap it, try hugging it — an armful at a time!"

They did. And how they loved him for so pleasantly teaching them how!

From 1914 until the time of his retirement, and his death 3 months later on March 18, 1947, Longfellow worked with devotion and enthusiasm in the nationwide water safety program of the Red Cross. The results were astonishing both in the prevention of death by drowning and in the growing participation of millions who were being taught how to enjoy the water in safety. Within his near half-century of crusading, the Commodore witnessed a tremendous upsurge in the popularity of swimming, boating, and other water activities to the point where an estimated 80 million Americans were participating in some form of aquatic recreation. He saw the nation's drowning rate cut in half — from 10.4 per 100,000 to 5.2. Thanks to the dedication and untiring efforts of those who followed his example and continued his work, by 1979 the drowning rate dropped further — to 3.0 per 100,000.

His efforts, enthusiasm, and foresight must continue to be carried on by his successors in the never-ending challenge of preventing serious injuries and the loss of life through aquatic accidents.

A History of Red Cross Water Safety Beginnings

1914 — Lifesaving instruction initiated
1922 — Beginner Swimming instruction initiated
1922 — National Aquatic and First Aid Schools initiated
1922 — First National Life Saving Conference held
1937 — *Lifesaving and Water Safety* textbook published
1938 — *Swimming and Diving* textbook published
1943 — Functional or Survival Swimming program initiated
1944 — Swimming for the Handicapped program initiated
1953 — Water Safety Aide program initiated
1957 — *Teaching Johnny To Swim* booklet published
1960 — Swimmer Aide program initiated
1961 — Swim and Stay Fit program initiated
1968 — *Swimming and Water Safety* textbook published
1974 — *Lifesaving: Rescue and Water Safety* textbook published
1977 — *Adapted Aquatics* textbook published

CHAPTER 2

THE EVOLUTION OF SWIMMING

"Every American A Swimmer,
Every Swimmer A Lifesaver!"
The Commodore

As practiced by man, swimming is an art. Fish, amphibians, waterfowl, and practically all quadrupeds are either born with the ability to swim, have instincts that enable them to acquire swimming ability very rapidly, or are able to use the same form of locomotion in water as they do on land and still make good progress.

Basically, humans are handicapped by structure and habit when they enter the water. Their natural position is upright and they propel themselves by thrusting against the ground with a relatively small area of the foot. Also, for the most part, they possess a narrow margin of buoyancy. The specific gravity of human beings is so nearly that of water itself that average people, when suspended motionless in the water, find that they submerge to about eye level. Unable to breathe at this level, they must necessarily make some lifting motions to raise themselves a little above their normal flotation level. If, in this vertical position, they attempt to make progress by using the same movements as they do when walking on land, the only possible result can be some up and down movement but little or no forward progress. Humans must therefore adjust to water as an element, learn to assume other than the vertical position, and, finally, employ different arm and leg movements.

In spite of not being an amphibious animal, humans have become amazingly versatile in the water, primarily because of their capacity to reason plus their possession of an important physical asset — a set of swivel or ball and socket joints in the shoulders and the hips — that permits a wide range of movement. As a result, they can swim on the front, the side, and the back, at the surface or underneath. They can swim forward, backward, or even sideways. They can somersault forward or backward or can rotate on the long axis of the body like a rolling log. In contrast, swimming animals are limited by their structure to far fewer patterns of swimming action.

Even though humans have devised a great variety of skills and stunts that have been given names such as dolphin, porpoise, seal-diving, swordfish, sealfish, and marlin, the physical actions employed by people are radically different from those of the animals that gave the skills their names. There is actually little that humans have been able to borrow from the animal world in the development of the art of swimming. Not understanding this fact was a deterrent to people's development of aquatics skills. A classic example is the kick employed in the breaststroke. All through history, learners were told to imitate the frog in using the legs for this stroke. However, when humans attempt to thrust backward against the water as frogs do, with the frog's widespreading, webbed feet, they make little forward progress. Yet even today the leg action in the breaststroke is mistakenly called the frog kick.

Through a slow process over the centuries, humans have had to learn and to discover their own principles and methods of water locomotion. People have learned from their predecessors, but for many years improvement was the result of trial and error only. During the modern era, improved facilities, clarity of water, and photographic techniques permitting stop-action and slow-motion filming of body movements in the water, especially under the surface, have all enhanced the understanding of how man swims most effectively. Scientific study and experimentation by qualified swimming experts have resulted in the application of the physical laws that govern body movements in the water to the point where people today are swimming more efficiently and effectively than ever before.

How and why humans actually took to the water is not known; however, the three motivating forces that influenced their immersion were undoubtedly economic necessity, comfort, and preservation of life in the face of danger. Economic necessity must have been the dominant factor. Humans derived much of their food supply from the many forms of marine life. Wading, reaching, and groping for food in shallow waters caused initial immersion and paved the way for the development of some forms of swimming movement. Seeking to escape the discomfort caused by the extreme heat during hot seasons and in tropical regions, they must have discovered early in their experiences that immersion in water allayed that discomfort. Immersion could also have been used by primitive people as a refuge from fire, animals, and other persons, in an attempt to preserve their own lives when in danger. Other motivations for immersion may have been cleanliness, as part of a religious rite, and quite possibly for sport.

While there is fragmentary evidence in literature and the visual arts that ancient peoples swam, before the sixteenth century no one, presumably, thought it necessary to describe the strokes used nor any method of teaching them. At that point, however, a few treatises on swimming began to appear in the literature of Europe. The first known work on swimming was written by Nicolaus Wynman, a German professor of languages, and was published in 1538. In 1587, a book on swimming, written in Latin by Sir Everard Digby and later translated into English, was published in England. About 1697, a Frenchman, Thevenot, wrote a book entitled *The Art of Swimming,* in which he described and illustrated a method closely resembling the breaststroke. This style of swimming gave unobstructed vision and, with the mouth and nose held out of the water, permitted free breathing. The underwater arm recovery eliminated splashing water in the swimmer's face and gave the swimmer good stability even in rough water. From Thevenot's description, it is evident that a breaststroke style had been in common usage for many years. English translations of his work became a standard reference and helped to establish this stroke as the method most commonly employed, a distinction it was to enjoy for many years.

From this point, the people of northern Europe went through the process of evolving a series of swimming strokes, turning from the breast to the side and progressing to an overarm sidestroke used extensively in England in the middle nineteenth century. With the introduction of competition, speed became an important factor and the hand-over-hand stroke came, belatedly, to Europe. It was introduced in England, in 1873, by John Trudgen, who had learned the style from South American Indians. This hand-over-hand stroke, also referred to as the alternating overarm stroke or trudgen stroke, soon caught the public fancy and was actually the forerunner in the development of the crawl stroke as it is known today. Each arm recovered out of the water by rolling the body from side to side and a scissors kick occurred following the stroke of one arm.

Until approximately the turn of the twentieth century, most of the attention had been given to the arm action, with almost total disregard to the action of the legs. Now, however, the increasing emphasis on competition spurred a search for styles of swimming and refinements in stroking that would produce even greater speed over measured distances than the trudgen stroke. Study and experimentation with the trudgen stroke showed that the negative recovery action of the legs discounted much of the positive thrust. Each leg kick provided a single forward thrust and the kick did not seem to blend with the alternating overarm stroke.

At this point, an Australian competitive swimmer, Richard Cavill, developed an up-and-down thrashing action of the legs that he combined with the alternating overarm stroke. This style was introduced in 1902 at the International Championships, where Cavill demonstrated its speed by swimming 100 yards in 58.4 seconds to set a new world record. The method became known as the Australian Crawl, and with this introduction of a form of the flutter kick, a new era in speed swimming began.

American swimming coaches and speed swimmers made further refinements in the breathing, kicking, and arm recovery techniques of the crawl. The success of their efforts was evident when, in 1906, C. M. Daniels became the first United States speed swimming champion of the world as he lowered the 100-yard record to 55.4 seconds. The Australian Crawl, with refinements, became known as the American Crawl.

The development of the crawl stroke was further influenced by the late "Duke" Kahanamoku, an Hawaiian, whose stroke was characterized by a truly vertical 6-beat flutter kick action of the legs. The "Duke" was an Olympic record holder and an Olympic Gold Medal winner for the 100-yard crawl in both the 1912 and the 1920 Games. Also influencing the stroke was another outstanding U.S. swimmer, Johnny Weissmuller, who dominated crawl sprint swimming throughout the years encompassing the 1924 and the 1928 Olympic Games. In 1927, Weissmuller swam 100 yards in 51 seconds flat in a 25-yard course, setting a record that was to remain unbroken for almost two decades. Weissmuller's style featured a deeper kick that allowed the chest and shoulders to ride higher; a rotating of the head, for inhalation, that was independent of the action of the arms; and an underwater arm action in which the elbow was bent slightly for greater positive action. Since champions have always had a large following, the popularity of both Duke Kahanamoku and Johnny Weissmuller not only contributed greatly to the development of the present-day crawl but also popularized the stroke so that it became the stroke to teach beginners.

During the 1920s, the Japanese made extensive use of slow-motion films that were taken of Weissmuller and other great swimmers to add further improvements to stroking mechanics. These improvements, coupled with a tremendous emphasis on training and conditioning, enabled the Japanese to dominate swimming in the early 1930s.

In the present day, more people are swimming for pleasure and more people are competing than ever before, and the continued lowering of swimming records is indicative that stroking mechanics are still being improved.

Before 1900, swimming on the back was more of a stunt than an actual stroke. Since the breaststroke was in high favor at the turn of the century, the backstroke that was performed at that time was an inverted breaststroke. With the development of the alternating overarm style on the front, this method was experimented with on the back and finally, combined with an inverted flutter kick, resulted in a stroke that was faster than the breaststroke. In 1912, the backstroke was recognized as a competitive event. The search for greater speed, combined with basically the same elements of study and experimentation that occurred in the development of the crawl stroke, has led to the refinements of the stroke as it is known today.

The history of the breaststroke is interesting and again points to the influence of speed swimming in its development. Even though other strokes have proved to be faster, the breaststroke has continued as a separate competitive event. In fact, until the recognition of the butterfly stroke as a separate stroke in competition, the breaststroke was the only one in which a prescribed style was required. However, since the breaststroke employed an underwater recovery of both arms and legs, this high resistance factor was a problem in developing more speed. In 1934, David Armbruster, then swimming coach at the University of Iowa, devised a variation that employed a double overarm recovery out of the water. This arm action resulted in greater speed but required greater training and conditioning. In 1935, a breaststroke style was introduced that incorporated the out-of-water arm recovery combined with a vertical dolphin or fishtail kick. Even though it was a faster method of the butterfly, the dolphin kick was declared in violation of the competitive rules.

For the next 20 years, champion breaststrokers used an out-of-water arm recovery (butterfly) with a shortened breaststroke kick. In the late 1950s, the butterfly stroke with the dolphin kick was legalized for competition, and the butterfly stroke and the breaststroke were then separated into two distinctly different strokes.

It can be seen that the quest for speed has greatly influenced how humans swim. By applying the same basic body mechanics that the competitive swimmer uses and by taking advantage of the experience and knowledge gained over the years, the noncompetitor should become a safer and more effective performer in the water.

SAFETY IN AQUATICS

CHAPTER 3

*"Water Is A Good Friend
But A Deadly Enemy!"*
The Commodore

Drownings in the United States have averaged between 7,000 and 8,000 yearly during the past few years. These statistics would seem to imply that the concentrated efforts of the Red Cross and other agencies in the field of water safety have not been successful. However, the number of yearly drownings alone does not give an accurate picture.

Millions of Americans have learned to swim since Commodore Wilbert E. Longfellow launched his "Water-proof America" crusade in 1914. The founder of the American Red Cross Water Safety Program built his campaign on the slogan "Every American a swimmer, every swimmer a lifesaver." Before his nationwide effort began, the drowning rate was 10.4 per 100,000 population. Today, as a result of the combined efforts of many agencies and organizations, the rate is approximately 3.0 per 100,000 population. When one considers the tremendous increase both in population and in participation in aquatics activities since the early 1900s, it is evident that water safety instruction and education have proved to be successful in reducing the number of fatalities.

Drownings can occur any place where there is water. National Safety Council statistics of drownings around the home show that individuals have drowned in bath-tubs, wells, cisterns, cesspools, and even puddles or pools of water, as well as in swimming pools. Only about 40 percent of the yearly drownings occur to people who are swimming or playing in the water. The remainder, or 60 percent, occur in the classification of nonswimming fatalities due to accidental falls into the water from docks, decks of pools, bridges, or shores, or recreational boating and fishing accidents, or accidents in the home or on home premises.

It is estimated that over 100 million individuals each year engage in some form of aquatic endeavor. No longer confined to the category of being a luxury, over 1,200,000 in-ground residential swimming pools are in existence today. The construction of water conservation facilities and dams and huge man-made lakes and reservoirs have created recreational aquatic facilities where none existed previously. The farm pond, which was originally intended for watering livestock, fire protection, and irrigation, has become today's version of the "ole swimmin' hole" in rural areas. There are now well over a million of these ponds, and the number grows steadily larger each year. Since many of these ponds are equipped with docks, floats, diving boards, and boats of varying types, and are even stocked with fish, they provide an outlet for aquatic recreation. Keeping pace with the growth of facilities has been the increased availability and refinement of the equipment needed for such activities as skin and scuba diving, water skiing, recreational boating, fishing, and surfing.

The need for everyone to be able to swim well enough to survive is evident. Nonswimmers and novice swimmers account for the majority of drownings. The large number of drownings of young children when left unguarded, even for a few moments, points to the need for more education for all adults and parents. Supervision at all times, especially when it concerns young children, is a must.

Since a majority of drownings occur because people violate or ignore good safety practices, an attempt will be made to categorize such recommended procedures under the following headings:
- Personal water safety
- Safety at home pools
- Safety at farm ponds
- Safety at beaches
- Hazards in the aquatic environment
- Disrobing in the water
- Boating safety
- Personal flotation devices
- Immersion hypothermia

PERSONAL WATER SAFETY
1. Learn to swim well enough to survive in an emergency.
2. Never swim alone and swim only with a buddy who has the ability to help when necessary.
3. Swim only in supervised areas.
4. Follow the rules set up for the particular pool, beach, or waterfront where you are swimming.
5. Learn the simple and safe reaching rescues.
6. Know how to administer artificial respiration.
7. Know your limitations and do not overestimate your ability.
8. Stay out of the water when overheated or overtired.
9. Stay out of the water during electrical storms. If at all possible, seek protection in an enclosed shelter. Trees **do not** provide protection.
10. Dive only into known waters of sufficient depth.
11. Do not substitute inflated tubes, air mattresses, or other artificial supports for swimming ability.

12. Always swim a safe distance away from diving boards and platforms.
13. Avoid long periods of immersion and overexposure to the sun.
14. Take instruction under qualified instructors before participating in such aquatics sports as skin and scuba diving and water skiing.
15. Call for help only when you really need it.
16. Remember that a nonswimmer or a poor swimmer should never attempt a swimming rescue. A swimmer untrained in lifesaving should swim to a victim in trouble only as a last resort and only when all suggested safe rescue methods cannot be used. If it is necessary to risk swimming to a victim, the rescuer should take a towel, a shirt, or any buoyant object to extend to the victim.

SAFETY AT HOME POOLS
1. Never permit anyone to swim alone. Constant and responsible supervision is a must. No child should be left unattended in the pool area even for the length of time it takes to answer a telephone.
2. Have adequate fencing and a gate with a lock to prevent children from unauthorized entry.
3. Keep basic rescue and lifesaving equipment always available.
4. Post emergency instructions and telephone numbers conspicuously.
5. Have an adequate first aid kit available.
6. Enforce common-sense safety rules at all times. At least one responsible person should know how to administer cardiopulmonary resuscitation and give intelligent first aid.
7. Clearly mark the deep and shallow sections. Separate the deep and shallow water by use of a buoyed line whenever weak swimmers or nonswimmers are using the pool.
8. Do not allow running, pushing, or boisterous play on the deck.
9. Encourage responsible parents or other adults to give water safety and swimming instruction to youngsters. A recommended text is the American Red Cross booklet *Teaching Johnny To Swim* (Stock No. 321126).
10. Make sure there is adequate filtration to maintain good clarity of the water. Consult the local health department for regulations on pool sanitation.
11. Do not permit bottles, glasses, or sharp objects in or around the pool area.
12. Observe applicable personal safety rules, such as not swimming when overheated or overtired or during an electrical storm and diving only in known and safe depths. Nonswimmers should not use inflated objects for support in water deeper than standing depth.
13. Small plastic pools should be emptied and turned over when not in use.
14. Protection devices such as a pool cover or an underwater alarm system may be considered by the pool owner.

SAFETY AT FARM PONDS
1. Never swim alone.
2. Mark off safe swimming areas with buoyed lines. Remove underwater snags, trash, bottles, and the like.
3. Avoid swimming areas immediately in front of steep-sloping banks.
4. Post warning signs at danger points.
5. Supervise children at all times.
6. Have the water checked and approved by the local health department and recheck it periodically if it is used for swimming.
7. If practical, erect an adequate fence and a gate with a lock to prevent unauthorized entry by children.
8. Keep basic rescue and lifesaving equipment always available.
9. Post emergency instructions and telephone numbers.
10. Have an adequate first aid kit available.
11. Enforce common-sense safety rules. At least one responsible person should know how to administer cardiopulmonary resuscitation, perform basic reaching rescues, and give intelligent first aid.
12. Have a responsible adult start water safety and swimming instruction for potential farm pond users. A recommended text is the American Red Cross booklet *Teaching Johnny To Swim* (Stock No. 321126).
13. Make sure that piers, rafts, and landings are well-built and securely braced.
14. Observe applicable personal safety rules, such as not swimming when overheated or overtired or during an electrical storm and diving only in known and safe depths. Nonswimmers should not use inflated objects for support in water deeper than standing depth.
15. If a pond is used for skating, add a ladder to the safety post as helpful emergency equipment.
16. To avoid accidents on the ice: **Never** skate alone, skate only on a safe thickness of ice, maintain supervision at all times, and skate in a restricted area.

SAFETY AT BEACHES
1. Swim in areas supervised by a lifeguard.
2. **Never** swim alone.
3. Check with a lifeguard regarding beach and surf conditions before swimming.
4. Report any unsafe beach conditions to the lifeguard.
5. If you are being pulled offshore by a rip current, do not panic and do not try to buck the current. Swim parallel to shore across the current and, once free, swim to shore.
6. Call or wave for help if unable to swim out of a strong current.
7. Never fake trouble or calls for help.
8. Never substitute the use of floating devices for swimming ability.
9. Do not use breakable objects on the beach, and, if any are found, pick them up and dispose of them in containers for your own protection and for the safety of others.

10. Do not dive into unknown water or into shallow-breaking waves.
11. Do not overestimate your ability by attempting long-distance swims. Swimming parallel to the shore is safer and provides just as much exercise.
12. Maintain continuous supervision of small children even where there are lifeguards.
13. Do not swim close to piers or pilings.
14. Avoid sand throwing or any kind of horseplay.
15. Do not engage in unnecessary conversation with a lifeguard.
16. Be a strong swimmer and be knowledgeable about ocean conditions before attempting body surfing or board surfing in deep water.
17. Observe applicable personal safety rules, such as not swimming when overheated or overtired or during an electrical storm.
18. Respect the judgment and experience of the trained lifeguards, follow their advice, and do not interfere with the performance of their duties.

HAZARDS IN THE AQUATIC ENVIRONMENT

Swimmers must be constantly alert to the hazards of the aquatic environment. Panic, exhaustion, and cramps are three conditions of personal danger. The action of the water and certain types of marine life present hazards to individuals. Information about these conditions and situations is contained in the American Red Cross publication *Lifesaving: Rescue and Water Safety* (Stock No. 321103).

DISROBING IN THE WATER

A majority of drownings occur to people who find themselves accidentally in the water. In most cases, especially in cold water, no effort should be made to remove the clothes. When safety is only a short distance away, the swimmer may decide to swim to safety. In this situation, the swimmer may elect to remove the shoes. In warm water, the swimmer may decide to remove the outer clothing and shoes, since water-soaked apparel impairs swimming efficiency. Swimming to safety should usually be considered as a last resort, except when the distance is short, or when the swimmer is confronted with a dangerous situation.

If no flotation device is available that can be used to support the swimmer in warmer water, a shirt can be easily inflated or the trousers can be removed and inflated. Methods of disrobing and using clothes for flotation devices are discussed in the American Red Cross publication *Lifesaving: Rescue and Water Safety* (Stock No. 321103).

BOATING SAFETY

Each year there are approximately 1,300 fatalities associated with boating activities. The vast majority of these fatalities (75 percent) are a result of capsizing, falls overboard, or collisions. The craft operator needs to know and to apply the following basic information in order to help reduce needless accidents and loss of life:

1. Nonswimmers should always wear a personal flotation device (PFD) while on board the craft. Everyone should wear a PFD if a storm is threatening, the water is rough, or during high speed operations.
2. In case of capsize or swamping, stay with the boat and wear a PFD. Try to right the boat, if possible, and climb back aboard.
3. In case of capsize, get out of cold water as rapidly as possible. If unable to do so, follow the directions that are discussed in the section entitled "Immersion Hypothermia," on pages 9 and 10.
4. Maintain a constant lookout in a full circle around the craft to avoid collisions.
5. Know the specific handling characteristics of the craft in both calm and rough waters, and when fully loaded or with just the operator aboard.
6. Complete a nationally recognized course of instruction that includes supervised on-the-water practice.
7. Consult an up-to-date local weather forecast prior to any boating outing.
8. Head for shore or shelter at the first sign of an impending storm.
9. Get information on local water conditions and any special hazards.
10. Leave a float plan with family or friends, telling them when and where you are going, and when you expect to return.
11. Know and obey the rules of the road.
12. Check and adhere to state and U.S. Coast Guard regulations.

Consult your Red Cross chapter for more complete information on boating-safety-education publications and courses.

PERSONAL FLOTATION DEVICES

Federal law requires that there be a U.S. Coast Guard approved personal flotation device (PFD) for each person afloat in a small craft. Common sense dictates that the device be worn — by nonswimmers and novices especially. The ability to don and use a PFD is a skill that can be learned and practiced easily in water of standing depth. Jumping and falling into the water with a PFD on should also be practiced. With the straps fastened securely, a buoyant vest can maintain a proper position for swimmers and nonswimmers in the water, and mobility can be acquired easily by kicking and moving the arms in almost any fashion simulating swimming strokes. A PFD may be used under the arms for support in the water even without being worn. When aboard a small craft, or when fishing from a pier or the shore, all nonswimmers and novices should wear a PFD. All boaters should remember that PFDs are lifesaving devices and are not to be knelt upon or sat upon for fear of destroying the device's intended usefulness.

Belt preservers of any kind are inadequate, since their buoyancy acts at the middle of the body instead of at the chest. A belt preserver will not support the face of a stunned or an unconscious person out of the water.

Descriptions of the five types of approved PFDs are as follows:

Type I — an approved device designed to turn an unconscious person in the water from a facedown position to a vertical or slightly backward position and to have more than 20 pounds of buoyancy. This device is recommended for offshore cruising and is acceptable for all sizes of boats. Example: A typical life preserver.

TYPE I

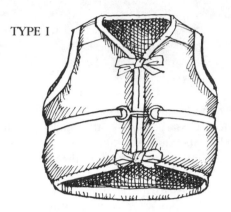

Type II — an approved device designed to turn an unconscious person in the water from a facedown position to a vertical or slightly backward position and to have at least 15.5 pounds or more of buoyancy. The Type II vest is produced in a variety of sizes and is undoubtedly the least expensive device available. Its only apparent drawback is the discomfort of wearing it over a prolonged period. Example: A typical buoyancy vest that has somewhat less of a buoyancy factor than a Type I.

TYPE II

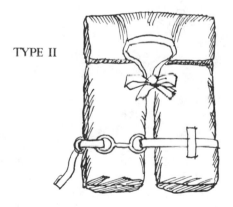

Type III — an approved device designed to keep a conscious person in a vertical or slightly backward position and to have at least 15.5 pounds of buoyancy. Although having the same buoyancy as Type II, the Type III has a lesser turning ability to allow for a comfortable design that does not hinder a person's movement in activities such as water skiing. This device is recommended for use in in-water sports and on boats used on lakes or on other bodies of confined water and close inshore on larger bodies of water. It is acceptable for all sizes of boats. Example: A special-purpose device.

TYPE III

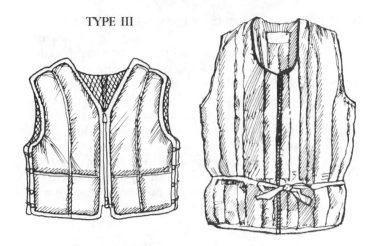

Type IV — an approved device designed to be thrown to a person in the water but not worn. It is designed to have at least 16.5 pounds of buoyancy. It is acceptable for canoes, kayaks, and boats less than 16 feet in length, and as a throwable device for boats 16 feet and over in length. Example: A buoyancy cushion or ring buoy.

TYPE IV

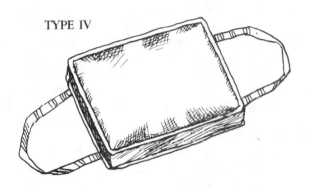

Type V — a PFD approved for restricted use. No PFD of this type is currently approved for use on recreational boats to meet mandatory carriage requirements. However, some Type V PFDs are approved as Type III devices that are satisfactory.

The U.S. Coast Guard is quick to point out that all PFDs for sale in stores must be in serviceable condition and legibly marked with the approval number. On boats, Types I, II, and III must be of an appropriate size for the persons who intend to wear them or are wearing them. They, along with a Type IV PFD, must be in good and serviceable condition, and they must be readily accessible.

IMMERSION HYPOTHERMIA

Hypothermia, a term used to describe a decrease in the inner (core) body temperature, can be brought about by exposure of the body to cold. Hypothermia begins when the body starts losing heat faster than it produces it. In cold water, the onset of hypothermia can begin within minutes, since heat is lost from the body to the water 25 times faster than in the air.

Most persons who find themselves in cold water

probably had no intention of being there in the first place; therefore, those planning to engage in any activity on or around cold water should wear a personal flotation device (PFD). They should also be especially aware of the dangers of suddenly and unexpectedly finding themselves immersed in cold water. Sudden immersion (1) will cause a feeling of intense pain and (2) will trigger an individual's gasp reflex that may cause the victim to inhale water.

One or both of these phenomena can totally disable the victim and cause panic. Without a properly worn PFD at the time of the accidental immersion, the victim can be overcome by either or both of the above phenomena to the point of being helpless and may drown.

To reduce the effects of hypothermia, **the first objective is to get out of the water as rapidly as possible.** When boating, the victim should get back aboard the boat or climb onto the hull if the boat is capsized, or the victim should attempt to climb onto a rock, a jetty, or a dock if it is possible to do so.

The following rules can apply when an individual **cannot** get out of the water immediately:

1. Do not perform survival floating (drownproofing), since this survival technique necessitates putting the head into the water and the head is a major heat loss area of the body. The head should be maintained above the water by wearing a PFD. If no support to the body is available, the head can be kept above the surface by treading water as slowly as possible, both to support the body in the desired position and to minimize the loss of body heat.

2. Do not remove any clothing, since clothes provide some insulation to other major heat loss areas of the body, such as the neck, the sides of the chest, and the groin.

3. Do not attempt to swim, since physical activity releases life-sustaining heat from the body through exercise and permits cold water to flow through clothing and to chill the body more rapidly. NOTE. In 50°F (10°C) water, even good swimmers find it difficult to cover distance in excess of one-half of a mile. Swimming to safety should be done only if the distance is short or there is imminent danger (waterfall, dam, etc.).

4. Wear a PFD, since it permits an individual to stay relatively motionless at the surface of the water.

5. If a victim cannot get out of the water and rescue is not imminent, additional protection against the cold can be obtained by adding flotation or clothing at the sides of the chest and to the groin area, or by assuming the H.E.L.P. or HUDDLE positions.
   a. **H.E.L.P. Position.** H.E.L.P. means Heat Escape Lessening Posture(s) and can be done as shown in the drawing (Fig. 1). Depending on the type

Fig. 1

of PFD and the flexibility of the individual, it may be necessary to lower the thighs to achieve a good balanced position in the water. Lowering the thighs may also help prevent cramping of the leg muscles.
   b. **HUDDLE Position.** The HUDDLE can be used if there are three or more victims in the water. The important factor in this procedure is to have the sides of the chests touching.

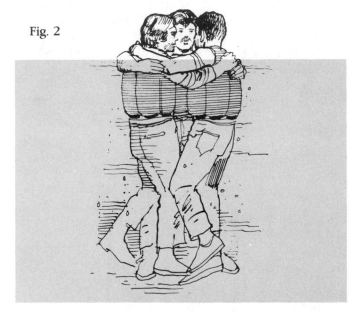
Fig. 2

NOTE. **Never** try to use the H.E.L.P. or HUDDLE positions in swift river currents or whitewater. These positions are last resort efforts to prolong survival time in still water. They are highly effective and can double one's survival time in water as cold as 50°F (10°C).

6. When individuals know that they are going into the water, they should try to enter as slowly as possible to reduce the "shock" of immersion in the cold water. They should make every effort to hold their breath until their mouths are clear of the water.

CHAPTER 4

GUIDELINES FOR TEACHING DIFFERENT AGE LEVELS

*"Entertain Them Hugely While
Educating Them Gently!"*
The Commodore

A major objective of the American Red Cross swimming and water safety program is to reach as many people as possible. This program is intended **primarily** for mass instruction of students who have usually become comfortable and adjusted to learning through group participation. For Red Cross purposes, this refers to individuals **six years of age and older.**

It is an acknowledged fact that children younger than six years of age (preschoolers) are receiving swimming instruction, and that water orientation programs for infants and tiny tots are being conducted. Many four- and five-year-old children are capable of learning aquatic motor skills when participating in **small** groups, but most children who are younger than four years of age require individualized assistance.

To use instructors and facilities most efficiently, and depending on the experience of the instructors, a ratio of 10 to 15 students to one instructor is recommended. Therefore, **formalized** Red Cross courses of instruction are **not** advocated for children three years of age or younger. **Formalized** courses for four- to five-year-old children, with a ratio of one instructor to approximately five students, can be conducted when deemed necessary or advisable by the respective Red Cross chapter. **Since the major goal is to provide mass instruction,** the information in this chapter about teaching preschoolers is limited.

WORKING WITH PRESCHOOL CHILDREN

In this text, the term *preschool* means "under six years of age" and *very young* means "three years of age and younger." In any work with preschoolers, much of the success that can be achieved will depend on the child's early experience with the water. This experience actually started when the baby was first introduced to water while getting a bath.

Preschool children present special problems. They are not well-coordinated and they cannot concentrate for more than a short time. Since they do not easily understand instructions and explanations, they need to be shown repeatedly. The very young learn mostly through imitating and responding to certain sensations.

Following are helpful suggestions to consider when teaching preschoolers and the very young:

1. The temperature of the water should be comfortable, ranging from 82° to 86°F (27.8° to 30°C). Indoor pool air temperature should be as high as, or slightly higher than, the water temperature.

2. The children should be healthy, rested, and in a good frame of mind.

3. Never hurry progress or show impatience. Try to keep the children from getting an accidental noseful and mouthful of water.

4. Keep the lessons short and enjoyable. Try to gauge the exact time to coincide with the interest and the fun factor.

5. A ratio of one aide to each child is recommended when teaching the very young. A parent can be oriented to be the aide. This procedure has proved very successful in Mother-Tiny Tot programs.

6. Parent orientation is important. Help the parents to understand their role in, and responsibility for, supervising the preschooler or the very young child in all his or her recreational aquatic activities, the limitation of swimming skills that the child can acquire, and the aim and the goals of the instructional program.

Simple games and stunts can be used effectively when working with many preschoolers. Most games are intended for groups, and learning skills through games is more enjoyable when playing with one or more companions.

The use of any flotation supports by preschoolers should be restricted to periods of instruction and **supervised** recreation. In recreational periods, if the wearing of artificial supports is allowed, the nonswimmers should be restricted to the shallow water area.

WORKING WITH ELEMENTARY SCHOOL AGE CHILDREN

Most elementary school age children take swimming instruction on a group basis. It is important, therefore, that children enrolled in such group instruction have developed a readiness and an acceptance for learning in a group situation.

To be successful, the instructor must gain the confidence of the group, since this is inherent in instilling self-confidence in the individual.

In all group instruction, safety and supervision should be built in. A lifeguard or other responsible person should be situated in a look-out position while instructional classes are in progress, since the instructor is not always located strategically to safeguard all the pupils.

Elementary school age children in the six- to eight-year-old bracket will usually make slower and more uneven progress than those who are nine years of age or older. While progress in a class of elementary school age children will, therefore, be uneven, the instructor should continue teaching at a pace that will keep the majority of the group active, interested, stimulated, and progressing. Use of the assembly line method of instruction (Chapter 15) allows students to progress at their respective pace of learning.

It might be necessary to give extra attention to the slower learners by using aides when available. The class members who are making the quickest progress can be assigned extra work and practice to keep them satisfied. All children need to feel that they are important members of the class, and all need constant encouragement regarding their progress. Since the progress of children in the nine-years-and-older bracket will be more even and steady, group instruction at this age level will usually result in a higher degree of success in learning motor skills.

The following are additional teaching suggestions:
1. Keep instruction fun. The use of games and stunts will enhance the learning of required skills and will keep the experience pleasurable.
2. When teaching skills, use terminology that children can relate to easily and that they can enjoy. For example, instead of saying "Put your face underwater," the instructor might say "Hide your face." The substitution of "Float like a log" for "Do a prone float" might give the children a better mental picture of what they are trying to do. Give skills familiar, exciting names. The object is to get the students to learn and to perfect the skills, not to have them know the technical names of the skills.
3. Keep the class busy and active. **Be ready to change to a new skill or to practice another skill before the students become restless and bored.**
4. Do not make fun of, ridicule, or threaten the learner.
5. Demonstrate skills slowly and correctly. It may be helpful to have a class member who is proficient in a skill to perform the demonstration for the other students.
6. Most importantly, always provide for the overall protection and supervision of the whole class.

WORKING WITH TEENAGERS
Teenagers present no special problems when they become motivated to learn how to swim. When an individual has reached this age level and is still a nonswimmer, the instructor must try to learn and to understand the reasons for it and must make an earnest attempt to counteract those reasons.
Being a nonswimmer at this age may be due to a lack of opportunity. On the other hand, some experience in the individual's background may be the cause. Fear of the water may be the result of a previous near-drowning experience or it may be an aftermath of simply viewing a water tragedy. Having heard a vivid account of a drowning tragedy or even repeated warnings from parents or other adults might be contributing factors. The instructor may make some progress in dissipating

these fears merely by bringing the causes out into the open. By firmly and clearly explaining the buoyancy of the body in the water, by outlining the ease and simplicity of swimming and stroking movements, and by stressing relaxation, the instructor starts the process of building confidence.

It is important that the learners have confidence in the instructor. The instructor builds this confidence by understanding the causes of their fears, by never forcing them to attempt a skill until they are ready, and by always realizing that, until the adjustment process is complete, fear is very real to the learner. Failure on the part of a student to successfully perform a simple skill should be met with encouragement, patience, and firm understanding, but never with ridicule.

Nonswimmers in the teenage group may attempt to avoid the opportunity to learn. Often this reluctance can be traced to social embarrassment and to a fear of ridicule. Instructors should attempt to motivate teenage nonswimmers or novices to become skilled swimmers at every opportunity, since they may then have the opportunity to participate in and to enjoy a number of recreational aquatic endeavors. Such related activities as boating, sailing, water skiing, skin and scuba diving, and body and board surfing can many times be the attraction that will motivate teenagers to overcome their reluctance and their fears.

WORKING WITH ADULTS
It is an established fact that most adults want to learn, do learn, and continue to learn despite the adage of not being able "to teach an old dog new tricks." Adults are different from children not only in body characteristics, but also in learning histories, reaction speed, attitudes, values, aspirations, anxieties, motivation, economic status, and responsibilities. What they choose to learn and how it is learned may alter through the years, but the capacity for learning persists. One of the primary considerations of adult learning is in having a teacher who is competent and prepared. Adult learners must not feel that their time is being wasted, but they, on the other hand, do not expect a super-human performance, knowing from experience that no instructor has all the answers and all the abilities.

Some adults may be proficient in performing some aquatics skills and may desire certification for a particular reason. Others may be comfortable in the water and may want to add to their knowledge of personal safety and to increase their enjoyment of their leisure time. Many are interested in swimming for fitness and health, as rehabilitation, or as a retardation of the aging process.

Adults can have the same types of fears and anxieties about learning to swim as those in younger age groups. Some of them may also have real concern that they won't be able to learn no matter how hard they try. A distinct advantage to the instructor is that almost all adults enroll in swimming courses because they want to learn. Adults who fear the water need understanding, simple and sensible progressions, and the freedom to try things their own way, or to get help from buoyant aids or other people if advice or support are needed. A reasonable degree of privacy, so that there is no threatening audience present, will help to keep anxiety at a low level.

Students having difficulties need to be reassured that, with the instructor's help, they will be successful if they keep trying. Adults are fully capable of learning a wide variety of new physical skills and of understanding many of the important principles involved. Instructors should know and be able to explain to the students the various physical laws and their application to swimming.

The amount of physical exertion during each class session must be suitable for the students. The level of physical condition may vary considerably with class members, and it may be highly desirable to allow students to establish their own practice procedures.

Senior citizens are able to relax and to learn more rapidly when the water and air temperatures are about 85°F (29.4°C). These temperatures are suitable for a class period that is approximately 50 minutes long.

All students learn more rapidly by having more than one lesson per week. Their endurance will increase following regular once-a-week participation regardless of the degree of improvement in performing swimming strokes.

Senior citizens may take more time in dressing and showering, in entering the water, in executing the first warm-up movements, in getting organized for instruction, and in achieving skilled performance. These characteristics must be handled with patience and understanding by the instructor.

It is important to use carefully chosen, logical teaching progressions, and a more informal approach in organizing and conducting the class. Adults should be involved to a greater degree in making decisions about what skills they might learn and how they might learn them. Understanding, patience, flexibility, and imagination must be used by the instructors, perhaps more so than with any other age group.

Skilled demonstrations will help many adults to learn. Others, with impaired hearing, lack of kinesthetic sense, or lack of flexibility, may learn more quickly by having the instructor explain a movement while manipulating a part of the student's body. Learning to swim while supported by a PFD or other attachable flotation device will speed up the learning process and make it more enjoyable. Individuals who lack range of movement in the hips, the knees, and the ankles will gain propulsion by using swim fins.

Many adults never learned to swim because of a great fear of the water. Instructors should learn to recognize some of the ways adults express their fears in order to better distinguish the difference between inability to learn and reluctance to learn because of fear. Alert instructors can spot problems by looking for the following "fear-signs":

- **Huddling** — Rounding the shoulders too much and making the chest concave, especially when performing the prone float.

- **Prenatal Position** — Drawing the knees up to the chest (or a tendency to do this).
- **Wiping** — Frequent wiping of the face, ostensibly to get hair or water out of the eyes.
- **Tenseness** — Holding the muscles taut, particularly in the shoulder area and also in the legs and the arms.
- **Fisting** — Making a fist with the hands or holding the thumbs across the palms with the fingers overlapping.
- **Lips** — Pressing the lips tightly together as if in concentration and biting the lips.
- **Movement** — Kicking and moving slightly when asked to float without kicking.
- **Performance** — Inability to keep the face in the water for more than 5 seconds. The teacher should be on the lookout for some interesting excuses here. Learners will often say that the chlorine is bad or the water got up their noses, but this phase of learning should not be glossed over because the instructor is taken in by such excuses.
- **Shivering** — A person who is frightened will shiver no matter how warm the water.
- **Elbows** — Keeping the elbows bent when hanging onto the gutter in the float position, or keeping the elbows bent in the prone float position while the instructor is guiding the pupil hand-to-hand.
- **Gripping** — Holding the instructor's hands tighter than necessary while learning the prone float. Teaching the prone float in this manner is not necessary for people who are not subject to fear. If the pupils trust the teacher, it's good for the pupils because they get the feel of moving forward. It also permits an evaluation by the teacher as to how frightened the pupil is and how fast that fear is beginning to dissipate. When the pupil begins holding on very loosely, the instructor may go on to a more advanced step.
- **Take-Offs** — Not pushing off of the side or bottom of the pool with the foot or the feet when going into the prone float and not keeping the head down at this time.
- **Strokes** — Stroking that is too short, too shallow, and/or too fast.

Motivating adult students to learn effectively should start even before they enter the water. It is important for the instructor to gain the confidence of the students and to instill in them the certainty that their safety is an integral part of the program. A brief introduction, both social and professional, is necessary at this point and should include a tour of the swimming area with an explanation of all the safety features and the reasons for them, an explanation of the rules and regulations to be adhered to and the reasons for their existence, and an explanation of what is to be accomplished (goals of the course). This can be a good time to explain and to have the students practice a rescue from land using a free-floating object. Adults should learn that the safest rescue methods for both swimmers and nonswimmers to use to help someone who is in trouble in the water are those that involve absolutely no personal contact with the victim.

Methods of getting the students into the water must be considered. These methods may vary depending on the type of facility, the skill level of the students, their flexibility and strength, and their possible physical disabilities. Some adults may need assistance. Many activities can be used to get the students accustomed to the water and these activities can vary depending on the skill level of the students.

Adult beginners need to become physically and mentally adjusted to the water. Games should be utilized. Dodge ball and volleyball (no net) encourage enjoyment and movements that cause students to get splashed and to get their faces wet. Walking, hopping, and running activities in waist-deep water promote splashing and an understanding of the water's resistance and buoyant effect.

Use games to get the students' faces in the water. Have them practice at home by putting their face in a sink filled with water. Recovering objects from the bottom at a depth that requires the students to put their faces in the water will help with adjustment. The ability to hold one's breath while the face is in the water and to exhale underwater are necessary skills to learn. Careful, patient teaching of breath control is important. Adults should be encouraged to help each other and to feel free to try it **their own way** once they are sure of what they have been asked to do.

Students need to learn how the water will support them and early lessons should center around experiences with buoyancy. Have them feel the support of the water by pressing an air-filled ball or a plastic bottle into the water, releasing it, and seeing it pop up, pushed up by buoyancy. Have the students crouch in waist-deep water until their chins are on the surface and then ask them to balance on one big toe. This enables them to feel the buoyant lift of the water. From this balanced position, the head may be gently bent forward so that the body tips forward, face in the water, into a simple relaxed float. Once the learners can float and hold their breath for 3 seconds or more, they are over the biggest hurdle. Recovering to a standing position is an important safety skill for adults and **it must be learned.**

Personal safety skills should be practiced during each class. The students should be able to turn over and change direction both to the left and to the right. It is helpful to have definite, specific points to swim to or a set course to follow.

Instructors must be ready to utilize the students' most natural manners of moving through the water. Students may be more successful in performing a simple side-stroke variant as opposed to the more difficult coordination necessary in the crawl stroke. The elementary backstroke should be included in the instruction, since this is another simple means of propulsion and is a good resting stroke as well. **The objective of all instruction for adult nonswimmers should be the development of sufficient skills to enable them to take care of themselves in deep water rather than the perfection of total performance.** Some adult beginners will want to learn the crawl stroke. In some cases, variations of the crawl, such as the trudgen or the trudgen crawl, may be learned more easily. No rigid or set progression should be used. Senior citizens generally show less interest in being able to develop good stroking form. They are more interested in being able to make comfortable progress through the water.

Learning to tread water gives students a feeling of security and confidence in deep water and creates a sense of accomplishment. Other activities, such as snorkeling, low-key games and races, inner tube water polo, simple synchronized swimming stunts, or simple water ballet routines, add to the students' participation and enjoyment of the water. Regular participation in the Red Cross *Swim and Stay Fit Program* is an excellent way to develop and to maintain good physical fitness.

Adults should learn artificial respiration and they should be encouraged to enroll in first aid and cardio-pulmonary resuscitation training courses. Many adults own boats or have friends who are boaters. They should be informed about Red Cross small craft safety courses and be encouraged to enroll in any appropriate course.

CHAPTER 5

ELEMENTS OF SUCCESSFUL TEACHING

"Don't Slap At The Water,
Hug It By The Armfull!"
The Commodore

The successful use of the many elements of instruction that are discussed in this chapter will contribute to the achievement of the major objective of the Red Cross instructional program. This objective is for the students to learn skills and safety information in an environment that is most conducive to learning. This program is **not** designed to produce highly skilled and highly trained **competitive** swimmers.

Understanding and helping the beginning swimmer to overcome fear of the water is vital. More advanced students may have a fear of failure. Some students may feel embarrassed because of their appearance in a bathing suit. It is vital that instructors remain constantly aware of these and other factors that can retard learning, and that they take the steps necessary to reduce or to eliminate these factors. Almost all instructors had difficulties in learning one or more aquatics skills at one time or another. They learned these skills only with the patient assistance of their instructor and because they had the opportunity to practice under proper supervision. As an instructor, you must recognize these feelings and needs that you had as a student and use them in working with your students. Some other helpful hints are:

- Get to know your students by name whenever possible.
- Use words and teaching approaches that are most appropriate for the ages and the abilities of the students.

TEACHING APPROACHES

There are several types of teaching approaches that can be used and they are discussed in the Red Cross publication *A Guide for Safety Services Instructors* (Stock No. 321090). All of them have some advantages and disadvantages. All of them can be learned by instructors and used in Red Cross instruction programs. All of them utilize the information that is presented in this chapter. Regardless of which approach is used, students should learn and practice skills with the body in the proper position for the stroke to be learned. Land practice is used primarily for students who need special help and practice. Major emphasis is given to the following teaching approaches:

Whole Approach

Research has shown that many students learn more rapidly by performing whole movements, such as a swimming stroke, rather than by learning parts of the stroke first. These movements can be learned with or without the use of flotation aids. A disadvantage of this approach is applicable to newly trained or inexperienced instructors. Since students learn at different rates of speed, they should be organized into subgroups according to their respective abilities. **Inexperienced** instructors often have difficulty in dealing with this situation effectively, but they are encouraged to use and to become comfortable with this approach, since it provides students the opportunity to progress at their own rate of achievement.

Progressive-Part Approach

Many students have difficulty in understanding and learning the parts of a stroke simultaneously. These parts are leg action, arm action, and breathing. Many students find it easier to learn a swimming stroke by learning one part first, then adding other parts. As an example, in learning the breaststroke, the students learn the kick first, then add the arm action while doing the kick, and then add the breathing with the arm and leg actions. The total stroke should be practiced as soon as possible by all students. Procedures to correct faults in the parts of the stroke are practiced by the students while swimming the full stroke. An advantage of this approach is that it allows students to concentrate solely on learning a difficult (for many students) part, such as the breaststroke kick, in the prone position. Sub-grouping of students may become necessary while using this approach.

Part-Whole Approach

In this approach, the students learn and practice all parts of a stroke independently of each other. After each part is learned, the students then combine them and practice the whole stroke. The advantage of this approach to instructors, especially those with little experience, is that they find it easier to control the group, since all or most students perform the same skill at the same time. The major disadvantage is that all students are forced to learn at the same rate, which thus inhibits the progress of both faster and slower learners.

LESSON PLANS

Lesson planning is discussed in the Red Cross publication *A Guide for Safety Services Instructors* (Stock No. 321090). A well-organized lesson plan for teaching swimming skills contains the following elements:

1. Warm-up drills if the weather or the water is cool.
2. A period of adjustment to the water for the students.
3. A review practice of selected, previously learned skills.
4. An explanation and demonstration of the new skill(s).
5. A practice period for the new skill(s) to be learned, including mass drilling, individual correction and comment, and repetition of the explanation and a demonstration of the skill(s) when necessary.
6. A tapering-off period that may include free swimming, stunts, games of low organization, informal competition, and additional help to students who are having difficulties.

One or more of the above parts of the lesson may be eliminated occasionally, or they may be rearranged, but usually the elements outlined should be utilized.

EVALUATING MOTOR SKILLS

Self-analysis by swimmers is very difficult when performing skills, especially swimming strokes. Hearing and vision are often impaired and the legs, the arms, and the head may not give adequate feedback to the brain to tell the students what these parts are doing. The students must rely on the instructor for the help that they need in improving their skill performance.

Although each swimming stroke requires the coordination of specific arm and leg patterns of movement, a good stroke is one that propels the swimmer through the water smoothly with a maximum of efficiency, while expending a minimum amount of effort and exchanging an adequate supply of air.

The stroke will become smoother and stronger when the coordination and the timing are improved. This is accomplished by:

1. Obtaining the proper coordination of all phases of the stroke including the breathing.
2. Making sure that the negative movements are made in a manner that will produce the least resistance to the water.
3. Coordinating the breathing with the stroke action so that the exchange of air pattern becomes an integral part of the timing for each full stroke, regardless of whether or not an exchange of air is made during each stroke.

Experience helps the instructor improve what is commonly called a "photographic eye." This is the instructor's ability to recognize faults occurring at any given point in the stroke pattern that inhibit the swimmer's efficiency. Many instructors erroneously correct the fault observed without further analysis. They are unable to obtain the desired results because they have failed to recognize the true cause of the fault. Once the major cause is eliminated, the observed pattern fault will usually disappear. Two examples are:

1. Telling a student to lift the legs and to kick nearer the surface in the crawl stroke when the major cause of the low position of the legs is the head being held too high. Correcting the head position will usually remedy the position of the legs.
2. Telling the student to relax when performing the crawl stroke. A major cause of tenseness is failure to get a regular and adequate exchange of air. Improving the breathing habits will contribute to relaxation.

The elements listed below should be considered in analyzing swimming strokes. Those listed under the heading "General" are usually analyzed first, and major faults within these elements are usually corrected first. Major faults, and then minor faults, are addressed for the elements under the heading "Specific." These are usually corrected **after** the faults within the elements listed under "General" are corrected.

General	Specific
• Body position	• Arms
• Coordination	• Legs
• Smoothness and relaxation	• Breathing

In addition to teaching experience, a thorough knowledge of the basic principles involved in each total stroke pattern is necessary to determine the major cause of the fault observed. The faults and the fault causes observed can be called "fault keys." The instructor must retain a record of these "fault keys" for each stroke performed by every member of the class from one session to the next in order to be able to measure the progress of the class members and in order to provide the necessary corrective procedures for each student during the following session. The required information can be recorded in a minimum amount of time and provides a permanent record of the strokes attempted, the "fault keys," and the stroke evaluations for every student in attendance. After the original information is recorded, additional information can be added at each class session, or as needed, for the skill level at which the stroke is being taught. The information recorded should include:

1. The instructor's evaluation of the stroke at the skill level being taught.
2. Symbols or notations of the "fault keys" in relation to the evaluation recorded.
3. Other pertinent information regarding the stroke.

Over many years, some instructors have developed their own systems for recording information about their students' skill performances. The system that follows was developed many years ago by retired Red Cross Safety Services staff member, William Blau. It is an excellent method of recording a considerable amount of information quickly. Instructors are encouraged to develop a form and a series of markings similar to the following material.

Name and/or Number	Stroke		Stroke		Stroke	

16

The suggested stroke evaluation and analysis form can be enlarged to contain more columns for names and strokes. An explanation of the form and its use follows.

1. The students' names and/or numbers are listed in the column at the left hand side of the form. The assignment of permanent numbers to class members is of value in some classes, since it provides a definite class order for group work as well as a simple method for periodic evaluations and final gradings.

2. The other double columns are used for stroke evaluation. The name of the stroke should be written in each column at the time of use as it may be desirable to change the sequence or to add new strokes from time to time.

3. The block with the crossed dotted lines at the left side of each double column represents the human body in the following manner:

HUMAN BODY

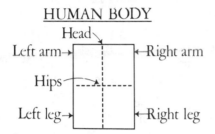

4. The open square at the right side of each double column is used for recording evaluation grades, "fault keys," and other pertinent data.

5. Examples of the data recorded in the "Human Body" section of the form are:
   a. A slant line in the bottom left or right hand corner shows on which side the sidestroke is performed, and an arc [)] in proper relation to the slant line shows excessive arch or forward bend of the body during the glide.
   b. An "S" on the leg indicates a scissors kick with the breaststroke or the elementary backstroke.
   c. A circle at the head or the hips shows that that part is too high and a square shows that it is too low.
   d. A check (✓) on the proper side in the arm area shows the point at which the inhalation is started during an overhand stroke, or it can be placed in the middle of the same area for the breaststroke.
   e. Crossed or parallel lines show the arms crossing over the center line during recovery and show the legs passing each other at the completion of the scissors kick.

   Numerous other symbols can be used but instructors should determine those that will reflect their observations in the simplest manner.

6. The open square section of the form must contain the overall evaluation of the stroke at the level being taught or there will be no meaning to the symbols, the "fault keys," or other pertinent data as they relate to the evaluation. An example of numerical grading is:
   4 Outstanding (Excellent)
   3 Above average (Good)
   2 Average (Passing)
   1 Below average (Weak)
   0 Fail (Incorrect stroke action)
   In addition to the evaluation grade, the following can be used:
   a. AP or KP to show lack of power in the arms or the legs (kick).
   b. AG, BG, or HG to show lack of glide caused by poor arm position, body balance, or head position.
   c. Others include WK (weak kick), T (timing), C (Coordination), and V (vibrating, which is a quivering action of the legs during the flutter kick).

7. The aforementioned information should enable instructors to use the form to whatever extent desired. However, the class must be organized properly for the evaluation of each stroke or the procedure will become time consuming and unwieldly. One method is as follows:
   a. Arrange the class in name or numerical order and announce the first stroke. (The student should be advised to swim at a given speed to avoid misunderstanding.)
   b. Have each student swim 10 or 15 yards and then return to the rear of the line.
   c. As the first swimmer reaches the 10- or 15-yard mark, the second swimmer starts, etc.

   At first, instructors may find that the swimmers are passing them at too fast a rate, but with a little practice they will be able to record the necessary information rapidly and conserve class time. If the pace is too fast for the instructors, or more detailed analysis is desired, the distance or the interval between swimmers can be increased.

TEACHING TO COURSE REQUIREMENTS

Individual skill requirements and combined skills tests are well-defined for Red Cross Swimming and Water Safety courses. Instructors should be continually aware of the progress of their students. The *Worksheet for Swimming Courses* (Form 5723) is used by instructors to maintain up-to-date records of their students.

The term "Teach-Testing" refers to teaching a skill, providing practice time for the students, and then testing the students on the skill. Students learn to swim by swimming and the majority of the class time must be devoted to the practice of skill improvement. A common pitfall in the use of the above form is in devoting an excessive amount of class time to testing students and recording their progress. Attempting to provide a rating mark such as an *X* (satisfactory), an *0* (unsatisfactory), or an *NI* (needs improvement) for every student for every skill wastes valuable class time. Instructors should provide a mark only for those students who perform a skill poorly or for those who were absent during the testing. Students' performances should be noted on the work sheet **during regular practice** as much as possible.

Guidelines for evaluating skill performances for basic swimming strokes are in Chapter 14. They are to be used by instructors to determine satisfactory from unsatisfactory skill performance.

CONDUCTING FINAL TESTS

The master lesson plan for a swimming course must include the time frames needed for conducting final skill tests. Poor planning can result in not having enough time or space to conduct and to complete the testing. Listed below are factors that must be considered and resolved:

1. **The type of course conducted.** The number of final tests varies with each course (i.e., the number of strokes to be evaluated, the distance for each stroke, and the combined skills test).
2. **Time and space requirements.** It is obvious that ten students in a class can be tested faster than a class of twenty students. Less time is consumed if five students swim at the same time as opposed to two students swimming at the same time. An average student may need at least one minute to swim 50 yards using the elementary backstroke. Two to three minutes may be needed for a 100-yard swim utilizing other strokes. Using these time-frame guidelines, instructors must then calculate the total time needed based on the number of students to be tested and the number of tests to be conducted. Space needs should be arranged for well in advance of final testing. The safety of the students must be provided for during the testing.

Retesting

A major objective is to pass deserving students. Students who fail a final test often request to be retested. Instructors should do so if they believe the student(s) can receive a satisfactory grade through having another opportunity. Retesting is also predicated on having class time and space available after all tests have been given to all students. Instructors must exercise good judgement and tact when allowing retesting. All students may want to be retested and this may be impossible.

GIVING DIRECTIONS

Some form of class organization occurs regardless of the teaching approach used, and some controls are used periodically by the instructor to help meet instructional objectives. Instructors must develop verbal and nonverbal methods of communication with students to maximize effective use of classtime for instruction and practice. Good directions or commands have the following characteristics:

- They are brief, clear, and easily understood. The students are informed of what is to be done, how to do it, when to start and stop, and where to swim.
- They include a command of preparation, such as "ready" (alerting students to get ready to perform an action), and a command of execution, such as "go" or "swim."
- They instruct the students as to who moves first, second, etc.

In a typical teaching situation (for example, the students have counted off into three waves and are holding onto the side of the pool), the instructor can use the information above as follows:

- Name the skill to be practiced (Scissors kick).
- Tell how the skill is to be practiced (Everyone on your left side, or right side, or either side).
- Tell where to swim and when to stop (One width and stop).
- Command of preparation (No. 1s, ready).
- Command of execution (Go).
- Continue with the rest of the class (No. 2s, ready, go, etc.).

Many instructors often teach three or four classes consecutively. There may be conflicting noise from other classes, poor acoustics from indoor pools, or the students in the class may be some distance away from the instructor during fluid drills. To save the instructor's voice and to maintain good class organization, the instructor must develop good nonverbal communication skills. Directions can be given by (1) pantomiming the skill to be performed, (2) indicating which wave is to move by the use of one or more fingers (command of preparation), and (3) beckoning with the hand when the designated wave is to move (command of execution).

ORGANIZING THE CLASS FOR SKILL DEVELOPMENT

Much of the average water safety instructor's teaching is done on the beginner, the advanced beginner, and the intermediate levels, where the classes are usually large and the interest span of the students is comparatively limited. Every minute must count if best results are to be obtained. A knowledge of the principles of class organization should enable the instructor to plan the work so as to provide the students with an opportunity to make the desired progress.

PRINCIPLES OF CLASS ORGANIZATION

In organizing the class for effective teaching and learning experiences, the instructor should always arrange the class so that:

- The safety of the students is ensured.
- Everyone can hear the instructions.
- Everyone can see the demonstration.
- Everyone will have an opportunity for maximum practice.
- Everyone will have an opportunity to be checked for skill improvement.

The most important factor is in providing for the safety of the students. Every effort must be made to prevent an accident from occurring. A lifeguard should be on duty during instructional periods. Rules, such as no running, no ducking, no horseplay, and no diving into shallow water, must be explained and enforced. Potential hazards are pointed out. All students must be accounted for at the start of a class period, periodically during the period, and at the close of the class. Instructors are never to leave the instructional area at the end of class until all students are accounted for and have left the area. The instructor(s) or a lifeguard must be in the immediate area of the pool or the waterfront before the students are allowed to enter.

The procedures used for learning and practicing skills in the water are determined by the skill to be learned, the skill level of the students, the size and shape of the facility, the extent of shallow- and deep-water areas available for practice, and the number, sizes, and ages of the students. The following factors are utilized by instructors to ensure successful learning, regardless of the type of teaching approach used:

- Students should, if at all possible, face away from the sun, bright light from windows, or distracting influence during the demonstrations.
- Students must be able to see and to hear during the demonstrations.
- Students must be able to hear and to see the instructions during practice sessions.
- Students must have the opportunity (1) to make the physical and mental adjustment to the water in relation to the skill to be learned, (2) to find and to maintain a good working position in the water as determined by the skill to be learned, and (3) to have maximum practice in order to develop the desired pattern of movement in terms of accuracy, coordination, speed, and expenditure of energy. This practice must include an analysis of each student's movements and the provision of appropriate and timely suggestions for improvement when necessary by the instructor, an aide, or a buddy.
- Students must have ample space in which to practice so as not to be interferred with by other students.

PATTERNS OF CLASS ORGANIZATION

Patterns of class organization are formations employed by the instructor to provide students with the opportunity to develop the desired skill. On the following pages are some of the more common patterns of class organization. Instructors should become thoroughly familiar with all of them. They include formations for discussions, demonstrations, drills in which the students remain in one spot (static drills), and drills in which the students move from one point to another (fluid drills).

Instructors must constantly strive to provide maximum opportunity for skill practice for all students during each class period. Failure on the part of the instructor to keep the students actively involved can cause the inactive students to become chilled, bored, and restless, which can cause disruptions and loss of class control.

Arranging the Class for a Discussion on Land
Formation: Semicircle (one or more lines).

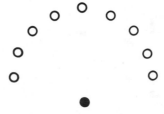

When Used: When speaking to the group.
Important Factors:
1. The sun should be behind the students.
2. The group should face away from distracting influences.
3. Wind coming from behind the instructor will help to carry his or her voice to the students.

Arranging the Class for a Demonstration in the Water
Formation: "L" formation (single or multiple lines).

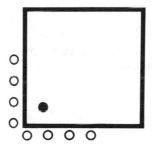

When Used: When the end and the side of the pool or the dock are available.
Important Factors:
1. The demonstrator should work in a "pocket" directly in front of the students.
2. If talking against the wind, the demonstrator should talk toward the water and allow the sound to be carried over the water.
3. Students should be close to and high enough above so as to look down on the demonstrator.

Formation: Single line.

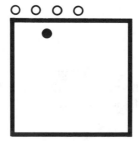

When Used: When working from a single runway or from the side of the pool or the dock when the group is small.
Important Factors: Same as for the "L" formation.

Formation: Multiple lines.

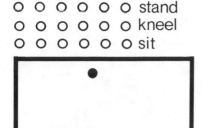

When Used: When working from a single runway or
the side of the pool or the dock when the
group is large.

Important Factors:

1. One group sits, the next group kneels,
and the third group stands.
2. Same as for the "L" formation.

Arranging the Class for Fluid Drills

Fluid drill formations are used to improve the skill
efficiency and the physical endurance of the students as
well as to evaluate them. These drills should be varied
to meet the needs of the students and the instructor.
The following factors should be considered when these
drill formations are used: The level of skill proficiency
of the students, their physical condition, the distance
to be achieved for each swim, the intensity level of
each swim, and the frequency and length of rest periods
between swims. Students should be comfortably tired
but **not physically exhausted** at the end of the class
period.

Formation: Wave.

When Used: 1. To divide a large group into smaller
units to provide maximum supervised
student practice.
2. To allow the instructor to observe fewer
students at one time in order to make
comments for skill improvement.

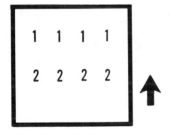

Important Factors:

1. The group is divided into smaller groups
known as No. 1, No. 2, etc.
2. The instructor must tell each group
what to do and when to do it. EXAMPLE.
"Side stroke. No. 1s. Ready. Swim."
3. Each group swims as a unit on the
appropriate command.
4. Each group swims to a designated point
and stops.

The wave formation is one of the most often used of
all fluid drill formations. Consequently, the instructor
should become skilled in organizing a class quickly. Some
of the major factors to consider are:

- To avoid loss of time, young children should be placed
into the positions desired by the instructor.
- For fluid drills (and static drills) on dry land or in
shallow water, have the students line up in one
straight rank. Have them count off according to the
number of groups desired, starting from one end.
Have the students turn their heads in the direction of
the count so that the next student can clearly hear
the number being called out. Depending on the
number of ranks to be formed, have the No. 1s hold
their positions, No. 2s step back two paces, No. 3s step
forward two paces, etc. For fluid drills (and static
drills) in shallow water, have the tallest students
nearer the deeper water and the shortest students
nearest the shallower water.
- For fluid drills in deep water, have the students line
up by holding onto the edge of the pool or the dock.
Have them count off using the procedures previously
discussed. Each student should remember his or her
number and who is on either side of him or her. By
keeping the proper positions, each student will have
sufficient space to practice as drilling continues back
and forth across the swimming area.
- With patience, perseverance, and the use of humor on
behalf of the instructor, the students should quickly
learn to move only on the appropriate command,
and to stop and to remain in place at the designated
location.

Formation: Stagger.

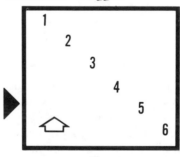

When Used: When it is necessary to watch students
individually and for final evaluation of many
skills. The students' safety must be provided
for.

Important Factors:

1. The group remains in a single line.
2. Signal the first student to start swimming.
If two instructors are available, start each
end of the line simultaneously.
3. The student next in line starts when the
swimmer just ahead reaches the spot
designated by the instructor.
4. The instructor should be able to follow
the progress of each student for a few
body lengths.
5. The instructor usually moves along the
deck so as to have a better view of the
swimmers.

Formation: Short- or long-course swim.

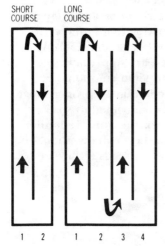

When Used: 1. For practicing distance swimming in an enclosed area that is narrow and long.
2. Builds stamina and permits individual attention to the students by the instructor.

Important Factors:
1. The swimming area is divided into smaller areas, with two lanes each for one or more areas (short course), or into multiple lanes (long course).
2. For the short course, divide the group by the number of areas available. One group is assigned to each area, by similar abilities if necessary.
3. For the long course, place the faster swimmers ahead of the slower ones.
4. Designate the number of laps (one length or width of the pool) to be completed before stopping.
5. The swimmers should keep a safe distance apart.

Arranging the Class for Static Drills on Land or in Shallow Water

Formation: Single line.

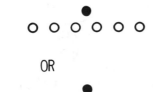

When Used: When the area is long and narrow or the group is small; either on land or in the water.

Important Factors:
1. The students should be far enough apart so as not to interfere with each other.
2. The instructor may stand in front of or at either end of the line.

Formation: Parallel lines.

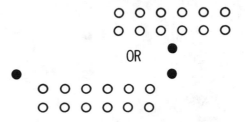

When Used: When the area is long and narrow and the group is large.

Important Factors:
1. Especially effective when the students work as buddies.
2. The instructor's position may vary as for the single line formation.

Formation: Multiple lines.

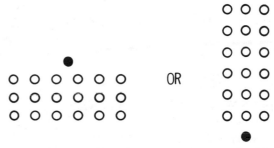

When Used: When the area is short and wide and the group is large.

Important Factors:
1. The students should be far enough apart so as not to interfere with each other.
2. The instructor must be seen by all students and vice versa.

Formation: Circle.

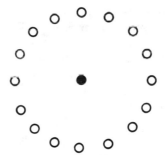

When Used: When the area is short and wide and the group is large.

Important Factors:
1. It is difficult to observe all the students at the same time with this formation.
2. The instructor must be certain that all students are able to see any demonstrations.
3. The instructor should have an observer outside of the circle for the safety of the students, or the instructor must turn around frequently to observe the students.

Formation: Semicircle.

When Used: When the group is small and the area is limited in length and width.

Important Factor:

- The same as for the semicircle formation on land.

Formation: "V" formation.

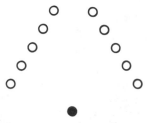

When Used: When the area is limited in width.

Important Factor:

- The students must be placed so as not to interfere with each other's vision or motion.

TEACHING AIDS

A wide variety of supports can be used in the learning process. Used correctly, they can speed up learning and make practice sessions more rewarding and meaningful for the students. In the initial learning stages, stationary and hand supports may be used, but they should be used sparingly and only until the students develop a feeling for the desired patterns of movement of the arms and legs. Stationary and hand supports are more effective for students having learning difficulties and who need individual assistance and practice. Instructors should use fluid (moving) drills, with or without the use of flotation aids, as soon as possible. Teaching aids can be grouped into four broad categories: Flotation devices, stationary supports, hand supports, and other aids, such as diving objects, swim fins, and face masks.

Flotation Devices

Flotation devices must be used properly in order for the learner to assume the correct body position in relation to the skill to be practiced and developed. These aids fall into two categories:

1. Those that are attached to the body or from which the body is suspended.

2. Free flotation aids that the student holds onto, such as a swimboard, cannister, pull buoy, or plastic jug.

For many years, the use of flotation aids attached to the body was not recommended for beginner swimmers until they had made the necessary physical and mental adjustments to the water. In recent years, however, many swimming instructors have reported success in having beginners use an attached device in the early stages of learning, especially when using the **Whole Approach** or the **Progressive-Part Approach.** The use of flotation devices by nonswimmers should be restricted to periods of instruction under proper supervision. Nonswimmers should be restricted to shallow water areas and they **should not become dependent on an aid.** Nonswimmers, and their parents, should be cautioned about the hazards of such aids if they are to be used during recreational swimming or while practicing skills without the supervision of a qualified instructor.

Support to the Body

For maximum effectiveness, a flotation device to support the body should—

- Provide maximum safety for the user.
- Support the body in the proper position for the skill to be learned.
- Be placed on the part of the body requiring support without interfering with the body parts that are to be moved.
- Be secured (attachable aids) so as not to slip or come loose.
- Be constructed so that it will not deflate accidently.
- Be easily inflatable and deflatable.

Examples of attachable aids are personal flotation devices (life jackets), "eggs" or "bubbles," inner tubes, and inflatable arm bands. An inexpensive and effective aid for supporting the body can be constructed easily and quickly by tying each end of a piece of rope, or canvas webbing, approximately 2 feet long, to the handles of two empty plastic containers, such as milk or bleach bottles. Water can be added to the containers to create added resistance or drag, thus forcing the student to work harder to overcome the resistance.

Examples and use of these devices, and the approximate area of the body where they should be placed, are shown below.

STROKES DONE ON THE BACK

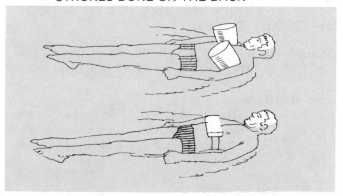

The use of plastic bottles or an inner tube to support the feet is for the use of **more advanced swimmers.**

STROKES DONE ON THE FRONT

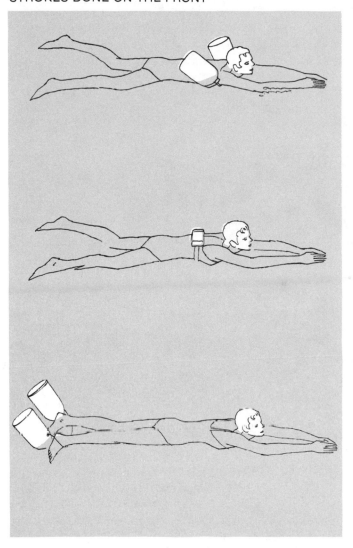

STROKES DONE ON THE SIDE

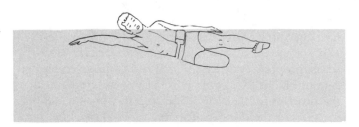

Free-Floating Supports

A variety of free-floating supports can be used to support the body, thus enabling the swimmer to practice with one or both arms, with or without breathing, and utilizing the various leg kicks. These supports can be grasped with one or both hands or can be held between the thighs or lower legs. Examples of these aids are swimboards, boat seat cushions, ring buoys, plastic containers, and pull-buoys that can be held between the legs.

FOR LEG KICK ON THE FRONT

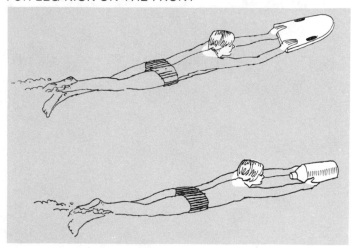

FOR LEG KICK ON THE SIDE

FOR STROKES ON THE FRONT AND THE SIDE

FOR LEG KICK ON THE BACK

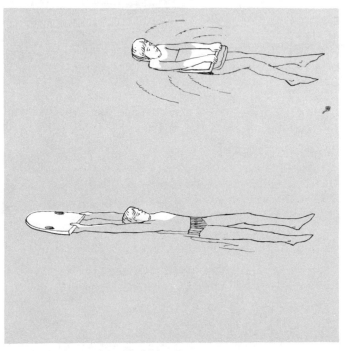

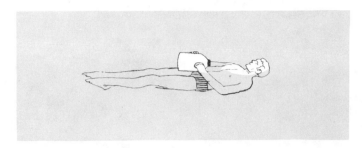

FOR ARM STROKE ON THE BACK

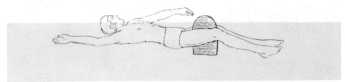

To prevent injuries to the body, swimboards (kickboards) should not be thrown or swung around nor should students push them under the water and suddenly release them.

Stationary Supports

Since learning usually occurs faster through the **Whole** or **Progressive-Part Approaches**, the use of stationary supports is generally employed for the student who is having difficulty and needs special attention. Examples of stationary supports are the deck or the side of a pool or a dock, the bottom of a shallow water area, and the ladders or the steps in a pool. Shown below are several ways the body can be supported to allow practice of leg movements.

PRONE POSITION

SUPINE POSITION

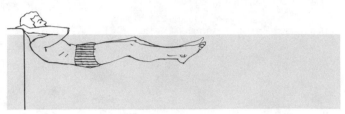

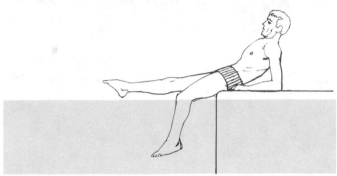

ON THE SIDE

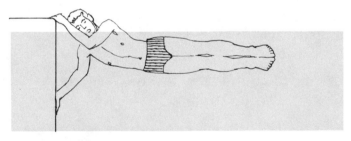

Practicing in this position is difficult for many students because of an inability to keep the hips and the legs near the surface.

It is important that students learn to bracket themselves properly in order to learn and to practice leg actions efficiently. Learning to balance and to control the position of the body while holding onto the side of the pool or the dock contributes to good body balance when swimming.

When bracketing the body in the prone position, it is generally easier for students to grasp the overflow trough with one hand while placing the other hand below the waterline and against the wall. The arms are extended and the head is kept low in the water to enable the hips and the legs to rise toward the surface. The chin can be kept in the water to allow for easy breathing, or the face can be in the water and lifted whenever a breath is needed.

24

To bracket the body on its side, the student grasps the overflow trough with the hand of the upper arm. The palm of the lower hand, fingers toward the bottom, is placed against the wall directly under the top hand and approximately 24 inches beneath the surface of the water. The depth of the lower hand depends a great deal on the length of the student's arm. The body is kept straight, stretched, and perpendicular to the wall, with the lower ear in the water. The lower hand provides most of the support and control for the body. Many students tend to sway forward or backward from the perpendicular position to the wall. This swaying action is counteracted by having the student slide the lower hand in the direction of the sway and by exerting pressure against the wall to push the body back into the proper position.

Hand Supports

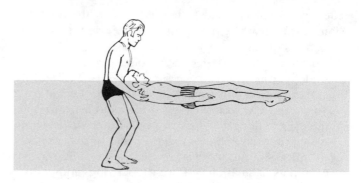

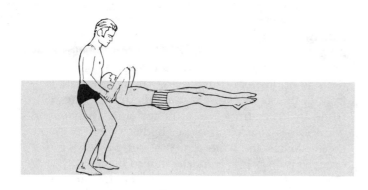

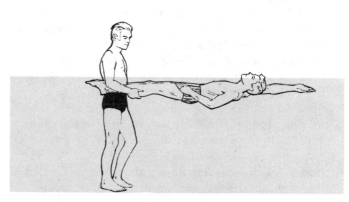

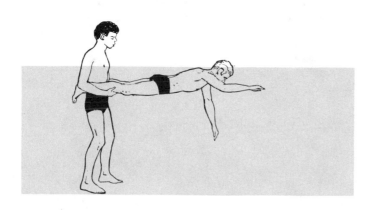

Hand support by the instructor, an aide, or a buddy can also be used effectively for students who need special assistance. This personal contact can be especially helpful for timid beginners, since it provides confidence to the learner. Support of the students should be primarily from the water, and the body must be in the proper position for the skill that is to be practiced.

The instructor's or aide's hands will need to shift positions to appropriately support the student's body when practicing arm and leg movements on the side. For student practice of arm movements on the front or the back, the student's legs must be supported in such a way as to permit the proper head position. Support from the hands under the student's shoulders is superior to placing the hands under the head. Hand support can be effectively maintained while the student moves through the water as a result of the actions of the arms or the legs.

Other Aids

Many types of aids, other than those previously discussed and shown, can be used to enhance the learning process and will help to "keep the fun in fundamentals." The

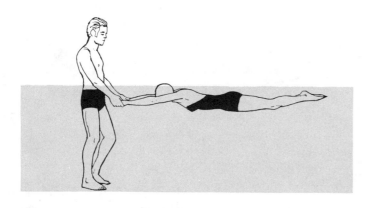

effective use of such aids is limited only by the imagination or the creativity of the instructor. Several types or categories of aids are discussed below:

- Objects of all types, sizes, and colors, which beginning students can dive or reach for, can be used effectively in the physical and mental adjustment to the water. They can be used in helping students to learn to open the eyes underwater, to hear underwater by "clapping" two appropriate objects together, and to experience the effects of the water in relation to body buoyancy. Examples of such objects are rubber rings and coins. These objects should contrast with the color of the bottom of the swimming area. They should also be made of a substance that will neither damage nor stain the bottom of a swimming pool.

- Toys and other objects will help the learning process, especially with young children. They can "blow" table tennis balls across the surface of the water; jump, dive, or swim through hula hoops; and throw or pass balls back and forth.

- A properly fitted face mask or eye goggles can help timid students overcome the difficulty of placing and keeping the face in the water, and can be useful when initially attempting to open the eyes underwater. They make swimming underwater much more enjoyable, since the eyes can be opened with no discomfort. A face mask can help many students to develop correct breathing patterns for the beginner stroke or the crawl stroke, but a mask must **never** cover the mouth. A face mask or goggles are effective for the instructor who may need to go into the water to observe the underwater actions of the arms or legs of the students.

- Swim fins can be effective in helping to develop the flutterkick or when employing the flutterkick when learning or improving the arm action of the crawl stroke and the backstroke. Because of the added propulsion from swim fins, a better body position is created for the beginners that is helpful in learning correct breathing patterns. Some of the precautions regarding the use of swim fins are (1) that students should not become dependent on them, and (2) the use of extra long or extra stiff fins, which may cause cramping of the muscles of the legs and the feet.

- Hand paddles can help more advanced students to establish correct hand positions and arm stroke mechanics and to create a greater awareness of the correct propulsive actions of the hands. They should not be used extensively, since damage to the shoulder joints may occur.

- A whistle, used sparingly and in short blasts by the instructor, can be a voice saver to get the attention of a class. When blown too often, the students may ignore it and it can cause confusion for the students in other classes that may be in close proximity.

- Music of an appropriate rhythm, through overhead and underwater speakers, can be used by more advanced students to help develop desired rhythmic patterns of movement.

- A lightweight reaching pole can be used to help improve the ability of the student when diving from the side of the pool or the dock. The pole is held in front of the student **and across his or her line of flight** by the instructor or a trained aide. The student will learn to control his or her body to achieve greater height and a more vertical entry by diving over the pole as it is gradually moved higher and closer to the student. Diving must be performed in deep water (minimum 10-foot depth) when using this teaching method. The pole should be lowered quickly when it is obvious that it will be struck by a student.

PHYSICAL LAWS APPLIED TO BODY MOVEMENTS IN THE WATER

Effective instructors of swimming and related aquatics skills must have an understanding of the human body, the physical laws or mechanical principles that affect motion, and the forces that produce or retard motion of the human body through the water. Understanding the effects of physical laws on the performance of swimming strokes and other aquatics skills enables instructors to gain insight into the causes of ineffective movements. This understanding also enables them to provide instructional techniques that contribute to effective performances by their students.

With few exceptions, humans must inhale and hold their breath in order to float in the water. The majority of people are able to float and most of them float motionless with the body at an angle to the surface (diagonal position) or in a near vertical position. That people are able to float is explained by Archimedes' principle—a body is buoyed by a force equal to the weight of the water that the body displaces. The body will sink if the weight of the immersed body is greater than the weight of the displaced water. Conversely, the body will float if the weight of the immersed body is less than the weight of the displaced water. The amount of buoyancy of an individual in the water is governed by the amount of air that is inhaled and held and by the composition of the body.

BODY COMPOSITION

The differences in the buoyancy of individuals will vary considerably depending on the relationship between the amount of heavier bone and muscle tissue and the amount of lighter adipose (fatty) tissue. Adipose tissue has a specific gravity of less than 1.0, which is the specific gravity of water. Anything having a specific gravity of less than 1.0 will float on the surface. Bone and muscle tissue have a specific gravity slightly greater than 1.0 and will tend to sink. Individuals, usually men, who are heavily muscled, who have heavier bone structure, or who have little body fat, have a larger proportion of lean body mass and a smaller percentage of adipose tissue and will have more difficulty floating. Most women have a greater percentage of adipose tissue relative to lean body mass than men and are likely to float more easily.

An easy test called the "jellyfish float" can be used to determine the degree of buoyancy of a swimmer. While in chest-deep water, the swimmer submerges to the neck, takes a deep breath of air, bends forward from the waist, places the head in the water, and bends the knees enough to get the feet off the bottom. The person holds the breath and relaxes as much as possible. If the person sinks, the swimmer's weight is greater than the buoyant force of the water. If a portion of the head or the back remains above the surface, the person can learn to float on the back with the face out of the water.

Individuals with marginal buoyancy will have to use explosive breathing while floating on their backs to keep their faces from submerging while getting an exchange of air. Explosive breathing means a rapid exhalation followed immediately by a rapid inhalation.

Little can be done to affect the weight of the individual. However, by inhaling more deeply, the area of the chest is expanded to a greater degree, which increases its **volume** without any significant change in weight. The result is that the weight of that segment of the body is spread over a larger surface area of the water, resulting in less weight per square inch and thus an increase in buoyancy.

The slight difference in the specific gravity of fresh water and salt water affects one's buoyancy in the water. Since salt water is slightly more dense than fresh water, it can support more weight. An individual who floats in fresh water will float slightly higher in salt water or will tend to float in a more horizontal position. The saltier the water, the greater the buoyant force.

CENTER OF GRAVITY AND CENTER OF BUOYANCY

The position in which a swimmer floats is determined not only by the overall composition of the body but also by the relative positions of the center of gravity and the center of buoyancy within each individual while trying to float. On land or in the air, the person turns or rotates around a point at the center of weight called the **center of gravity.** In the water, however, the person rotates around a point in the chest region called the **center of buoyancy**.

The center of gravity of a person lying horizontally on the surface of the water with the arms at the sides of the body is at the center of all weight and is located somewhere in the pelvis. Since the body segments are of different weights, the distance of each segment from the center of gravity of the body plays a role in determining the exact location of the center of gravity.

When a person is lying horizontally on the surface, gravity tends to act on each body segment individually to pull it down. The buoyant force of the water will support each segment horizontally if the specific gravity of each part is less than 1.0. Some body segments may be more buoyant than others. An arm might float, but a leg, with its heavier bone structure, might not.

The primary upward (buoyant) force of the water is directed through a point in the chest area called the center of buoyancy of the body. The air in the lungs makes the chest area, with its light bone structure and very light muscle structure, the most buoyant part of the body. Consequently, the chest tends to float at the surface.

A motionless float occurs only when the center of buoyancy is aligned directly over the center of gravity. With persons of average build, these two centers are aligned in a somewhat parallel position to the surface of the water when the person attempts to float in the horizontal position on the back with the arms extended along the sides of the body. In this position in the water, the average person has more body weight located in the hips and the legs than in the head and the shoulders. The force of gravity pulls the hips (center of weight) and the legs downward. The buoyant force of the water acts as if it were pushing upward on the chest area (center of buoyancy). These opposing forces cause the body to act like a teeter-totter. The body starts to rotate forward as the hips and the legs move downward. When the center of gravity in the pelvis has rotated to a point directly below the center of buoyancy in the chest, the person should float motionless. However, as the legs sink during the forward rotation of the body, their downward momentum increases. This increased velocity of the legs, plus their weight, may cause the body to submerge, since the force of buoyancy is insufficient to overcome the force of gravity and the downward movement of the legs.

This tendency for the legs to pull the whole body under the water means that beginners should not be taught the back float from a horizontal position but from a vertical position where the feet will tend to rise to the person's normal floating position. The learner should be in water of shoulder depth. When the head is laid back so that the back arches gently and the arms are extended outward from the shoulders, the water will begin to support the body. Without any push-off, the feet will rise to the normal floating position for that person. Through practice the swimmer will learn which of the three positions is the normal one for him or her — horizontal, diagonal, or vertical.

HORIZONTAL

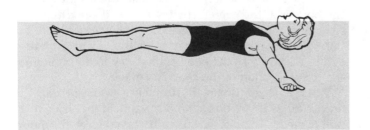

DIAGONAL

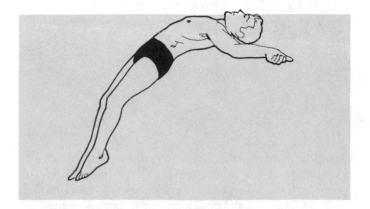

VERTICAL

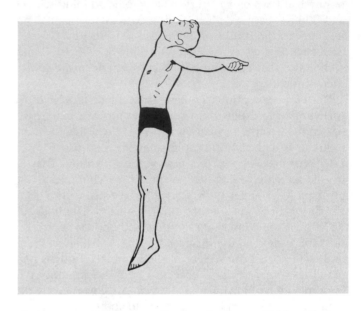

Swimmers who float motionless in the vertical or the diagonal position can learn to float in a more horizontal position by changing the positions of their arms and legs. These swimmers may want to learn to alter their normal floating position in order to demonstrate the back float in more than one position or merely to increase their overall aquatics abilities.

Changing Floating Positions

To assume a more nearly horizontal body position, diagonal and vertical floaters will need to adjust the positions of their arms and legs so that the center of buoyancy and the center of gravity will move closer together.

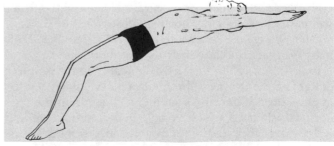

To move the center of gravity slightly closer to the chest, the swimmer fully extends the arms directly beyond the head, which helps to raise the legs.

To move the center of gravity slightly more toward the chest, the swimmer bends the knees and draws the heels toward the buttocks. These actions help the thighs to rise toward the surface. To bring the thighs even closer to the surface, the swimmer bends the wrists and raises a part of the hands out of the water. The weight of the hands out of the water helps to overcome the weight of the legs, which enables them to rise closer to the surface.

Most of these adjustments will have to be made for the vertical floater. Making only one or two changes may result in a horizontal position for the diagonal floater. Marginal floaters will have to use explosive breathing to keep their face from submerging while getting an exchange of air.

LAW OF INERTIA

The law of inertia states that a body remains at rest or in uniform motion unless acted upon by some external force. External forces that offer resistance and impede forward momentum cannot always be eliminated but they can and should be minimized for most effective stroking. These resistance forces are classified as **frontal resistance** and **eddy resistance (drag).**

The implications of the law of inertia are clear in swimming. There is always a trade-off involved between the duration of rest in the glide portion of a stroke and the amount of propulsive effort necessary to overcome the body slowing down because of the resistance forces of the water. If speed is the main concern, as in competitive swimming or approach stroking for a rescue, the glide portion is shortened to maintain a constant speed. If swimming for relaxation or distance is involved, then the glide portion can be lengthened to provide a longer rest period. However, the glide portion should not be held until forward momentum ceases, since extra effort is required to re-establish forward motion. This situation is comparable to pushing a car by hand. Once the car starts moving, it takes less effort to keep it moving than the initial effort it takes to start the action.

Frontal Resistance

Keeping the body in as near a horizontal plane as possible while swimming reduces frontal resistance. A body, or portion of a body, that is angled downward presents a greater frontal surface area to the water and causes a subsequent increase in the amount of frontal resistance. Examples of poor body position are (1) "sitting" in the water while stroking on the back, or (2) swimming with the head high, which causes the legs to drop while stroking on the front. With the legs in a dropped position, some of the propulsive force of the kick must be used to lift the body, resulting in a loss of effective forward movement.

Frontal resistance is also reduced by keeping the body straight and streamlined and by minimizing the cross-sectional area of the upper body (shoulders) by gliding with the arms stretched forward of the body with the hands together. Rolling the body from side-to-side on its long axis while swimming the crawl stroke also reduces the amount of cross-sectional area of the shoulders that is presented to the water.

Eddy Resistance (Drag)

A layer of water flows down the body while it is in motion. The negative effects of this laminal flow (drag) of water are reduced by keeping the body as straight and as streamlined as possible. A swim cap and a swimsuit of smooth material will also help to minimize this resistance.

LAW OF ACTION AND REACTION

Newton's law of action and reaction states that for every action there is an equal and an opposite reaction. By pushing water backward with the hands or the feet, the swimmer moves forward. Some of the effectiveness of the backward force may be lost because of water slipping around the arms and the hands or the legs and the feet if they are not positioned properly during their propulsive movements.

A force directed away from the desired line of travel of the body will result in a loss of effective forward movement. In the crawl stroke, pressing water with the hands to the outside of the long axis midline of the body will cause the shoulders and the legs to move in the opposite direction. A result of this bending of the body is an increase in resistance and a reduction of kicking efficiency, since the hips and the legs are out of proper alignment. Twisting the head and the shoulders to one side because of improper breathing habits, or recovering and entering the hand in the water across the long axis midline of the body in the crawl stroke or the back crawl stroke, will cause the body to bend out of proper alignment. Pushing downward with the hands while swimming most strokes causes the upper body to rise, resulting in wasted energy and retardation of body motion in the desired direction.

A further application of this law to swimming implies that if the underwater recovery actions of the arms and the legs are too vigorous, the water will "push back" with equal force, resulting in retarded momentum forward. The resistance of the water to the body during the underwater recovery (negative) action of the arms and the legs should be minimized by —

- Using somewhat slower and less forceful movements than their respective propulsive actions.

- Keeping them close to or in line with the body to reduce the amount of surface area of the body segment that is "pushed" against the water.

LAW OF ACCELERATION
The law of acceleration states that the velocity of a body is proportional to the force applied and occurs in the direction in which that force acts. Simply stated, the harder the swimmer presses backward against the water, the faster the swimmer will move forward. An increase in the velocity of the swimmer in the desired direction is also dependent upon the swimmer maintaining a good body position and smooth, well-coordinated, and efficient movements of the arms and the legs.

LEVERAGE
In stroking, the entire arm and the hand act as a third-class lever. Force is applied between the fulcrum (shoulder joint) and the resistance of water to the surface of the arms and the hand. The law of levers states that the product of the force times the length of the force arm is equal to the product of the resistance times the length of the resistance arm.

The **force** is the muscle force applied; the **force arm** is the distance from the shoulder joint to the point where the force is applied (about 2 inches from the shoulder joint where the muscles involved are inserted). **Resistance** is mostly water resistance; the **resistance arm** is the distance from the hand back to the fulcrum.

Flexing the elbows as the arm moves through the water shortens the resistance arm, with the result that the same propulsive effort can be affected with only about half the force applied compared to when the arm is straight.

RELAXATION AND BREATHING
In addition to physical laws that govern body movements in the water, two other factors — relaxation and breathing — also affect swimming performance.

Relaxation
Swimmers attempting to propel themselves are never completely relaxed. The aim of skilled swimmers is to relax those muscles that are not contributing to a desired movement. Activating muscles that need not be used during a stroke can actually inhibit the desired movement as well as hasten fatigue. The actions and movements of beginners in the water are usually awkward, tense, and tiring, since they use many more muscle groups than necessary.

Breathing
The importance of proper breath control while swimming cannot be overemphasized. Persons who do not get a regular, sufficient supply of oxygen will soon tire. Rhythmic breathing for facedown strokes can be learned and perfected when practiced constantly.

In all strokes, inhalation and exhalation must be done in a manner that will result in minimum interference with stroking rhythm and that will minimize any change in correct body position.

Proper breathing techniques are also important for health reasons, especially for strokes performed in the facedown position. Water that enters the sinus cavities or the inner ear canals through the nasal passages can lead to infection. While exhaling under water, some air should be exhaled through the nose, at a pressure equal to or greater than the pressure of the water inward, in order to prevent water from entering the nasal passages.

In the strokes where the face is carried beneath the surface, the interval when air is inhaled is short; therefore, air must be inhaled quickly through the mouth. The exhalation begins through the mouth and the nose as soon as the face re-enters the water, and continues, slowly and steadily, until the next inhalation. If some air remains before the next inhalation is ready to be taken, it should be expelled quickly as the mouth is clearing the water.

Some highly skilled swimmers who possess good breath control do not exhale until just before they are ready to take another breath, at which time they expel the air rapidly through both the nose and the mouth. This is referred to as **explosive breathing** and prolongs the period of greater buoyancy, since more air is retained in the lungs for a longer period of time. However, this style of breathing is not introduced in Red Cross courses, since learning to breathe regularly (rhythmic breathing), as previously described, is very important in developing smooth, efficient, and well-coordinated swimming strokes.

ADAPTING STROKES TO BODY CHARACTERISTICS
No two swimmers will perform the same swimming strokes in an identical manner, yet both swimmers may perform the same stroke with equal efficiency. Differences in body characteristics, such as buoyancy, flexibility and range of movement in the body joints, length of the arms and the legs, size of the hands and the feet, and the speed of movement of the arms and the legs, affect the ability of individuals to perform swimming strokes. It is vital, therefore, for the instructor and the student to understand that a proper pattern of movement for each stroke **must be adapted to the swimmer.** Use of the laws and principles in this chapter will lead to smooth, relaxed, effective strokes for almost every swimmer.

CHAPTER 7

TEACHING THE BEGINNER SWIMMER

"Keep The Fun In Fundamentals!"
The Commodore

Becoming a skilled performer in the water requires the learning of basic fundamental skills that are contained in each of the following categories:

- Physical and mental adjustment (entering the water, breath control, seeing underwater, and hearing underwater).
- Rhythmic breathing.
- Buoyancy, body position, and relaxation (prone float, jellyfish float, prone glide, and back glide).
- Propulsive movements (prone glide with kick, back glide with kick, arm stroke and breathing in prone position, arm stroke on the back, and combined stroke on the front and on the back).
- Personal safety (turning over, changing directions, leveling off from a vertical position, and jumping entries into the water).

Many beginning swimmers may learn the basic fundamentals, except for floating, while learning swimming strokes through the use of the **Whole Approach** or the **Progressive-Part Approach.** Many other beginners learn these fundamentals best by practicing them individually. Regardless of the learning approach used, it is imperative that these basic fundamentals are mastered, since they constitute the foundation upon which skilled swimming is based. (NOTE. The games and stunts found on pages 36-40 and in Chapter 16 can be used successfully to help the students learn the skills contained in this chapter.)

PHYSICAL AND MENTAL ADJUSTMENT

When nonswimmers enter the water for the first time, they go through a new and unique experience that requires considerable adjustment to be made both physically and mentally. The water is much cooler than the bath water they are accustomed to. Even water temperatures of from 80° to 82°F (26.7° to 27.8°C) will feel cool on the body and will cause the breath and the pulse to quicken. When the body is submerged in neck-deep water by either wading or crouching, the learners will experience some slight difficulty in breathing because of added pressure of the water to the chest and, secondly, they will feel a noticeable loss of weight because of the effects of buoyancy. The effects of temperature, pressure, and buoyancy to the body are the first experiences that nonswimmers must adjust to.

Many nonswimmers will have some fear of the new element. Most fears are unfounded but they are real to the individual. The first step in the adjustment process should be to dissipate this fear and to instill confidence in each of the students. The nonswimmers should understand that they will be in the shallow water area until they are able to swim and that their safety will be protected at all times. If the learners are old enough to understand, it should be clearly explained and demonstrated that they possess a certain amount of body buoyancy that will help them to stay on the surface of the water. Emphasis should also be placed on the ease and the simplicity of swimming. In addition, the learners must be impressed with the fact that they will learn if they follow the instructor's directions and if they will try the skills and the new experiences without hesitation. When the instructor has succeeded in getting the beginners to overcome their fear of the water and to have confidence in him or her, a good beginning has been made that can do much toward shortening the learning process.

Beginner skills and methods of learning them are discussed in the following pages. This information is supplemented by "Games and Stunts for Beginners," which begins on page 36 in this chapter, and in Chapter 16, "Games and Stunts." The games and stunts listed are but a few of those that can be used. They can be adapted to different age levels and new ones can be devised by instructors and their students. The types of games that can be created to help the learning process are limited only by the imagination and creativity of the instructors and the students.

Entering the Water

If there is a gradual slope, ramp, or steps, the learners can wade to about thigh-deep water, scoop water with their hands, and then wet down the arms, chest, neck, and face, thus gradually getting wet all over. At poolside, the same process of getting wet all over gradually can be accomplished by having the class sit on the edge of the pool deck, reach over, and go through the wetting down process. The class should then be shown how to lower themselves into the water, which in some cases may be neck or chin deep. In such cases, some assistance from the instructor or an aide may be advisable.

There are many adjustment activities that can be done if the water is shallow enough. Sitting on the bottom, for example, with their hands placed behind them, the learners may tilt backward slightly and let the legs rise. Still in the same depth water, they may attempt to lean back and submerge the head as far as the ears. They may roll from the back position onto the side and then onto the front position, and may even splash and kick with the legs while turning. They may crawl along the bottom and then add a kicking movement. All of these simple skills should be repeated a number of times, since they help the nonswimmers get the "feel" of the water and give them a feeling of initial accomplishment.

Another activity for nonswimmers is simply walking in water that may be chest or neck deep. This may have to be initiated by having the pupils keep one hand in contact with the side of the dock or the pool or the overflow trough. Next, they should walk without holding onto the side of the pool. In some cases, instructor help and guidance may be advisable. The walking phase should progress to the point where it is done with both arms and hands in the water to assist in maintaining better balance.

Adjustment activities are helpful in many ways. They help make the water more enjoyable for nonswimmers. In addition, they unconsciously involve the learners in a series of simple skills, the performance of which helps them to learn a great deal about adjustment, buoyancy, and body balance.

Listed and described below are some additional teaching suggestions that might be of assistance in working with beginner swimmers:

1. Have the students form a line and hold hands either on the beach or in waist-deep water in a pool (shallower if possible). This will encourage the timid students to participate in the activities to be introduced. The instructor stands between the students and the deep-water area.

2. The instructor, facing the students, walks backward slowly, encouraging the students to follow. The students walk slowly toward chest- or shoulder-depth water and stop. Ask them what they felt during the walk. Have them turn around, link hands, and walk slowly back to shallow water. Repeat two or three times until the students feel comfortable and relaxed. NOTE. Some very fearful students may not participate at first. Don't force them to. Allow them to watch the group activities. Some may join later. Some students will need individual help from an aide or from the instructor during playtime near the end of the session. Do not allow nonparticipating students to wander away from the area.

3. Repeat 2; students walk "out" and "back" without holding hands. Repeat again, increasing the speed of the walk. Talk to the students. Create an atmosphere of fun.

4. Introduce a game such as the "Friendly Dolphin." Have the students form a line in chest-deep water, facing the shore or the shallow end of the pool. Upon a signal from the instructor (Friendly Dolphin), who stands in deeper water, the instructor submerges and the students race toward the shallow end. The instructor swims underwater and tries to touch as many students as possible. This game is a good lead-up activity to getting the students' faces wet.

Breath Control

With the face out of the water, breathing is an instinctive and normal process. Being able to breathe regularly while the face is in the water has to be practiced many times before it becomes instinctive. It should be taught in easy stages with a great deal of practice at every lesson. The process involves breath holding with the face submerged, exhaling underwater through the mouth and nose, bobbing, and finally, rhythmic breathing.

Breath holding that will lead into rhythmic breathing should be introduced early in the learner's experience and should continue to be a regular part of every practice session. The initial objective is to get the nonswimmer to hold the breath comfortably with the face underwater.

The first step is simply to take a normal breath, close the mouth, and slowly lower the head parallel to the water until at least the face and ears are submerged. After raising the face from the water, some students may feel discomfort from water running down the face. These students can use their hands to wipe excess water from the forehead and hair. Blinking the eyes will help to remove the water from them. Rubbing the eyes may lead to irritation. When children are hesitant to take this step, the instructor can have them cup water in their hands and then wash and rinse their faces.

Familiarity with the process in using a home washbasin may help children overcome their initial reluctance. Submerging the face and head should be repeated many times. As soon as possible, the number of seconds that the head stays submerged should be gradually increased.

The next step is to learn how to exhale in the water. Learners can practice by inhaling, compressing the lips, and forcibly exhaling in a manner similar to blowing out a candle. Blowing bubbles using a slower exhalation tends to give better control, stresses breathing out through the mouth, and keeps water from entering the mouth. While some air may be exhaled through the nose, emphasis should be on exhaling through the mouth.

Bobbing is introduced after the students are able to raise the head to breathe and then to exhale comfortably and slowly with the face submerged. The students can be paired off to practice bobbing. Facing each other and holding hands in waist- to chest-deep water, one partner takes a breath, submerges, and exhales. When this partner stands up to get a breath, the other partner submerges and exhales. Playing "teeter-totter" adds enjoyment to the learning process. Students can practice bobbing by holding onto the overflow trough. Through practice, the students should learn to breathe comfortably at least 25 times while bobbing up and down in a rhythmic pattern.

Seeing Underwater

Interspersed with breath-control skills is practice in opening the eyes underwater. The beginner has a tendency to keep the eyes tightly closed, but experience will quickly prove that one is able to see quite well underwater and even enjoy it. Vision may be somewhat blurred; however, exercises, such as counting the extended fingers (underwater) of a partner and locating and retrieving objects in shallow water, will help the learner to adjust. For convenience, balance, orientation, and **safety,** keeping the eyes open when the face is underwater is a must. Use of a properly fitted face mask or eye goggles will help timid students to overcome their reluctance to open their eyes underwater.

Hearing Underwater

Rounding out the physical and mental adjustment skills is learning that sounds can be heard underwater. Sounds from a motorboat can alert skin and scuba divers to possible danger and can prevent them from surfacing into the path of the boat. Synchronized swimmers often rely on listening to music from underwater speakers to help them perform their routines properly. Hearing underwater can be introduced to the students by having them submerge and by having the instructor clap two pieces of metal together underwater, or the instructor can also submerge and exhale forcibly through the mouth. The students can play a game by pairing off, submerging, opening their eyes, and blowing bubbles at each other.

RHYTHMIC BREATHING

Rhythmic breathing is simply breathing in series or in specific rhythm — inhaling through the mouth as the face turns to the side and starting to exhale underwater as the face turns downward. Adequate ventilation of the lungs at regular intervals is vital to continuous swimming, and breathing practice should be started early in the learning process and continued at every opportunity. The aim is to get the learners to perfect the rhythmic breathing cycle until they can continue for 5, 10, 20, 30, 40, or even 50 times without stopping and still get adequate ventilation.

Rhythmic breathing can be practiced while doing kicking drills with the body in a bracketed position, while kicking with one arm extended to the front or with both arms at the side while using a fluid drill, or when synchronized with the arm actions of the beginner stroke or the crawl stroke. Most beginners find it easier to learn this skill initially by using a stationary drill in shallow water. The students should practice in the prone position as soon as possible, since there may be little transfer of learning from a standing or crouching position to moving through the water in the prone position.

Standing in chest-deep water, the learners lean forward and place the side of the face in the water so that the ear is submerged. They then inhale quickly through the mouth and begin to exhale as the head rotates to the facedown position. They continue to exhale slowly as the head reaches the facedown position and as the head rotates back to its original position. The final bit of air is exhaled as the mouth clears the water, another breath is taken, and the cycle is repeated. Rhythmic breathing is practiced first on one side for a few cycles and then on the other side. The learners will soon determine which is their natural breathing side. The breathing should be in a continuous, rhythmic sequence.

Practice at home can be done by using a large wash-basin or a tub of water placed on the floor or on the ground. Additional practice can occur when taking a shower, by turning the face away from the stream of water and inhaling and then exhaling while the water is directed over the head and face.

Many of the common faults of rhythmic breathing and corrective suggestions for them are found in Chapter 8, "Analyzing and Teaching Basic Swimming Strokes."

BUOYANCY, BODY POSITION, AND RELAXATION

Many of the skills that the learners have been practicing from the time of their first entry into the water have given them some feeling of the lifting effect of the water. The floating and body position skills should prove to the learners that water will support them with little or no effort.

The majority of beginners initially believe that it is necessary to stroke continually with the arms and the legs to keep from sinking. Every effort should be made to dispel this belief. Success in this regard can be accomplished by constant emphasis and practice of breath control, relaxation, and body position. As soon as the learners experience the effect of the body's natural buoyancy, they are ready to start adding the stroking movements that can result in moving through the water as opposed to the effort expended toward trying to prevent sinking.

Prone Float

Shallow water of from 2 to 2½ feet in depth is ideal for learning the prone float. Lying extended in a prone position and supported by having their hands on the bottom, the learners take a breath, place the face in the water, and slowly lift the hands from the bottom and extend the arms in front of the head. If the toes are still on the bottom, a **gentle push** will usually raise them toward the surface, allowing the whole body to be suspended in a prone float position. Learners who are leg heavy will find that their legs will slowly sink until the feet touch the bottom. The instructor should explain to them that they will find their balanced floating position after practicing in deeper water. Emphasis is placed on having the students fill their lungs with air and then relaxing in the floating position.

The prone float may also be taught by having the learners crouch in chest-deep water until the shoulders are submerged. The arms are extended to the front, a breath is taken, the face is placed in the water, and the learners **gently** push from the bottom or the side of the pool into a prone float position. The **slight** push from the side or the bottom may help the less buoyant learner to achieve the feel of the prone floating position.

Recovery from the prone float to a standing position is accomplished by drawing the knees under the body, pushing the arms downward, and, when the body has shifted from the horizontal to the vertical, straightening the legs, lifting the head, and standing up. Use of a partner helps the beginner to gain confidence in the initial learning stage. Most students will be able to stand up easily following a demonstration by the instructor of the recovery to a standing position. This recovery is learned rapidly when the students are learning to float while holding onto the overflow trough. They draw their knees toward the chest, pull their body toward the wall as the head lifts and the hips drop, and then they place their feet on the bottom and stand up.

The overflow trough in a pool can be used very effectively in learning the prone float. In chest-deep water, the students face the wall, crouch until the shoulders are in the water, place the fingers on the trough, take a breath, and place the face in the water with the arms straight, and fully extend the body and the legs away from the wall. The students stand when a breath is needed. Repeat this exercise several times with the students gradually increasing the time the breath is held. Emphasize total relaxation while floating. The students should learn to float nonsupported as rapidly as possible by gently pushing away from the wall once the float position is achieved.

To help overcome the fear of those students who are reluctant to have their feet come off the bottom, the instructor can use the following technique: Grasp the student's outstretched hands lightly and pull him or her across the water slowly. Repeat and gradually reduce the amount of hand contact until the instructor can let go and the student floats or glides unaided. Talk to the student during these exercises. Remind the student to relax his or her body and the grip on your hands. Tell the student when you are going to release hand contact and that you are there to assist if help is needed. Keep the student's trust and confidence in you.

Jellyfish Float

This floating position can be helpful to beginners in learning about the buoyant effect of the water and it can also be a basic starting skill for learning the prone float. Since the jellyfish float employs a facedown and totally relaxed body position, it is a fundamental skill for survival floating.

From a standing position in about chest-deep water, the learners bend forward and place the hands comfortably on the thighs. They then take a breath and bend further forward from the waist until the face is submerged. The hands then slide down the legs close to the ankles. If this is done slowly and in a relaxed manner, the feet will usually float free of the bottom, and the body will be floating with a portion of the back or the head showing above the water. As the skill is mastered, the arms and the legs hang suspended and relaxed in this position. To regain footing, the learners slowly raise the head and the upper body toward

the surface, allowing the feet to settle on the bottom. Emphasis must be placed on moving slowly, and the learners should not attempt to stand until the feet are securely placed on the bottom and the body is balanced over them. A partner or the instructor should be standing by during the learning process to help the beginners gain confidence and to assist them to stand if help is needed.

To go from the jellyfish float to the prone float, the learners slowly raise the arms forward and extend the legs backward until the body is in a fully extended prone position. Recovery to the standing position is accomplished using the procedures previously discussed under "Prone Float."

Prone Glide

The prone glide is a very important fundamental skill and should be mastered. Learning the proper body position in the prone glide contributes greatly to the students' establishment of a proper body position for strokes performed in the facedown position. To perform this skill, the students inhale, place the face in the water, and push off from the side of the pool or the dock. During the glide, the arms are stretched and extended forward of the head with the thumbs touching, the head is submerged to about the hairline, and the legs are straight and together, with the toes pointed.

Continued practice, with emphasis on longer breath holding and a more vigorous push-off, will result in a glide of several body lengths with ease. Good head position and a streamlined body position should be continually emphasized in the practice sessions. Using terms, such as "make yourself long," or "look like a long, slender log" will help the students to develop the desired streamlined position.

Back Glide

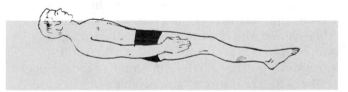

Learning correct body position for the back glide should be mastered by beginners, since efficient stroking on the back depends, to a great extent, on correct body position.

In chest-deep water, the learners crouch and submerge until the shoulders are in the water. They lie back, place their ears in the water, and then push off easily and glide on the surface with the arms at the sides. The face is parallel to the water or the chin is tucked slightly, depending on the buoyancy characteristics of the learner. The glide is taken with the body in the streamlined position.

The learners recover to the standing position when the momentum from the glide ends. To recover to a standing position, the student draws the knees toward the chest, tucks the chin, and draws the head forward. When the head is over the hips, the student places the feet on the bottom, lifts the head, and then stands. Sweeping the arms forward while standing will help the student to maintain good balance.

Some students will attempt to push off too hard during the initial learning, which can cause water to wash over the face. Others may push off with the head extended backward, which can cause the head and the upper body to plane under the water. Others may fail to straighten the body following the push-off and will glide with the body in the sitting position, which creates added frontal resistance. Other students may glide with the legs apart or with the arms away from the sides. All of these potential problems are easily recognized and corrected by instructors.

As practice continues and the learners improve, they will be able to push off a little more vigorously to increase the length of the glide.

PROPULSIVE MOVEMENTS

Prone Glide With Kick

The description and learning procedures for the flutter (crawl) kick combined with the prone glide are found in Chapter 8, "Analyzing and Teaching Basic Swimming Strokes," in the section on the beginner stroke. Common faults and corrective techniques for this kick are discussed in the section on the crawl stroke, which is in the same chapter.

Back Glide With Kick

After learning the back glide, the students add the flutter (crawl) kick on the back. The description, learning techniques, common faults, and corrections for this kick on the back are found in Chapter 8, "Analyzing and Teaching Basic Swimming Strokes," in the section on the back crawl stroke.

Arm Stroke and Breathing in the Prone Position

The arm actions, breathing, and coordination of the beginner stroke and the crawl stroke are covered in detail in Chapter 8, "Analyzing and Teaching Basic Swimming Strokes."

Arm Stroke on the Back

An easy and efficient arm action for most beginners to learn on the back first is called winging. From the glide position, with the arms fully extended along the sides of the body, the recovery is made by drawing the fingertips up along the sides of the body to about the lowest ribs. The fingertips extend outward, and the hands push outward and then backward simultaneously in a circular motion toward the feet, ending with the arms in the glide position.

The recovery movements are done slowly, followed by a more vigorous pushing action of the hands. The arm action is practiced in conjunction with the back glide, with the student nonsupported or supported by a flotation aid attached to the body. The inhalation should occur during the recovery of the arms and the exhalation during the pressing actions of the arms, since this breathing pattern is the same as for the elementary backstroke.

Combined Stroke on the Back

From the back glide, the learners start the leg action and then add the winging movement of the arms. Since there is no breathing problem as long as correct head and body positions are maintained, this beginner's stroke on the back is easily coordinated.

Continued emphasis should be placed on making all movements as easy and relaxed as possible so that the learners will maintain a comfortable, proper body position and will be able to make some progress through the water. This is a valuable resting stroke for beginners, since it enables them to stay afloat, breathe freely, and move easily through the water, all with a minimum of effort.

PERSONAL SAFETY

Turning Over

When the learners can swim on the front and on the back, an important safety skill is the ability to change from one position to the other with ease. Students should learn to rotate the body to both the left and right sides when turning over from the front onto the back, and from the back onto the front. Turning over should be performed confidently with good form in water of approximately chest depth before it is done in deep water.

To turn onto the back while swimming the crawl stroke or beginner stroke, the body must rotate 180° on its long axis. To initiate the turnover, the swimmer stops stroking and turns the head away from the forward extended arm. A breath is taken as soon as the mouth clears the surface of the water. The head continues to turn followed by the body and the other arm turning in the same direction. At the completion of the turnover, the arms are either alongside of or extended outward from the sides of the body, the head is back with the ears in the water, and the hips are near the surface. During the turnover, the arms are kept under the surface. The weight of an arm that is lifted from the water will press the body downward, which will upset the desired body position. Once on the back the student may float or resume swimming using any known stroke on the back.

Instructors must emphasize the importance of the students getting a breath quickly and keeping their hips near the surface while turning. Students who assume a sitting position at the completion of the turnover may not be able to get another breath when needed. This can create difficulties for beginner students in deep water.

Turning over from the back to the front is performed as follows: If, for example, the learners wish to turn over to the left, they take a breath and hold it, rotate the head to the left, draw the right arm across the chest, and the body will rotate in the desired direction. As soon as the turnover is completed, they reach forward with one arm and start stroking to maintain a horizontal body position. Turning onto the front can be practiced from the back float, the back glide, and while swimming the combined stroke on the back.

Changing Direction

Changing direction is a simple but important safety skill for beginners. While swimming the beginner stroke or the crawl stroke, the learners reach in the direction that they want to go with the forward arm and turn the head in the same direction. Repeated stroking enables them to make a simple, wide turn. Continued practice will enable them to shorten the turn, which should be practiced in either direction. Some students learn to change directions quickly and safely by merely swimming, stopping, spinning around, and resuming stroking. Beginners must be able to change directions confidently in chest- to neck-deep water before trying it in deeper water.

Leveling Off From a Vertical Position

Getting into the horizontal position from the vertical position is a safety skill that should be mastered before the learners are allowed to jump into or to swim in deep water.

The skills involved can readily be learned by following a simple sequence of steps. First, standing in neck-deep water, the learners lean slightly forward and, with a minimum push against the bottom, swim to the horizontal position and continue on to shallower water.

Next, standing in neck-deep water, the learners sink under the surface and lean forward slightly. They place the head between the arms, which are extended to the front, then push off **gently** from the bottom, and kick and pull the body diagonally up to the surface using the arm and leg actions of the beginner stroke. They continue to swim for a few feet after reaching the surface.

Finally, under good supervision, the learner swims out into deep water, stops kicking, allows the feet to sink until the body is in a vertical position, then swims to a horizontal position, and continues to the edge of the pool or to shallow water. Repeat this drill several times to enable the learners to gain confidence in their ability to level off into the prone position. For purposes of safety, only one student per instructor should perform these skills in deep water.

Jumping Entry Into the Water

The methods of teaching beginners to jump into deep water are contained in Chapter 11, "Analyzing and Teaching Entries Into the Water."

Summary

The majority of teaching by Red Cross instructors occurs in the Beginner and Advanced Beginner courses. It is very important that beginner students learn to perform the skills well that are discussed or referred to in this chapter, since they provide the foundation for more complex skills. These skills should be learned through the use of appropriate games as much as possible. Remembering the Commodore's advice to "Keep the fun in fundamentals" contributes to an enjoyable learning experience and helps to motivate students to want to continue instruction. Instructors should make every effort to encourage their students to continue instruction beyond the beginner level, since students who pass the Beginner course are, after all, only reasonably safe while in, on, or around the water.

GAMES AND STUNTS FOR BEGINNERS

On the following pages are listed and described some games and stunts to use with the students in order to prepare them for learning to swim. The first series of games and stunts can be used for getting the students adjusted to the water.

Adjustment to the Water

- **The Friendly Dolphin** — The class stands in line, side by side, facing the dolphin (the instructor). The students walk slowly forward, turn, and run to the starting point when the dolphin swims underwater to catch them.
- **Dodge Ball** — The players choose sides. Group one forms a large circle around group two in the shallow end of the pool. The players in the outside circle have one or two volley balls or water polo balls, with which they attempt to hit the players in the middle of the circle. The players within the circle may walk, swim, or duck under the water to avoid being hit. As soon as a player is hit with the ball, he must join the outside circle and assist in hitting the players within the inner circle. When all have been hit, the groups change places and repeat the activity. The last two players to be hit in the game are captains and get to choose up sides for the next contest.
- **Poison Frog Relay** — The group joins hands in a circle. A floating object is put in the center of the ring to serve as "poison." As soon as the whistle is blown, all pull and try to pull another person into the "poison." Anyone touching it must either drop out or stay in to serve as "additional poison." Each time a player is "poisoned," the ring is reformed and the play is continued until there are a designated few (usually six) left in the circle. They become the winners. No ducking is allowed. Players who break the grip when the "poison" is about to touch them are "poisoned" by rule of the referee.
- **Follow the Leader** — The group is divided into sets of two and the partners hold hands and walk, jump, or hop while going forward and backward in waist-deep water. This can be done by following the leader (instructor or student).
- **"Ring Around the Rosey" or "Mulberry Bush"** — The students form a circle, hold hands, and then circle and bob while singing or chanting. Place three or four students inside a hula hoop and play "Ring Around the Rosey."

Breath Holding; Opening the Eyes Underwater

The following games can be used to get the students to place their faces in the water, to exhale underwater, and for "bobbing" and for opening the eyes underwater.

- **Tunnel Ball** — Arrange the class, in chest-deep water, into two ranks with an equal number of students in each. At a signal from the instructor, a volley ball or a soccer ball is passed backward, between the legs, from student to student. The winning rank is the one whose last member receives the ball first.

- **Treasure Hunt** — In waist-deep water, scatter brightly colored objects on the bottom. Ask class members to see how many objects each one can pick up. Repeat several times. Vary the "hunt" by asking certain members to pick up objects of a specified color.
- **Opening Eyes Underwater** — The students spread their legs, take a breath, place their face in the water, wiggle their toes, and open their eyes to see.
  GAME: The students buddy up and one buddy takes a breath, places the face in the water, and opens the eyes while the second buddy extends one to five fingers under the surface for the partner to "count how many."
- **Blowing Ping Pong Balls** — The students blow ping pong balls across the surface of the water from one side of the pool to the other. The instructor can create races between the students.
- **Motor Boat** — The students place their faces in the water, blow, and make a sound like a motorboat. They then lift their heads, inhale, and repeat the exercise. The idea is to see who can produce the loudest motor.
- **Crash Dive** — At a signal from the "captain," the students submerge. The "submarine" who stays underwater the longest becomes the next captain.
- **Indian Dance** — The students circle and chant. At the "chief's" signal, the "braves" submerge and hold their breath.
- **Hula Hoops** — Place about six hula hoops or inflated innertubes next to each other in a straight line. Have some students hold them in place. The remaining students, one by one, duck under and come up through each hoop to breathe. Repeat until all the students have participated. NOTE: Tape or tie the inflation valve of the tube to the tube in order to prevent the students from injuring themselves.

Bobbing and Rhythmic Breathing

- **Jumping Jack** — The purpose is to learn underwater exhaling in a rhythmical fashion, which will be essential later on when learning swimming strokes. Two children hold hands. One jumps up like a jack-in-the-box and takes in a breath, and then squats underwater, exhales, and comes up again. The other child then does the same. Repeat the cycle several times.
- **Ostrich Tag** — This game is an important one, designed to perfect the breathing technique as it will be used in swimming. The children pretend they are ostriches pursued by a hunter who is after their heads. To escape, the "ostriches," standing in chest-high water, lean down and bury their heads in the "sand," which in this case is facedown in the water. Periodically, the "ostriches" have to come up for air to see if the hunter is nearby. Consequently, they turn their faces to the side, take in air, turn back, and exhale. All this must be done in a slow, steady motion like the swinging pendulum of a clock. The hunter, who can

be the instructor or another child, moves among the children trying to tap an ostrich as he comes up for air. A child who is caught becomes the hunter. Practice until the pupils can breathe rhythmically at least 10 times without stopping.

Buoyancy and Floating

- **Underwater Anagrams** — For children old enough to spell three-letter words, this game works wonders in demonstrating buoyancy. Using fingernail polish or water-proof paint, print the letters of easy words, such as CAT, DOG, or BOY, on square asbestos tiles, one letter per tile. Place the tiles facedown on the pool bottom. Let the children take turns flipping the tiles over in an effort to form a word. Score a point for completion of a word and a one-point penalty for misspelling.
  The game is played in waist-deep water. The rules are that no person can squat or bend their knees, but must remain stiff-legged while turning over the tiles. As the students bend at the waist, the water will tend to lift up their feet. Then move the game out to chest-deep water where the students will not be able to touch the tiles, since their feet will come upward. With the legs and the arms dangling and the face in the water, the children are in the jellyfish float position. Just persuade them to relax — "go limp like a jellyfish or an octopus" — and they will be floating.
- **Falling Timber** — While in the jellyfish float, have the children extend their arms and legs straight to position the body like a floating log. Be sure the limbs are close together, for children have a natural tendency to keep them apart.
  Now let them pretend they are falling trees. Standing in at least waist-deep water, they stretch their hands high above the head to represent branches, take a deep breath, and, as a buddy yells "timber," they fall forward into a prone float. The buddies can then give them a gentle push on the feet to make them glide like a log down the river. Be sure the students are not heading toward deep water.
- **"Old Wooden Head"** — The students are asked to imitate "logs." The student who remains a log (prone float) the longest is dubbed "Chief Wooden Head."
- **Floating Items** — Have the students do the prone float, eyes open, while imitating various animals, "leaves on a pond," butterflies, or inflatable toys. Have part of the class pretend that they are driftwood or corks while the rest of the class "picks up" (helps "floaters" recover) the driftwood.
- **Back Float and Recovery (Fainting)** — On land, one partner sits down with the other partner kneeling behind him or her. The instructor talks about fainting, asking the different class members who are in a sitting position to show what they think fainting looks like and telling them that their partner will catch them as they lean back or go into a faint. Have all the students who are seated go into a faint, following the example of the one who demonstrated the best faint by more or less throwing their arms to the side and completely

relaxing. Now have the other partners take their turn at fainting. The class then goes into knee-deep water and goes through the same routine. Call attention to the fact that they go into a floating position on the back as they lean back, relax, and take a deep breath. The class then moves into waist-deep water (shallow water if in a swimming pool). In most swimming pools, the knee-deep water drill would have to be eliminated. Here, the one partner, going into a faint, leans or falls back into the other partner's arms and pretends to go to sleep. The partner will provide support by placing his or her hands under the other partner's armpits or shoulder blades. (The "supporting" partner can help to raise the floater's hips, when necessary, by extending one leg under the floater and nudging the hips upward with the foot.) The partner who is being pulled pretends to be a steamboat. The floater's stomach is the passenger deck, so it has to be kept high. To recover, the floater brings the knees up toward the chest and tucks the chin and draws the head forward to look at imaginary Xs on his or her knees. When the Xs are almost directly below the eyes, the floater places the feet on the bottom, raises the head, and stands. Scooping the arms forward will help the floater to maintain good balance while standing.

Gliding

- **Porpoise Touchball** — The object is to teach the students to glide under their own power. Pretending to be porpoises, they crouch in the water up to their mouths with their hands extended high above their heads. Standing in front of each "porpoise" is another student, holding up a beach ball or a balloon. The "porpoise" springs up and tries to touch the ball. Each touch scores one point. From this game, they can progress to "porpoise football," in which two or more children line up in a crouched position as before. Instead of jumping upward, they spring forward and do a prone glide through the water to a predetermined goal line. The first one to reach the goal scores a touchdown.
- **Human Surf Board** — The students glide for distance in the prone position.
- **Sea Horse Race (Prone Glide)** — Pair up the students. One student assumes the prone glide position. The partner grasps the "glider's" hands and tows him or her across the pool. The instructor can then conduct races across a given area of the pool.
- **Sea Horse Race (Back Glide)** — Pair up the students. The "tower" grasps the partner under the armpits and pulls the "glider" across the pool. Conduct races but avoid the "glider's" face being pulled under the water.
- **Torpedo (Back Glide)** — Pair up the students and have one buddy push the other partner's feet (straight legs) for a glide.

Kicking

- **Steamboat (Prone Position)** — Explain how a steam-

boat has a paddle wheel that pushes it through the water. Pretend that the children are steamboats lined up at a dock. They grasp the side of the pool with their hands, their legs extended out in the water. Have them move their legs up and down slowly and alternately, keeping them straight but not stiff. Bending the knees too much, however, reduces leg power.

One child now becomes a tugboat that tows the steamboat away from the harbor into waist-deep water. All the time the child keeps kicking. Eventually, the tugboat turns back and the steamboat proceeds on its own, doing what is known as the prone glide and kick.

"A steamboat must take on more fuel in order to keep moving and people must take in air to keep them going." With this statement, the instructor can introduce the idea of combining rhythmic breathing with the kicking. Have the students practice breathing and kicking at the same time until they can cover at least three to five body lengths. A steamboat race can be run as an incentive.

- **Take a Trip** — The students, in a prone position, visit three or four different stations prearranged by the instructor.
- **Torpedo With a Brain** — The students, in a prone position, go through an obstacle course to reach and "blow up" the instructor.
- **Push of War** — Pair up the students. Facing each other in a prone position, they hold onto opposite ends of a kickboard or ring buoy and start kicking. The one who pushes the other backward first is the winner.
- **Motor Boat** — The students imitate motor boats, first pressing the motor button, usually located in the forehead, before executing the prone kick glide.
- **On the Back** — On land, the students line up in parallel lines, facing one another, about 5 feet apart, and kick inflated balloons to each other, first with one leg and then the other. Then, from a standing position, have a contest to see who can kick the balloon the farthest. Call attention to how they are kicking "up" when kicking the balloon, and how the knee is bent before it starts to kick forward and upward. Have the students relax the leg after it kicks upward. Standing in waist-deep water, they do the same kick. Then have one partner hold the other in a back float position, standing at the head. The student who is floating practices a slow and deliberate backward and upward kick to the surface of the water. To help develop the skill further, conduct relay games with the students holding onto a swimboard or a similar floating device. Remind the students that they are to imitate steamboats and that kicking pushes the water backwards as would the paddle wheel of an old river steamboat.
- **Newspaper/Magazine Race** — The students, on their backs, hold the newspaper or a magazine out

of the water. Kicking a prescribed distance, the
student who reads aloud and "tells the most" wins.

Arm Strokes

- **Touching Fish** — This game is designed to teach the
arm action for the beginner stroke. In waist-deep water,
the students bend forward from the waist and place the
chest in the water. One arm is extended forward of the
body and the other arm is extended behind the body,
just under the surface. The forward hand touches a
"fish" (6 to 8 inches under the water) and then pulls
slightly down and then backward along the side of the
body with the arm bent. As the arm starts to pull, the
other arm bends and is drawn forward underwater to
touch a "fish." Repeat with an alternating arm action,
touching a "fish" each time. Have the students walk and
pull themselves across the pool, first with their faces out
of the water and then with their faces in the water. Add
rhythmic breathing to one side. Next, the students practice the arm movements and then coordinate the arm
movements with the breathing, after pushing off into a
prone glide. Finally, they add the kick. NOTE. **Emphasize arm action** with (1) the palm of the hand almost
straight and the fingers together during the pull, (2) the
arms and the hands staying beneath the surface, (3) the
hands pulling back to the thighs, and (4) the arms
reaching forward to a fully extended position.
- **Wheelbarrow Race** — With this game, the students
can test their new beginner stroke. One student,
pretending to be a farmer, holds the legs (underwater)
of another student who is the wheelbarrow. The
wheelbarrows propel themselves by using the arm
actions of the beginner stroke, slowly at first, like
farmers sneaking softly through the field to avoid
Indians. Later, as they become more proficient, races
between teams can be held.
- **Touch Relays** — The pupils swim to certain objects,
touch them, and return to the starting point.
- **Out of Water Recovery** — This should be optional
and only for those students who can do a better than
average beginner stroke. Other students should continue practicing the beginner stroke.

  The instructor asks, "Have you seen the sun come
up in the morning? It goes across the sky and, ping,
goes down in the evening." The instructor's hand
represents the sun. Standing in waist-deep water and
bent forward from the waist with one arm extended
behind the body, the instructor lifts the hand out of
the water and then places it in the water forward of
the body. "Have you noticed, just before the sun comes
up, it gets light. What is that? ("Daybreak,") "That's
right. And right after the sun goes down, it stays light
a little while. This is called twilight. Now, let's pretend
the elbow is the light before the sun comes up and
just after it goes down." The instructor demonstrates
the high elbow lift to bring the hand (sun) out (the
hand stays below the elbow) and demonstrates the
hand reaching forward in a small arc, then going in the
water with the elbow following. "Now, let's all bend
over and try it with one arm, several times first, then

with the other arm. Now, alternately, one hand is
the sun, the other the moon. We are now ready to
have one partner go into a prone float while the other
partner holds the legs as in a wheelbarrow race."
The student in the prone position practices the arm
stroke slowly and deliberately with the elbow high
on recovery.

- **Row, Row, Row Your Boat** — Sing the tune while
winging on the back. Add a kick for a coordinated
stroke on the back.
- **Battleship** — The position of the ship in port is
explained to be on the back looking for airplanes.
The ship leaves port and starts its engines by kicking.
After the "Fleet" is underway, the students add winging
for more speed.

Turning Over

- **Log Rolling (Prone Position)** — The students push
off into a prone glide and roll over onto the back
(don't lift the head). Repeat and add extending the
arms out to the sides and floating on the back. Push
off into a prone glide and then roll over twice to the
right and then twice to the left. A game suggestion
is **Destroyer.** Look for jet airplanes while on the
back and then look for atomic submarines while
on the front.
- **Log Rolling (Back Position)** — Use variations of the
above games. During the roll over to the left (or
right) onto the front, emphasize bringing the arms
forward of the head in order to start swimming in
the prone position.

Changing Direction

- **Merry Mix-up** — The instructor starts all contestants
from the same point. The objective is to swim to a
point 25 yards away. The group starts off with the
beginner stroke or the crawl stroke. At one blast of
the whistle, the group reverses directions; 2 short
blasts, they roll over and do the combined stroke
on the back; and 3 short blasts, they do the beginner
stroke or the crawl stroke. It will prove to be a lot of
fun, especially if the contestants end up back where
they started from instead of at the finish line.
- **Changing Direction** — "Did you ever see a dog
chase its tail and go around in a circle? You don't want
to go in a circle, but you may want to change the
direction in which you are going. If so, you do some-
thing like a dog. We humans turn our heads to the
way we want to go and make our arms go in the same
direction. Or let's pretend we are riding a bicycle and
want to make a turn. We put out our hand the way
we are going to turn, then turn the handle bar that
way." Demonstrate by putting the right hand out in
front of the body and pulling it to the side and backward, which causes the body to turn to the left.

Leveling Off

- Under the supervision of the instructor or an aide,
the students (one at a time) walk out to neck-deep
water, turn, and face shallow water. With a very little
push from the bottom, the students swim to the prone

position and continue swimming back to shallow water.

- **Follow the Leader** — The leader swims to water about 6 feet deep, comes to a vertical position, tries to touch an object on the bottom with the toes, and then levels off and swims back to the starting point.

Jumping Into Chest-Deep Water

- **Christen the Ship** — The instructor taps a pupil on the shoulder to "launch" him or her, and then the pupil jumps into the water, pushes off from the bottom, and glides for a distance.

Introduction to Deep Water and Leveling Off

- **Down Periscope, Up Periscope** — Jumping (or diving) into deep water can be preceded by having the students push themselves underwater (down periscope) by using the pool ladder and then climbing

back up the ladder (up periscope) to get a breath. The student inhales and submerges on the instructor's signal. The instructor may also go down to watch the student's efforts and to provide confidence to the student. (This game is practiced with a one-to-one student-teacher ratio.) The student should have the eyes open underwater. As the student's confidence builds, add the following:

- "Climb" down at least three rungs of the ladder, then climb back to the surface.
- From underwater, the student lets go of the ladder and floats to the surface. Repeat this exercise two or three times.
- Repeat the above, and then have the student pull and kick his or her body into a horizontal position on the surface (back and/or front).

CHAPTER 8

ANALYZING AND TEACHING BASIC SWIMMING STROKES

"Water Unlocks Inhibitions!"
The Commodore

BEGINNER STROKE

The objective of the American Red Cross Beginner course is to equip the beginner swimmer with basic water safety skills and knowledge in order to make the individual reasonably safe while in, on, or about the water. The skills contained in the Beginner course provide the foundation for learning more complex swimming strokes.

The beginner stroke is an important skill in helping to meet the above objective. This stroke is not the old "dog paddle" or "human stroke." It is essentially the crawl stroke with an underwater recovery of the arms. By keeping the arms underwater, most of the common problems the beginner has in attempting to learn the crawl stroke are overcome. These problems are —

- Establishing and maintaining a good body position.
- Learning effective rotary rhythmic breathing.
- Learning to relax and to conserve energy.
- Developing good stroking coordination.

The beginner stroke is less complex than the crawl stroke and is easier to learn. This is especially true for young individuals whose neuromuscular abilities inhibit the learning of complex motor skills and for older adults who have limited flexibility in their joints, especially in the shoulders.

Some students who enroll in a Beginner course can already perform the crawl stroke with varying degrees of proficiency. It may not be necessary for all of these students to learn the beginner stroke, since they will be able to improve the crawl stroke through additional instruction and practice; however, some of these students may be able to improve the crawl stroke more rapidly after learning the beginner stroke. Experience will dictate to the instructor which approach will be best for these students.

Breathing rhythmically to the side in the crawl stroke is the single most difficult part of any swimming stroke for most swimmers to master. Ideally, this method of breathing should occur in the beginner stroke, and the beginner swimmer should strive to become reasonably comfortable and proficient in performing rotary rhythmic breathing. However, because of the great difficulty in mastering this form of breathing, it is permissible for the beginner swimmer to perform rhythmic breathing by lifting the face forward to inhale, then lowering the face into the water to exhale. The student should strive to keep the chin at or near the waterline during inhalation in order to keep the body as horizontal as possible.

In summary, the beginner stroke affords the beginner swimmer a good opportunity for survival in an aquatic emergency situation, since this stroke provides effective forward movement with a lesser degree of energy use than may be expended while using the crawl stroke. These benefits are vital in helping to meet the objectives of the Red Cross Beginner course, especially the objective "to make the individual reasonably safe while in the water."

Body Position

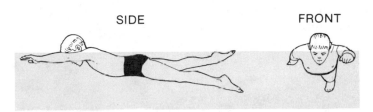

SIDE · FRONT

The body is in the prone position, nearly horizontal to the surface of the water. The body is straight, the head is aligned with the body, and the hips and the legs are positioned just below the surface of the water. The body and the head will roll slightly from side to side to allow for an easier and more effective inhalation and for more effective propulsive movements of the arms.

Leg Action

SIDE

The leg action is commonly called the flutter kick, which is an alternating up and down movement of the legs. The action of the legs provides some forward propulsion, but serves mainly to stabilize and to balance the body. The legs are kept almost straight and the ankles and the feet should be relaxed. The lifting and the lowering of the legs originates at the hips. The legs and the feet are kept under the surface at all times. A more detailed description of the flutter kick is found under "Crawl Stroke (Leg Action)," page 47.

Arm Action

All movements of the arms are performed underwater and in opposition to each other. As one arm is recovering, the other arm is pulling. When properly coordinated, the swimmer is constantly sliding forward on one extended arm while the other arm is pulling and pressing backward.

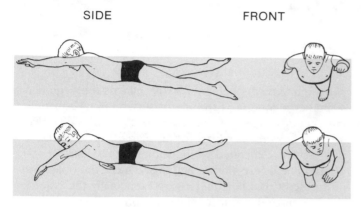

SIDE   FRONT

The arm action starts with one arm extended forward of its shoulder and the other arm extended backward along the side of the body. As the forward hand starts to pull, the opposite hand begins to recover.

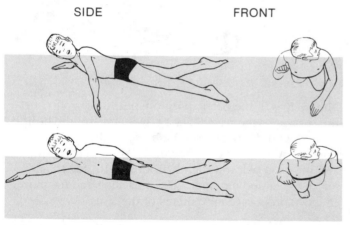

SIDE   FRONT

The palm of the hand and the forearm press backward along the midline of the body to about the thigh. During this action, the arm is bent and the elbow is kept higher than the hand but lower than the shoulder. The opposite arm recovers by lifting the elbow slightly as the hand is drawn forward along the side of the body. As the hand nears the armpit, the elbow drops slightly, and the fingers lead the arm to a fully extended position forward of its shoulder.

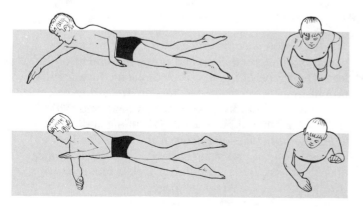

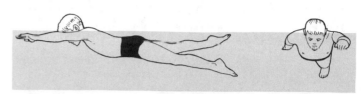

After reaching full extension, the hand immediately starts its pulling action as the opposite arm starts to recover.

Breathing

SIDE   FRONT

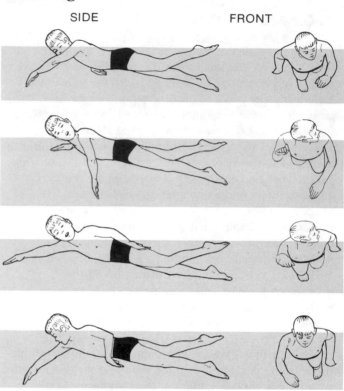

Breathing may be performed in more than one way. Ideally, rhythmic breathing occurs on one side of the body only. The head begins to rotate slowly toward the arm on the breathing side as it starts its pulling action. The head continues to rotate until the mouth is clear of the water, and inhalation begins when the arm on the breathing side is about halfway through its pressing action. At the completion of this pressing action, the arm starts its recovery and the face rotates back into the water. Exhalation begins as the face enters the water, and is slow and continuous and is completed when the next breath is ready to be taken.

Ideally, one breath should be taken and exhaled during each complete stroke cycle. However, because of the difficulty in mastering rhythmic breathing, it is acceptable for the beginner swimmer to breathe at least every two to three strokes.

A breath may also be taken by lifting the mouth just clear of the water as the forward extended arm begins to pull. As soon as a breath is taken, the face is placed back into the water and exhalation occurs as described for rotary rhythmic breathing. A disadvantage of this method of breathing is that lifting the head causes the hips and the legs to drop, which upsets good body position.

Coordination

During the arm and breathing actions, the legs maintain a fairly continuous flutter kick. The number of kicks can vary from two to six during each complete cycle of the arms.

BEGINNER STROKE

Suggested Learning Approaches

Whole Approach — Students are supported by wearing a PFD or another supporting device, such as inflatable arm bands, or are suspended from improvised water wings positioned in the upper chest area. NOTE. Although not mandatory, it is recommended that most students first become physically and mentally adjusted to the water.

1. Explain/demonstrate the stroke, with emphasis on several slow motion demonstrations with the head up and the mouth free of the water.

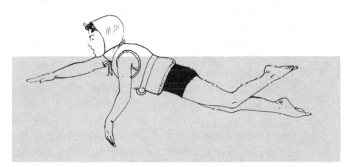

2. The students practice, starting with the head-up position to allow for easy breathing. Introduce the facedown breathing patterns after the students have gained confidence and are making reasonably good progress through the water. The chin may be lifted or the head rotated to the side for the inhalation. **Stress** slow, steady exhalation with the face in the water. Practice opening the eyes under the water during the exhalation.

3. Gradually reduce the amount of flotation (i.e., PFD to improvised water wings) **until the students are ready to swim without a supportive aide.** The students should learn to inhale, preferably to the side, at least every two to three strokes.

Progressive-Part Approach — Introduce this approach after the students have learned the prone float and the prone glide.

1. **Leg Action**
   (a) Explain/demonstrate the kick while bracketed to the side of the pool or the dock and while in a prone glide position. **Stress** keeping the legs almost straight and using the hips and the thighs to initiate the upward and downward movements.

   (b) The students, in the prone glide position and using a supporting aid to the upper back area, kick as far as possible with the mouth clear of the water to permit easy breathing. Correct major errors as necessary. Repeat the kicking practice until most of the students are making fairly good progress through the water.

   (c) The students, supported as in (b), add breathing to kicking. Have the students rotate (preferred) or lift the head and inhale while continuing to kick. The students breathe as often as necessary, and practice slow exhalation underwater. Repeat the drills to improve stamina, endurance, kicking mechanics, and breathing patterns.

   (d) The students, arms extended to the front, practice kicking and breathing, with or without the use of a swimboard as a supportive aid. All final practice is done without a supportive aid.
   NOTE. After learning the prone glide, many students are ready to learn and practice the kick without the use of a supportive aid. Also, some instructors may choose a learning approach involving the following steps:
   (1) An explanation/demonstration of the kick.
   (2) The students practice while bracketed to the side of the pool or the dock.
   (3) The students push off into a prone glide, hold their breath and kick until a breath is needed (do not hold the breath too long), stop, stand and inhale, and push off and resume kicking. Repeat as often as necessary until the leg action is satisfactory.
   (4) Repeat the drill, adding rhythmic breathing to the side (preferred) or have the students lift their heads to breathe. Stress slow, steady exhalation underwater.

Alternative Learning Procedures — The following procedures are also useful for students who are having major problems.

1. **Leg Action**
   (a) The students practice the kick while bracketed to the side of the pool or the dock, or they support their bodies in the horizontal position by placing their hands on the bottom of the shallow water area. The instructor may count out loud rhythmically and have the students kick to the counts.

   (b) The students practice the kick while lying on the deck with the legs extended out over the water. (This drill should be used only as a last resort.)

2. **Arm Actions and Breathing (Student Supported)**
   (a) Explain/demonstrate the underwater action of the arms. Emphasize a long pulling/pressing action of the arms, and drawing and sliding each arm forward to the fully extended position.

   (b) The students, supported by a PFD or an attachable device to the upper back area, practice arm actions while executing a slow, easy flutter kick. The mouth is kept clear of the water to permit easy breathing.

(c) Repeat (b) and add placing the face in the water and performing rhythmic breathing to the side (preferred) or by lifting the face forward to breathe. Have the "problem" student practice lifting the head to breathe and then exhaling underwater until the student can breathe and exhale comfortably at least every second to third stroke. Then have the student practice breathing to the side. NOTE. For rotary rhythmic breathing, have all students practice breathing on one side for a period of time, then practice breathing on the other side. Through continuous, alternate side breathing, each student will learn on which side it is easiest to breathe. Practice until the student can breathe comfortably at least once every two to three strokes.

(d) Repeat (c) with the students nonsupported. Daily practice is needed to improve coordination, breathing patterns, endurance, and confidence.

3. **Arm Actions and Breathing (Student Non-supported)** The instructor may elect to use the following learning sequences and use No. 2, above, for the students who are having difficulty with No. 3.

(a) Use 2(a), above.

(b) The students practice arm movements while holding their breaths with their faces in the water. Using a slow flutter kick, the students stop as often as necessary to breathe and then resume swimming. The students repeat the exercise until the arm movements are satisfactory.

(c) Repeat (b), adding rhythmic breathing. Use procedures in 2(c).

(d) Practice daily to improve the breathing pattern, stroke coordination and relaxation, endurance, and confidence.

Part-Whole Approach — This approach is useful when few or no supportive aids are available for use by the students. It is also useful for the students who are having problems learning any parts of the stroke or the coordination of the stroke using the **Whole** or

Progressive-Part Approaches. Introduce the following skills after the students are mentally and physically adjusted to the water.

1. **Leg Action**

(a) Explain/demonstrate the kick as discussed in the **Progressive-Part Approach.**

(b) The students practice the kick while bracketed to the side of the pool or the dock or by supporting their bodies in the horizontal position by placing their hands on the bottom if the water is shallow enough. The students practice to rhythmic cadence set by the instructor, e.g., "1-2-3-4, 1-2-3-4," or "up-down, up-down," etc. The initial practice can be done with the students' faces in the

water or with their mouths just clear of the water to permit easy breathing. Correct major errors as necessary.

(c) The students practice and improve the kick after pushing off into a prone glide. When a breath is needed, they stop, stand, inhale, push off into a prone glide, and resume kicking. Correct students' errors.

2. **Arm Actions and Breathing**

(a) Explain/demonstrate the arm actions.

(b) The students stand in waist-deep water, bend forward from the waist, and practice the arm stroke, first with their faces just clear of the water and then with their faces in the water, taking a breath whenever necessary by raising their head and then placing their faces back into the water. Their eyes should be open underwater.

(c) Repeat 2(b), above, while slowly walking across the instructional area.

(d) The students push off into a prone glide, add an easy flutter kick, and then the arm stroke. The breath is held with the face in the water. When a breath is needed, the students stop, stand and breathe, and then resume stroking. The instructor corrects arm action errors as necessary. Repeat the practice until the students can swim 20 to 25 feet nonstop, without breathing.

(e) Explain/demonstrate rotary rhythmic breathing (to one side) with the arm action.

(f) The students, with their faces in the water, practice the arm action with rhythmic breathing, using sequences 2(b) and 2(c), above.

(g) The students, preferably with support to the body, first practice the arm actions and breathing with minimal kicking, which will help stabilize a good body position. They then practice the full stroke without support to the body, with emphasis on the arm stroke and breathing. Encourage breathing at least once every two or three strokes. Repeat until all students can swim comfortably and with reasonably good coordination for 40 to 50 feet in water of standing depth.

BEGINNER STROKE

**Common Faults: Cause(s), Effect(s),
Corrective Suggestions
Body Position: See Crawl Stroke, Common Faults
Leg Action: See Crawl Stroke, Common Faults**

Arm Action:

1. **Drops elbow or uses straight arm during initial propulsive movement.** Causes loss of efficient forward propulsion. May also cause upper body to rise from the downward pressing action of hand and forearm. While swimming, body supported or nonsupported, face in water, eyes open, student watches problem arm(s) during first half of arm pull. Student concentrates on bending arm and on keeping elbow higher than hand during pulling action. Use of eye goggles or face mask will help student's vision.

2. **Pressing action of hand backward stops under chest.** This reduces effectiveness of forward movement of body. While swimming, have student concentrate on pushing hand toward feet until thumb touches outside of thigh (left hand, left thigh; right hand, right thigh).

3. **Pulls too far across imaginary longitudinal center line of body.** This can cause excessive body roll and is usually caused by poorly developed rhythmic breathing habits. Student rolls body and head excessively in order to get mouth clear of water to get a breath. During this body roll, arm on nonbreathing side pulls across long axis midline of body. Suggested corrective techniques are: Rotary rhythmic breathing

practice while bracketed to side of pool or dock, similar practice while supported by buddy or by flotation aid to upper part of body, and practice at home in tub of water or in kitchen sink. When taking a shower, practice breathing by turning head away from stream of water to inhale and rotating head back under water to exhale. NOTE. Stress head rotation to side to breathe, with minimal body rotation, in all of the above suggested drills.

4. **Recovers arm with elbow wide of side of body.** This can bring about added frontal resistance from forearm pushing against water. Corrective suggestion is to have student "scrape" inside of upper arm against side of body during initial recovery movements.

Breathing: See also Crawl Stroke, Common Faults

1. **Holds breath; does not exhale underwater.** Use Common Faults (Arm Action), No. 3, with emphasis on exhaling slowly between each inhalation.

2. **During "forward" breathing, lifts head too high.** Upsets body position, and causes hips and legs to sink. Practice "forward" rhythmic breathing while kicking in prone glide position. Emphasize lifting head and jutting lower jaw forward until chin is at waterline.

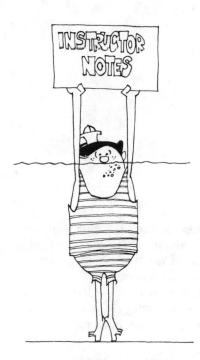

CRAWL STROKE

The crawl stroke is the fastest and one of the most efficient of all swimming stokes. The ability to perform an effective, smooth crawl stroke is a mark of a skilled swimmer. This stroke employs the flutter kick, which is a misnomer, since the legs do not actually flutter up and down. The need to develop a perfect six-beat crawl is no longer given the emphasis it received for many years. The use of two- or four-beat kicks and two- or four-beat cross-over kicks have proved to be very effective in modern day competitive swimming.

Body Position

SIDE   FRONT

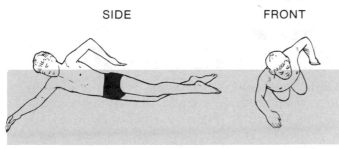

The swimmer is in a prone position, nearly horizontal to the surface of the water. The body is straight, and the hips and the legs are maintained in a position just below the surface at all times. The head is aligned with the body, with the waterline approximately at the hairline, but this position will vary somewhat with individual differences in swimmers. The body and the head will roll from side to side to allow for maximum propelling efficiency of the arms and for effective inhalation and also to permit free and easy recovery of the arms because of reduced frontal resistance.

Leg Action

The leg action is commonly called the flutter kick, which is an alternating up and down movement of the legs. The kick originates from the hips with resultant undulating actions of the lower legs, the ankles, and the feet. The length of the legs and the degree of flexibility in the hips, the knees, and the ankles can affect the range of motion of the legs and the effectiveness of the kick. In the kicking action, a relaxed ankle and foot will produce a toeing-in effect naturally. The toeing-in results from the anatomical structure of the ankle and the foot, the water pressure, and the desired relaxation of the ankle and the foot. Forward propulsion stems from water pressure against the top of the foot on the downward beat and against the bottom of the foot on the upward beat. The leg action contributes significantly to good body balance and stability, in addition to providing forward movement for the body. Over-kicking will simply lead to fatigue and will retard overall stroke effectiveness.

Breathing

SIDE

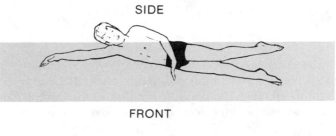

FRONT

The swimmer's head remains in line with the spine throughout the stroke. Inhalation through the mouth occurs when the arm on the breathing side is one-half to three-quarters of the way through its backward pressing action. In order for the mouth to properly clear the water for inhalation, the head must rotate independently of the shoulders.

During inhalation, the cheek opposite the breathing side is nearly flat to the water. With the head properly positioned, and depending on the swimmer's speed, inhalation can actually take place with the mouth just below surface level, in a trough of air that is created by the flow of water about the head. As the arm on the breathing side begins to lift from the water, the head rotates to a facedown position and exhalation begins as the mouth is in the water. Exhalation is through the mouth and the nose and is smooth and continuous until the next inhalation is taken. An inhalation and an exhalation occur during every stroke. Most good swimmers learn to breathe well to one side of the body. It is desirable to learn alternate side breathing for convenience, added safety, to develop a balanced stroke, and to permit the competitive swimmer to more readily observe other contestants during a freestyle race.

Arm Action and Coordination

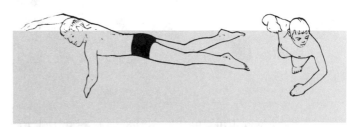

The hand enters the water almost directly forward of its shoulder, fingertips first, thumb side of the hand rotated downward slightly, with the elbow bent and higher than the hand. The opposite arm is about halfway through its pressing action, with a definite bend in the elbow and with the hand under the midline of the body. This arm accelerates to the completion of the pressing action from this position.

The entry hand slides forward and downward to the catch position. When this position is reached, the arm is fully extended, the opposite arm has almost completed its backward pressing action, and the inhalation is almost completed.

From the catch position, the forward arm and hand start to pull backward toward the long axis center of the body. The elbow is kept higher than the hand and lower than the shoulder during propulsive movements. The opposite arm begins to recover when the forward arm starts to pull.

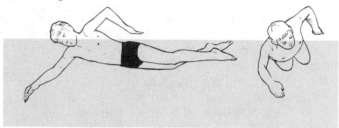

At the completion of the backward thrust of the arm on the breathing side, the elbow is immediately lifted upward and forward out of the water as a continuation of the momentum established from the rounding-off action of the hand. An easy, rolling motion of the body and the shoulders will facilitate the recovery movements of the arms and will contribute to effective propulsive movements. During this recovery action, the lower hand is pulling backward and the amount of bend in the elbow is increasing.

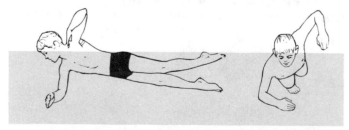

When the lower arm and the hand are pressed back to a point just below and in front of the shoulder, the elbow achieves maximum bend. The palm is kept positioned so as to keep maximum pressure against the water during its entire backward push. The opposite arm is about halfway through its recovery. The forearm and wrist are relaxed and the elbow is higher than the hand, with the hand slightly outside the elbow and near the water.

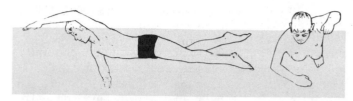

The lower arm begins to accelerate its pressing action backward toward the feet as the opposite arm completes its recovery. As the hand enters the water, the head and the body start their rolling actions onto the side of the entry arm. Except for the inhalation, the arm actions as described above are then performed on the opposite side of the body.

CRAWL STROKE

Suggested Learning Approaches

Whole Approach — Students may be nonsupported or supported by a PFD or a similar flotation device attached over the hips or the abdomen or suspended from improvised water wings placed under the hips or the lower back.

1. Demonstrate the stroke several times in slow motion.
2. The students practice without breathing.
3. The students practice with rhythmic breathing.
   NOTE. Many students will learn the crawl stroke more quickly and with greater ease if they learn the beginner stroke first.

Progressive-Part Approach — This approach is divided into three sequences, each sequence based on the student's prior skill attainment.

1. **Sequence A** This sequence is effective for the students who can perform the beginner stroke satisfactorily, including rhythmic breathing to the side.

   (a) Explain/demonstrate the over-the-water recovery movements of the arm. **Stress** rolling the body and lifting the arm out of the water with the shoulder; keeping a high elbow and a relaxed forearm, wrist, and fingers, and keeping the hand near the water; having the fingers enter the water first in front of the shoulder at about two-thirds arm extension with the elbow slightly higher than the hand; and letting the hand lead the arm to a full extension to the catch position.

   (b) The students practice the beginner stroke and then add (a), above, with no breathing. The students swim three to four crawl strokes while holding their breath, and then stop, stand, take a breath, and repeat the crawl stroke. Keep repeating until the arm actions are reasonably correct. The number of strokes may be increased slightly, but not to the point where the students become uncomfortable while holding their breath.

   (c) Add rhythmic breathing to (b), above. The students breathe on the side that was most comfortable while performing the beginner stroke. **Stress** that the students start rotating their heads to the side as the arm on the breathing side starts to pull, start inhaling when the pulling arm is about halfway through its pressing movement backward, and start exhaling as the face rotates back into the water as the breathing side arm begins to recover.

(d) Provide an opportunity during each lesson for stroke practice, especially for Beginners, Advanced Beginners, and Intermediates. Students at the Intermediate through Advanced Swimmer levels should become proficient in breathing on one side and reasonably proficient in breathing on the other side.

2. **Sequence B** The following suggested procedures are for students who do not know the beginner stroke, but can perform the prone glide with flutter kick. Practice the crawl stroke in shallow water until the students can swim about 20 yards continuously, confidently, and with reasonably good form.

(a) Explain/demonstrate the crawl stroke arm action.

(b) The students inhale, push off into the prone glide, add the kick, and then the arm movements. The students swim until a breath is needed. (Do not encourage holding the breath too long.) The students stop, stand, breathe, and repeat the drill until the arm movements are satisfactory.

(c) Explain/demonstrate arm actions with rhythmic breathing (to the side). Explain that most students find it easier to breathe on one side than on the other.

(d) The students practice the full stroke, breathing to one side for a prescribed distance (i.e., one width), and then breathing on the opposite side. Practice alternating sides (one side for a pre-scribed distance) until the students determine on which side it is easier to inhale.

3. **Sequence C** For use by students who do not know the beginner stroke, but can perform the prone kick glide. It is important that the students complete steps 3(a) through 3(f), which follow. When possible, the students should also complete step 3(g), since this style of swimming provides a more rapid turnover cycle of the arms. The slightly slower turnover rate of the arms in step 3(f) does permit the noncompetitive swimmer to perform the crawl stroke with considerable ease and efficiency.

(a) The students start in the prone glide position with the arms extended forward and hold onto the near edge of a swimboard, seat cushion, or similar flotation aid with both hands. The students hold their breath, place their face in the water, push off from the bottom or the side of the pool, and start kicking (flutter). The students release one hand, reach for the catch, execute propulsive and recovery actions, and grasp the board (entry). The students raise their heads for a breath whenever necessary. The students then repeat the

actions with the opposite arm, and end by grasping the board. Repeat the alternating arm drill until the mechanics of all arm movements are reasonably accurate.

(b) Repeat the above, adding rhythmic breathing to one side. Repeat until the students' breathing patterns are reasonably accurate and they breathe with some degree of comfort. Alternate the breathing sides until the students learn on which side it is easiest to breathe.

(c) Repeat (b), substituting a popsicle stick, or similar aid, for the swimboard. Repeat until the students perform this drill easily. **Stress** that the hand (and arm) grasping the popsicle stick must be kept in a forward, extended position almost directly in front of the head until the opposite hand grasps the stick.

(d) Repeat (c), eliminating the popsicle stick. The recovering hand touches the opposite hand (positioned directly forward of the head) before it starts its pull. Repeat until the students perform this drill with ease.

(e) Modification of (d). A split second before the fingertips of the recovering hand touch the wrist of the opposite arm, the gliding arm starts its pull. The entry of the hand and arm is as described in the stroke description. Through practice, and the instructor's help, the students will develop the "feel" of this "hand-to-wrist" timing. Repeat until the students perform this drill easily and effectively.

(f) Modification of (e). The extended (gliding) arm starts its pull when the recovering hand is passing to the side of the head. Repeat until the students perform the stroke easily, correctly, and smoothly.

(g) Modification of (f). The students start the pull of the forward hand as the opposite hand starts to recover.

Part-Whole Approach — Introduce this approach after the students have learned the prone glide.

1. **Leg Action**

(a) Explain/demonstrate the kick while bracketed to the side of the pool or the dock and/or while in a free-floating prone glide position. Stress keeping the legs almost straight and using the hips and thighs to initiate the upward and downward movements.

(b) Have the students practice the kick while bracketed to the side of the pool or the dock, or by supporting their bodies in the horizontal position by placing their hands on the bottom if the water is shallow enough. Have the students practice to a rhythmic cadence set by the instructor (e.g., "1-2-3-4," "1-2-3-4," or "up-down," "up-down"). The initial practice can be done with the student's face in the water or with the mouth just clear of the water to permit easy breathing. Correct major errors as necessary.

(c) Have the students practice and improve the kick after pushing off into a prone glide. When a breath is needed, they stop, stand, inhale, and then push off into a prone glide and resume kicking. Correct the students' errors. Repeat the kicking practice until most students are making fairly good progress through the water.

(d) Have the students practice the kick while lying on the deck with their legs extended over the water. (This drill should be used **only** with the student who is having great difficulty in learning the kick by using the above procedures.)

2. **Arm Actions and Breathing**

(a) Explain/demonstrate the arm action. Emphasize high elbow recovery with a relaxed forearm, wrist, and hand, and having the fingers enter the water first, forward of their respective shoulder, with the arm almost fully extended and with the elbow slightly higher than the hand.

(b) The students stand in waist-deep water, bend forward from the waist, and practice the arm stroke, first with the face just clear of the water, and then with the face in the water, taking a breath whenever necessary by raising the head and then placing the face back into the water. Their eyes should be open underwater.

(c) Repeat (b), above, while slowly walking across the instructional area.

(d) Have the students push off into the prone glide, add an easy flutter kick, and then the arm stroke. The breath is held with the face in the water. When a breath is needed, the students stop, stand and breathe, and then return to stroking. Correct arm action errors as necessary. Repeat this practice until the students can swim 20 to 25 feet nonstop, without breathing.

(e) Explain/demonstrate rotary rhythmic breathing (to one side) with arm action.

(f) The students, with their faces in the water, practice the arm actions with rhythmic breathing to the side, using sequences 2(b) and 2(c), above.

(g) The students, preferably with support to the body, practice the arm actions and breathing first, with minimal kicking to help stabilize a good body position. They then practice the full stroke without support to the body and with emphasis on the arm stroke and breathing. Through continuous, alternate side breathing, each student will learn on which side it is easiest to breathe. Practice until the students can breathe comfortably at least once every two or three strokes. The students must practice this stroke each class period to improve coordination, endurance, and confidence, and to learn to breathe during every complete stroke.

Suggested Alternative Learning Procedures — The first 4 of the following drills are to be used primarily as basic drills for the student who is having considerable difficulty in overcoming problems using the afore-

mentioned approaches; the remaining 2 drills (Nos. 5 and 6) are to be used with more advanced students.

1. The student stands in waist-deep water, bends forward from the waist with the chest in the water, and practices arm movements with or without rhythmic breathing.

2. The student, bracketed to the side of the pool, practices rhythmic breathing to the side while doing the flutter kick.

3. The student, in a prone position, practices rhythmic breathing to the side while kicking and holding onto a swimboard or similar flotation aid, and with the arms fully extended to the front.

4. The student improves the underwater propulsive movements of the arms for the crawl stroke while swimming the beginner stroke.

5. The student, in a prone position, with the arms at the sides, kicks and practices rhythmic breathing.

6. The student, holding onto a swimboard with one hand, kicks and practices movements of the other arm with or without rhythmic breathing.

Common Faults: Cause(s), Effect(s), Corrective Suggestions

Body Position:

1. **Head is too low in water.** Hips and legs ride too high in water. Feet and lower legs come out of water during kick. Raise head until hairline is about at waterline. Also see **Breathing Faults.**

2. **Head is held too high.** Neck is tense and there is excessive arch in the back, causing legs and feet to drop and causing added frontal resistance. Relax neck by dropping head until waterline is between eyebrow and hairline.

3. **Bending at waist.** Legs and feet will drop, causing added frontal resistance. Emphasize "stretched" body. Tighten stomach muscles. Prone glide with flutter kick, arms extended forward, will help develop feel for correct body position.

4. **Excessive body roll, especially to breathing side.**
(A) May be caused by head being too low in water, forcing swimmer to roll excessively to get breath of air. This can be corrected by raising head.

(B) May be caused by tense neck muscles, head held too high, improper breathing, some fear of having face in water, or fear of not getting face and mouth sufficiently clear of water to get a breath. This can be corrected by lowering head and relaxing neck muscles. Practice rhythmic breathing in shallow water (stationary drills) or fluid drills using supportive device.

(C) May be caused by lack of flexibility in shoulder joints. Lack of body buoyancy in some persons can cause body to ride low in water.

NOTE. Many persons, especially males, will need to roll more than the average swimmer in order to satisfactorily recover their arms or to breathe.

5. **Body too flat to surface of water.** Lack of body roll decreases efficiency of propulsive action and recovery of arms. Have student roll to each side during stroke.

6. **Bobbing up and down.** Upper body is raised by pressing downward with hand and forearm during reach for catch and/or initial stage of propulsive action. Body lowered, especially hips and legs, by pressing upward with hand during final stages of propulsive action. Corrective suggestions include emphasis on "spearing" action of hand and arm from entry to catch position (start pressing action of hand **back toward feet** after catch position is reached); pushing water back toward feet until arm is almost straight. Stationary drills in shallow water will allow student to watch correct propulsive movements of arms and hands.

7. **Body twists when breathing.** Caused by breathing too late or twisting head (and shoulders) to place chin near shoulder. Emphasize keeping head in line with spine. Rotate head so that student looks directly to the side. Use bracket drill or kicking with arms at sides or kicking with nonbreathing side arm extended to front and with other arm extended alongside body.

Leg Action:

1. **Excessive knee bend.** Kicking primarily from knee. Can cause lower leg and foot to come of water. Emphasize kick starting at hip and flowing through knee to foot. Suggested corrections include having student kick with straight legs (very few will actually kick with straight legs, or will soon allow knee to bend slightly because of fatigue) and bracketing swimmer against side of pool or dock. A buddy or aide holds his or her hands just under surface of water and above swimmer's thighs. Swimmer tries to touch aide's hands by lifting thighs while kicking upward. Another suggested correction involves having swimmer lie on one side of the body while holding onto side of pool or while supported by flotation device. Student watches and practices kick as if each leg is kicking a football on its forward movement. Emphasize that hips initiate backward and forward movements of legs. Flutter kicking on the back may be another helpful suggestion.

2. **Uses "bicycle" or "pumping action."** Draws knees forward toward hips, then thrusts feet backward. May be caused by bending at waist. If so, correct body position first. Correct by using drills as in No. 1, above. Also emphasize lifting legs up and breaking surface of water with heels.

3. **Hips wiggle back and forth; "quivering" legs; little or no effective forward movement.** Caused by tense gluteus muscles or tenseness in buttocks. Try to have student relax these muscles. Kicking while lying on one side of body will help. Practice wide, swinging back-and-forth action of legs. Use of swim fins may help.

4. **Irregular rhythm in kick.** Propulsive action of one leg is accented more than other leg. Correct by having aide count in a rhythmic manner or by using words

such as up-and-down and up-and-down, etc. Pupil practices to this rhythm.

5. **Thrash of legs too deep.** Excessive movement downward will cause added frontal resistance. May be caused by a too slow kick. If so, a faster tempo will usually shorten range of movement. Have student practice to cadence set by aide or buddy or have aide or buddy place and keep their hands 3 to 4 inches below swimmer's thighs. (Body and legs must be nearly horizontal to surface of water.) This will prevent swimmer's thighs from going too deep and will help swimmer develop feel of correct depth.

6. **Ankles, knees, and/or hips too tense.** Can cause fluttery, quivering action of legs and an ineffective kick. Practice wide, swinging kick while lying on one side of body. Use of swim fins may help develop flexibility and relaxation in ankles. CAUTION. Over-use of fins may cause cramps in feet or legs.

7. **"Hooking" toes at end of downward beat.** Caused by relaxing or allowing ankle to bend (dorsi-flex). Will negate forward motion and may cause swimmer to go backward. Correct by keeping toes pointed but not to the point of causing tenseness, fatigue, or cramping of feet. Kicking while lying on one side of body will help, since this will allow swimmer to watch action of foot at end of forward (downward) sweep (beat).

Arm Action (Recovery):

1. **Elbows, hands, or fingers drag through the water.** This causes resistance and slowing down of tempo of recovering arm. Correct by lifting elbow higher. (May need more body roll.) Have student roll to each side and look at each arm as it recovers to ensure hand is out of water. Swimmer must also develop feel of flinging hand forward so that there is no delay in recovery.

2. **Tenseness; rigidity in forearm and wrist.** Causes fatigue. Wrist may be bent excessively so that palm of hand faces directly upward. Have student watch each arm during initial recovery movements. Have swimmer shake fingers or shake water off of each arm while it is in air.

3. **Wide, sweeping action of arms.** Causes lateral motion of shoulders and subsequent lateral reaction of hips and legs. Correct by practicing high elbow recovery with relaxed forearm and wrist. Dragging thumb through armpit may help.

4. **Hands cross imaginary centerline of body for entry.** Causes twisting of shoulders and lateral sway (reaction) of hips and legs. Also causes negative, sideward action of hand from entry point back to respective side of body, prior to starting effective propulsive action. **Corrective suggestions:**

(a) Student swims and endeavors to enter left hand at 10:00 o'clock or 11:00 o'clock or right hand at 1:00 o'clock or 2:00 o'clock. (Student pretends to reach for and to grasp a $5 bill, an apple, etc.)

(b) It may be helpful to have student raise head

slightly, keep eyes open while underwater, and observe point of entry of hand.

(c) Have student stand in waist-deep water, bend forward from waist, eyes out of water, and watch as problem arm(s) is placed back in water at end of recovery. Hand should enter water at a point forward of and between respective cheek and shoulder.

5. **High, vertical, straight arm recovery.** Causes tenseness of arm, wastes energy, and may cause entry of forearm before hand. Use corrective techniques as for Nos. 1 and 2.

6. **Elbow or forearm enters water first.** Usually caused by over-reaching and by dropping elbow or shoulder or by bending wrist and elevating hand just prior to entry. All of these actions prevent hand from reaching catch position quickly. Correct by keeping elbow slightly bent and higher than hand upon its entry. Full extension of arm takes place **underwater.** Have swimmer imagine that forearm is the shaft of a spear and that fingertips are the point of the spear. Fingertips (point of spear) enter water first, followed by rest of arm (shaft of spear).

7. **"Smashing" arm or hand into water at entry.** Creates air bubbles under surface. Entry hand grasps air and water at catch position. Causes slippage and loss of efficiency at start of pull. Stress that fingers enter water first. Use corrective suggestions as in No. 6, above.

8. **Reaches too far forward for entry.** Usually caused by extending elbow and entering water with arm straight. Natural shoulder position is placed forward and out of proper alignment. Results in lack of effective pull because of poor alignment of muscles that are used for arm pull. Correct by use of "spear" technique, No. 6, above. Start entry of fingers near head and slide hand and arm underwater to catch position. Gradually lengthen entry point of hand until desired entry position is reached.

Arm Action (Propulsion):

1. **Pulling and pushing with arms too straight.** May cause body to bob up and down. (See No. 6 under "body position.") Causes loss of efficiency through inefficient use of leverage. Use fluid or stationary drills that enable swimmer to concentrate on correct mechanics of propulsive actions of arm. Practice correct arm movement while swimming beginner stroke.

2. **Pulls too far across imaginary long axis center-line of body.** Upsets body position. May cause excessive body roll. (Body roll may also be caused by improper head position and/or breathing. See faults and corrections under **Body Position** and **Breathing.**)

3. **Drops elbows.** Causes loss of efficiency. Use stationary drills in shallow water and use fluid drills. Have student look at pulling arm with elbow kept higher than hand. Use of hand paddles will help to develop

feel of maintaining correct water pressure against palm of hand.

4. **Doesn't accelerate arm during push phase.** Causes loss of efficiency. Practice accelerated tempo from middle to end of push phase. Use stationary drills in shallow water and fluid drills with and without support to body.

5. **Stops backward press forward of hip joint.** Causes loss of propulsion and effective forward movement of body. Also causes difficulties for effective arm recovery. Stress pressing hand backward until arm is almost fully extended.

6. **Presses hand backward and downward too far, and then upward until arm is fully extended to rear.** This causes hips to be pulled downward and upsets good body position. Often caused by pulling too deep. Pulling arm may be too straight. Emphasize bent arm (about 90°) at midpoint of propulsive phase. Emphasize pressing backward toward feet, not downward and then upward. Practice movements of one arm or both arms while swimming beginner stroke. Improve movements of problem arm while holding onto swimboard with opposite hand.

Breathing:

1. **Holds breath; doesn't exhale while face is in water.** Leads to fatigue and jerkiness in stroke. Rhythmic breathing practice needed. Use fluid or stationary drills, with or without support to body. No arm movements.

2. **Breathes while looking backward.** Upsets good body position, leads to excessive roll of body away from breathing side. Practice extending head and jaw slightly forward while rotating head to side, then look directly to the side to inhale.

3. **Lifts head; looks forward to breathe.** Upsets good body position. Use stationary and fluid drills to develop correct head position and breathing pattern to side.

4. **Waits too long to inhale.** Swimmer becomes a "late" breather, may inhale insufficient amount of air, and may tire quickly. Correct by having student start rotating head to the side when arm on breathing side starts its pull. Mouth should clear water for a breath when pulling arm is one-half to two-thirds of the way through its propulsive action. Corrective suggestions would be stationary, shallow water drills with student bent forward from waist with face in water, practicing arm and breathing movements, followed by fluid drills. Initial support to mid-body may be needed for "problem" student.

5. **Takes too long to inhale.**
(A) Body remains on the side too long. Body position is upset, effectiveness of propulsive actions of legs may be reduced. Pull of nonbreathing side arm is delayed. Practice quick inhalations using bracket drill, or prone kick glide with nonbreathing arm extended to front, or prone kick glide with both arms at sides (more advanced students).
(B) May be caused by rotating head to side too

slowly. Student practices quick rotation of head, taking a quick and adequate breath, and rotating head to facedown position quickly. Use prone kick glide with arms at sides of body to practice breathing patterns, followed by full stroke practice. More advanced students should rotate head independently of, and quicker than, speed of rotation of body on its long axis.

(C) May be caused by continuing to exhale after mouth is clear of the water and before breath is taken. More advanced students should learn to exhale remaining air explosively as mouth clears the water. Use drills, 5(B), above.

6. **Inhales while face is pointing upward.** Causes excessive body roll. Head position may be too low in water during stroke. Raise head position. May be holding breath and not exhaling properly and needs time to exhale and inhale concurrently while face is out of water. Practice breathing while bobbing and while holding onto side of pool with body in prone position. Also practice while using prone kick glide. Stress starting exhalation as soon as face returns underwater.

7. **Body twists when breathing.** Caused by lateral head movement and tucking of chin toward shoulder and armpit. This causes shoulders, hips, and legs to be thrown out of straight alignment. Use corrective suggestions as for Nos. 2 and 5(A).

8. **Inhalation and entry of hand of recovering arm are simultaneous.** Causes jerkiness in stroke. Delay clearing mouth from water until entry hand nears catch position. Emphasize synchronizing of head rotation with action of pressing arm (see No. 4, preceding). Use shallow water, stationary drills. Also,

practice coordination of head rotation and arm pull using beginner stroke.

9. **Inhaling too much air (more than is needed).** This may be caused by fear of not getting enough air. It may also be related to taking too long to inhale (see 5(A) and 5(B)). Excessive inhalation can cause tenseness and tiring. Suggest use of progressive drills (stationary drills in shallow water and fluid drills while supported and nonsupported) to develop good breathing habits.

10. **Physical problems.** A student having persistant difficulties in breathing may have a problem such as asthma or a closed nasal passage. Discuss these potential problems with older student or with parents of younger student.

Coordination:

1. **Catch-up stroke.** Excessive gliding on forward extended arm. Hand of recovering arm almost catches up with hand of gliding arm. Causes loss of continuous, effective, forward momentum. Speed up action from entry to catch position to start of pull. Pulling arm should be at least one-half way through its propulsive action when opposite hand enters water. Suggested corrective method would be to use **Progressive-Part Approach,** Sequence C, steps (f) and (g).

2. **Windmilling of arms.** This wastes energy and produces a jerky, uneven stroke. Use **Progressive-Part Approach,** Sequence C, steps (a) through (g), to develop better timing of arm movements.

3. **Jerky, uneven stroke.** Can usually be overcome only through considerable practice and correction of any faults already listed.

ELEMENTARY BACKSTROKE

This stroke was mentioned in the first swimming book of any record (*Colymbetes,* by Wilman, 1537).[*] It requires little physical effort as it is presently performed. Breathing is easy with the face being continually out of the water. This stroke can be used whenever the swimmer wants to recover from strenuous effort and still be able to make slow but effective progress through the water. It can be used for recreational and survival swimming or when the swimmer desires to exercise different muscle groups. This stroke employs paired movements of the arms and legs that are performed under the surface of the water.

Body Position

SIDE

FRONT

REAR

In the starting or gliding position, the body is in a horizontal, supine position. For most swimmers, the head is submerged to about the level of the ears, leaving the face clear of the water at all times. The back is almost straight, with the legs and hips slightly lower than the head and shoulders. The arms are extended along the sides of the body with the palms touching the thighs, and the legs are fully extended and together. The hips remain near the surface of the water at all times during stroking movements.

Leg Action

From the glide position, the legs recover by bending the legs and separating the knees gradually as the heels are drawn downward and toward the buttocks. The feet are relaxed and the heels are almost touching during this movement. At the end of the recovery, the knees are as wide as or slightly wider than the hips, and the ankles flex (dorsi) and rotate the feet outward into their catch position.

[*]American National Red Cross, *Swimming and Diving.* Philadephia: The Blakiston Co., 1938, p. 100.

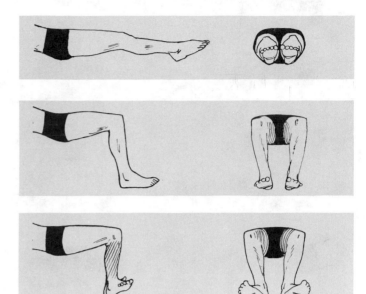

The propulsion begins by sliding (sculling) the feet sideways. When they reach a point under the knees, the knees rotate inward slightly, and the feet complete their propulsion phase using a rounded outward, backward, and inward movement. At the end of the propulsive actions, the ankles and feet come together, ending with the toes pointed and the legs straight and together. The feet accelerate their movements from the start of their thrusting actions backward to the completion of the kick.

Alternative Leg Actions

The following variation of the breaststroke kick is slightly less efficient than the kick described above. This loss of efficiency is due to the loss of propulsion from the pressing or sculling movements of the feet away from the midline of the body. The coordination of the elementary backstroke is the same when this kick variation is used.

SIDE   REAR

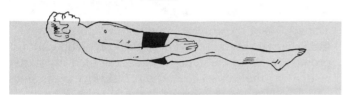

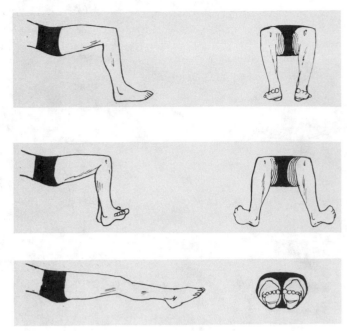

The legs recover by bending the legs and drawing the heels downward and backward to a point under and just outside of the knees. During this action, the knees separate until they are as wide as or slightly wider than the hips. The amount of knee spread will vary between swimmers because of individual differences. The recovery action is done easily and rhythmically, keeping the back, hips, and thighs in nearly straight alignment. At the end of the recovery, the knees rotate inward slightly as the ankles flex (dorsi) and rotate outward to place the feet in their respective catch positions for their propulsive movements. The feet press backward with a slightly rounded motion, ending with the legs straight and together and with the toes pointed (ankles plantar-flexed). The kick starts slowly and then accelerates to the completion of the thrust.

Another variation of the kick can be used by those few students who, because of limited rotation ability in the hip or knee joints, cannot perform either of the above kick variations effectively. In this variation, all leg movements are performed in a plane almost horizontal to the surface of the water. This style of kick is the least efficient method and should be used only by individuals having movement problems in the hips or knee joints.

Recovery of the legs from the glide position is achieved by bending them and separating the knees laterally as the heels are drawn toward the buttocks. During this action, the heels or soles of the feet are kept close to each other and the back and the hips are kept in alignment. At the end of the recovery, the ankles dorsi-flex and rotate outward. The toes lead the legs to their fully extended positions outside the hips. Without pause, the legs press backward and inward forcibly, ending together in the glide position.

To properly coordinate the elementary backstroke when using this kick variation, the legs start their recovery when the hands reach the lower area of the ribs during their recovery. This change in timing of

the recovery of the arms and legs is due to the longer and slower range of movement of the legs in this variation of the breaststroke kick.

Arm Action

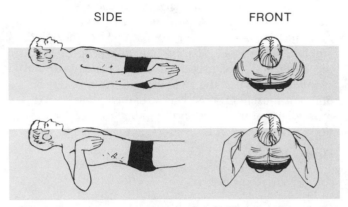

The actions of the arms are continuous and smooth from the start of the recovery to the completion of the propulsion. From the glide position, the recovery starts by drawing the palms or the thumbs slowly up the sides of the body to about the area of the armpits. A breath is taken during this action.

Without pause, the wrists rotate outward so that the fingers are pointing away from the shoulders with the palms facing somewhat toward the direction of the feet. With the fingers leading, the arms are fully extended to the side, to a point where the hands are about level with the top of the head. Without pause, the palms and the inside of the arms press simultaneously back toward the feet in a broad sweeping action, parallel to the surface of the water, ending with the arms and hands in the glide position. The arms may be straight or slightly bent during the pressing action. Exhalation occurs during the thrusting movements.

Coordination

SIDE	FRONT	REAR

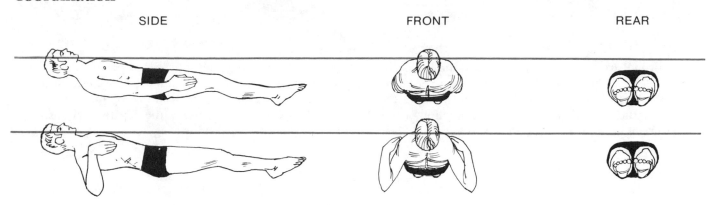

From the glide position, the stroke starts by recovering the hands to about the armpits, while the legs remain straight and together.

As the wrists begin their outward rotation, the legs initiate their recovery movements.

The heels continue to drop as the arms begin their extension to the side. When the arms are midway through their extension, the heels should be almost directly beneath the knees.

As the arms are completing their extension, the legs are completing their recovery and are ready for their thrusting action.

Coordination

SIDE   FRONT   REAR

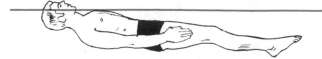

The propulsive actions of the arms and the legs start simultaneously. Because of their shorter range of movement, the legs will finish their thrust slightly before the end of the thrust of the arms. At the completion of the propulsive actions of the arms and the legs, a glide is taken with the body in a streamlined position. The next stroke begins while there is still momentum from the previous stroke in order to avoid having movement come to a complete stop because of the negative actions of the recovery of the arms and the legs.

ELEMENTARY BACKSTROKE

Suggested Learning Approaches

Except when using the **Whole Approach,** the leg action or the arm action can be introduced first to the students. Some instructors believe that the leg action should be taught first, since it is more difficult to learn than the arm action. Other instructors believe that the arm action should be taught first, since the learner can then use the arms to help balance the body while learning the kick. The instructor will learn through teaching experience which part of the stroke he or she would introduce first to the students.

Whole Approach — Students may be nonsupported or supported by a PFD or a similar flotation device attached over the hips or the abdomen, or suspended from improvised water wings placed under the hips or the lower back.

1. Have a slow motion demonstration and explanation by the instructor or an aide in the water. Repeat four or five times to allow the students to develop a mental feeling (picture) of the stroke movements.

2. The students practice in wave formations. Emphasize slow, easy movements. Make corrections of major errors as necessary (body position first, then the coordination, then the arms or the legs). The students swim the total stroke while concentrating on correcting faults in one of the parts of the stroke.

3. The students practice without support (if support is used first).

4. Those students having particular difficulty in improving a part of a stroke may need individual help. See the **Part-Whole Approach** for learning suggestions.

Progressive-Part Approach — Students may be nonsupported or supported as for the **Whole Approach.**
1. Explain and demonstrate the arm action and the

breathing. See the **Part-Whole Approach** for teaching suggestions.
2. The students practice, using the suggested sequences in the **Part-Whole Approach** (Arm Actions).
3. Explain and demonstrate the leg action and the stroke coordination.
4. Have the students practice the full stroke. Correct major errors as necessary (body position, coordination, leg action). Have the students swim the total stroke while concentrating on correcting the major error(s) and then the minor error(s).
5. The students continue practice without support (if support is used initially). NOTE. The **Part-Whole Approach** may have to be used by the student who has great difficulty in learning the leg action through the **Progressive-Part Approach.**

Part-Whole Approach — Suggested learning sequences are given below in the order that should prove to be most effective.
1. **Arm Actions**
   NOTE. These actions are an extension of the skill "winging," which the student learns in the Beginner Swimmer course.
   (a) Explain and demonstrate the arm action.
   (b) The students practice, either nonsupported or supported by a buddy or a flotation device and then without support. Correct errors as necessary.
   (c) Emphasize slow, accurate underwater movements, a proper breathing pattern, and a proper body position.
   (d) The use of words by the instructor, such as "draw" (recover), "extend," "press," "draw, inhale" or "draw, breathe," and "press, exhale" or "press, blow," may be helpful in the initial learning stages.
2. **Leg Actions**
   (a) Explain and demonstrate the leg actions in the

water (preferred) or while sitting on the edge of the pool with the legs extended over or in the water (optional).

(b) The students, in the water, practice to commands from the instructor and then without commands. The students are supported by a buddy or by a flotation device. On command, the students recover the legs and hold this position. Next (on command), have them flex the ankles (dorsiflex) and rotate the feet outward to the catch position. Next, on the command of a word such as "press" or "kick," the students **gently thrust** the feet to the side and then backward and inward with a smooth, continuous action to the glide position. Repeat the drill, using commands, and then without commands, until correct movements are achieved.

(c) The students practice while using fluid drills, either nonsupported or supported, and the instructor makes corrections as necessary. As soon as the leg movements are correct, the students should begin to accelerate the action of the feet during the thrust backward. Final practice is done without support to the body.

(d) The following drills enable the more advanced students to develop a longer range of leg motion, which, for most swimmers, will increase the effectiveness of the propulsive movements. Holding the arms extended along the sides of the body, the swimmers attempt to touch the fingertips with the heels when the feet are in position to deliver their thrust backward. The back and the hips must be kept in good alignment during this drill.

(e) Many of the above sequences can be used to teach the variation of the kick in which the legs and the feet remain nearly horizontal to the surface throughout all their movements. Use of command words, such as "recover," "set the feet," and "extend and thrust (or kick)," can be used. The students then practice without commands. Stress that the back and the hips should be kept in good alignment, especially during the recovery, since some students will show a tendency to sit in the water as the legs are recovered.

3. **Optional Stationary Drills (Legs)**

(a) The students practice while lying on the deck of a pool or the dock, with the legs extended over or partially in the water.

(b) The students practice in shallow water, keeping the body near the surface by placing the hands on the bottom.

(c) The students are bracketed, their backs to the wall, body in a vertical position, with their legs extended, and their feet not touching the bottom. The students bend their legs and spread their knees to just outside the hips as their heels are drawn up the wall to just outside the knees. They set their feet to the catch position and gently thrust their feet toward the bottom of the pool, keeping their heels in contact with the wall, until their legs are in a glide position, or the students bend their legs and spread their knees as the heels are kept nearly together and drawn up the pool wall toward the buttocks. With the feet set in the catch position, the feet slide sideways to just outside the knees and thrust gently down the wall to the glide position. Have the students look at their feet and knees during drilling to check correct positions and movements. NOTE. These learning procedures may lead to some students raising the knees out of the water when first practicing the kick in the supine position. Emphasize dropping the feet and keeping the knees just under the surface of the water.

4. **Coordination**

(a) Demonstrate and explain stroke coordination.

(b) Have the students practice, preferably non-supported.

- Keeping the legs straight and together, the students inhale as they recover their hands to the armpits. Use words or phrases such as "draw your thumbs (or finger tips) up your sides."
- They recover the legs and set the feet in their catch positions as the arms extend away from the sides of the body.
- The arms and the legs press backward simultaneously, ending in the glide position. Emphasize holding the arms and hands along the body and keeping the legs stretched and together with the toes pointed. Glide for 3 to 4 seconds before starting the next stroke.

5. **Coordination (Using the Kick Variation With the Horizontal Leg Movements)**

(a) Demonstrate and explain stroke coordination.

(b) Have the students practice, preferably non-supported.

- Start the recovery of the legs when the hands reach the lower ribs during their recovery. Continue the recovery of the hands to the armpits and draw the heels toward the buttocks.
- Rotate the wrists for extension of the arms and rotate the ankles outward.
- The extension and the thrust of the arms and the legs are simultaneous. The emphasis is the same as in the third part of 4(b), above.

(c) An alternative practice position is standing on the deck or in chest-deep water, with the students coordinating one leg and both arms.

Common Faults: Cause(s), Effect(s), Corrective Suggestions

Body Position:

1. **Hips/legs too low in water.** Head may be too high

or there may be excessive arch in the back. Effect of this is added frontal resistance. Adjust head position and straighten body alignment.

2. **Legs too high.** Thighs/knees break surface of water, especially during recovery of legs. Caused by head being back too far, or by piking at hips during leg recovery. Adjust position of head and/or hips.

3. **Not streamlined during glide.** Causes resistance; retards movement of body. Stress stretching of body parts; keeping arms at sides, legs together, toes pointed. Practice on land or while lying on bed, and while doing back glides in the water.

4. **Head too far back.** May cause face to submerge or may cause excessive arch in back. Tilt head forward with chin slightly tucked.

5. **Extreme arch in back during thrust of arms.** Face may submerge. Caused by pressing too hard or pressing downward with the arms. See corrections for **Arms (Thrust)**.

Arms (Recovery):

1. **Hands recover from thighs or hips directly into extended position.** This causes added resistance. Emphasize dragging thumbs or fingertips up the sides to armpits, rotating wrists, sliding hands/arms to extended positions. Land drill or buddy support in water will help, as will practice using fluid drill with body supported or nonsupported.

2. **Recover in front of chest.** May cause water to wash over face. Correct by keeping fingertips touching seam of suit and side of body.

3. **Fast, jerky movement.** Emphasize slow recovery.

Arms (Extension):

1. **Pushes water with hands and lower arms.** Caused by not rotating wrists outward and having fingers lead the arms during extension. Effect is added resistance. Correction can be achieved by emphasizing rotation of wrists outward and by dropping elbows before starting extension.

2. **Lifts hands and/or lower arms out of water.** May be caused by recovering hands from hips directly to extended positions or not rotating wrists and having fingers lead the extension of the arms. Effect is that face may submerge. Corrective action is to stress correct recovery movement or rotation of wrists at start of extension and keeping hands underwater during extension. Land drill or buddy support in water will help.

3. **Hands reach too far back behind head.** May be caused by desire for long, strong pull to compensate for weak kick. Also caused by inability to "feel" proper position of arms and hands or lack of understanding of initial, correct instruction. For corrective action, emphasize sliding hands away from body in a line almost perpendicular to shoulders. Have student rotate head to see where hand is going. Use fluid drills and stationary drills on land or in shallow water.

Arms (Thrust):

1. **Presses/thrusts too hard.** Often done to compensate for weak kick. Emphasize easier press. Improve kick.

2. **Presses/thrusts too deep.** This may cause lifting of chest from initial pressing action or pulling down of hips at end of thrust. Stress keeping arms parallel to surface throughout press.

3. **Stopping thrust before hands reach thighs, or letting the arms drift to the sides.** Emphasize thrusting all the way to sides of thighs and holding arms and hands at sides for glide.

Breathing:

1. **Holds breath.** Causes tenseness and fatigue. Emphasize breathing every stroke.

2. **Inhales on thrust of arms.** This makes it harder to inhale because of chest compression. Stress inhalation on recovery of arms.

3. **Inhales through nose.** May get water in nose. Emphasize mouth breathing. If water enters mouth during inhalation, blow it out and quickly take another breath.

Legs (Recovery):

1. **Knees break surface of water during recovery.** Usually caused by flexing hips. Check body position. Keep back and hips straight. Also caused by a very buoyant person keeping head too far back. Correct by tilting head forward slightly, and rounding back and shoulders slightly to lower hips and legs.

2. **Too fast and jerky.** Emphasize slow, controlled movement.

3. **Feet not drawn back far enough.** May be due to lack of flexibility in knee joint. Stretching exercises may help. To help increase range of movement of the lower part of legs, have student, in supine position, nonsupported or supported by buddy or flotation device attached to body, extend arms below and outside of hips and attempt to recover legs so that heels touch fingertips.

Legs (Propulsion):

1. **Scissors kick (thrusts with top of one foot).** Usually the result of the following causes:
   a. Improper body position during recovery and thrust; hips not level to surface of water. If scissors with right foot, body has rolled onto left side, or vice versa. **Corrective suggestions:**
      (1) Practice with body supported, using static and/ or fluid drills, and concentrate on maintaining proper body position.
      (2) If (1) doesn't work, and rolling is to left side, have student roll slightly onto right side during recovery. Continue drill until student "feels" correct hip position.
      (3) If (2) doesn't work, have buddy stand at side and grasp both hips of student. Buddy resists any attempts for rolling of body. Repeat until student "feels" correct position of hips. This drill may have to be repeated a number of times if student has continued problems.

b. Failure to flex and rotate ankle outward (point toes away from midline of body). **Corrective suggestions:**

(1) In slow motion, with instructor checking, repeat deck and bracket drills until desired pattern of movement is achieved. Emphasize stopping at end of recovery, "setting" the feet, then executing slow thrust.

(2) Instructor or buddy may have to hold student's feet and move them throughout full range of movement.

2. **Kicks outward forceably; legs drift together.** This causes loss of effective propulsion. Fault is more prevalent when student uses variation of kick in which legs move in a horizontal plane throughout all movements. Emphasize continuous, slow outward and forceful backward and inward movements until ankles touch.

3. **Start of thrust, knees separate to a position outside of feet.** This causes loss of rotation of lower leg around knee joint and loss of effective propulsion. Emphasize keeping knees as wide as or slightly wider than hips during thrusting action. With flotation support to hips or waist, have student raise head high enough to watch legs while practicing kick in slow motion. Gradually increase tempo of kick as correct knee postions are established. Then practice without support to the body.

4. **Lack of effectiveness; mechanics correct.** Knees may be too wide or narrow. Adjust knee position(s) until most satisfactory position is attained. Emphasize continued acceleration of feet throughout thrust. Lack of flexibility in knees or hips may prohibit adequate thrust. Student may do better with a variation of kick in which all leg movements are performed nearly horizontal to surface.

5. **Legs move in different planes.** One leg horizontal to surface of water, the other (lower leg) as shown and described under **Breaststroke (Leg Action).** Select one variation and have student watch all leg movements while practicing and sitting on edge of pool or dock, or in front of a mirror, followed by practice in the water.

Coordination:

1. **Starts leg recovery before arm recovery.** Or, arms finish thrust before legs finish. Or, legs finish thrust too soon before arms finish thrust. All three faults may be corrected by practicing proper coordination on land or in shallow water with signals or commands from instructor or partner.

2. **Sits during recovery of legs; straightens body on thrust of legs and arms.** Causes jerky stroke. Emphasize keeping back and hips almost straight and using knee joints like hinges during recovery of legs. Stationary, shallow water drill may be advised. Instructor may have to hold swimmer's hips to prevent overflexing during recovery.

Glide:

1. **Too short.** This can prohibit rest between strokes and can cause lack of overall smoothness. Have student count 1-2-3-4 (3 to 4 seconds) before starting next stroke.

2. **Too long.** Swimmer loses total momentum; may start to sink if nonbuoyant; may incur body roll if very buoyant. Can be corrected by less gliding.

3. **Feet drift apart or knees bend.** Can cause loss of streamlined look. Emphasize keeping legs straight and together, toes pointed.

INSTRUCTOR NOTES

BREASTSTROKE

The breaststroke is one of the oldest forms of swimming and for many centuries it was considered the best stroke to be taught to beginners. In many European countries it is still a very popular stroke for recreational swimming, since it is often performed with the head up, which permits easy vision and breathing and permits the swimmer to converse with others. It is one of the four strokes used in competitive swimming. Other than competition, it is basically a resting stroke and is useful for survival swimming. With certain modifications, it is also useful in some lifesaving situations.

Body Position

SIDE

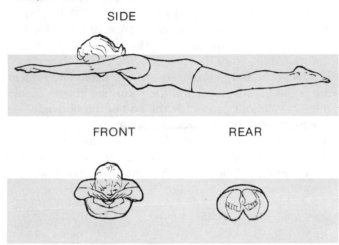

FRONT   REAR

During the glide, the body is streamlined, and the legs are stretched and together. The arms are nearly straight and extended in front of the head with the thumbs touching. The palms are down and are 6 to 8 inches below the surface of the water. The head is positioned so that the waterline is about at the hairline. The back is straight and the body is flat and nearly horizontal to the surface of the water, with the hips and legs kept just below the surface.

Leg Action

Two basic methods of performing the breaststroke kick in the prone position are illustrated and described. The first method is the most efficient because of the sculling actions of the feet during their initial propulsive actions. An acceptable breaststroke kick requires that all similar movements of the legs and feet be performed simultaneously, in the same manner, and in the same plane. These movements are called paired movements and are performed below the surface of the water.

SIDE   REAR

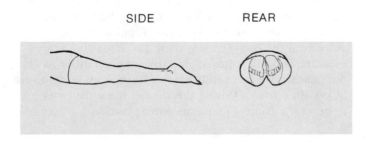

SIDE   REAR

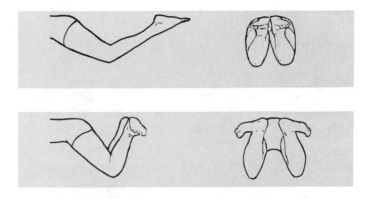

From the glide position, the recovery of the legs starts by bending the hips and knees, and by gradually separating the knees as the heels are drawn up the midline of the body toward the buttocks. The heels are kept near the surface during this action. At the end of the recovery, the ankles flex and rotate outward to position the feet for their propulsive actions. Most swimmers will achieve greater kicking effectiveness by drawing the feet as far forward as possible without upsetting good body position. Because of individual differences, the amount of spread between the knees at the end of the recovery will vary, as will the distance from which the heels are drawn toward the buttocks.

SIDE   REAR

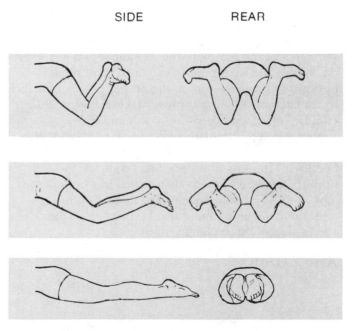

Using a continuous, circular action, the feet press sideways to a point just outside the knees and then backward. The pressing or sculling actions of the feet sideways produces some forward momentum as well as momentum to the feet for their thrust backward. The pressing actions start slowly, then accelerate to the completion of the kick. Propulsion results from the pressure of the water against the soles of the feet and the inside of the feet and lower legs. The kick finishes with an extension of the ankles, a slight lifting of the legs and feet, and with the legs and feet ending together in a streamlined position.

SIDE   FRONT

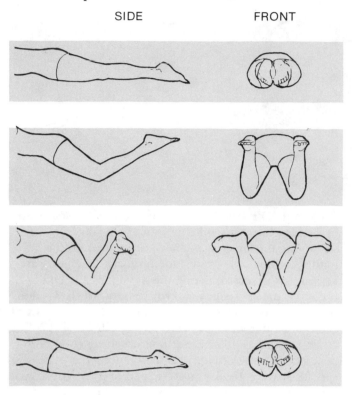

An alternative method of performing the breaststroke kick is accomplished by varying the recovery movement of the lower legs. During the recovery, the feet are drawn toward the hips, ending with the knees spread to about the width of the hips with the feet above and just outside the knees. The ankles then flex (dorsi) and rotate outward to place the feet in the proper position for their thrust backward. The feet press backward using a slight circular action, ending with the feet and legs together in a streamlined position. This alternative method is slightly less efficient than the method previously described because of the loss of the sculling actions of the feet from the midline of the body to a line just outside the hips. However, many students are able to learn to perform this method more quickly because of the elimination of the sculling actions.

Arm Action

SIDE   FRONT

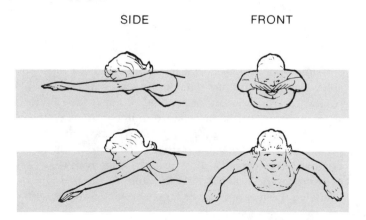

SIDE   FRONT

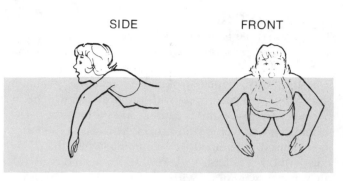

From the glide position, the propulsive actions of the arms start by positioning the hands so that they are angled slightly downward and the palms are turned outward to about a 45° angle to the surface of the water. With the arms straight, the palms press or scull sideward and somewhat downward until the hands are wider than the shoulders. From this position, the elbows begin to bend and the wrists rotate so that the palms and fingers are pointing downward and the palms are almost facing the feet. Without pausing at the end of the outward sweep, the hands and forearms pull backward and inward slightly, ending when the elbows and hands are slightly forward of the chin. During this pulling action, the elbows are kept higher than the hands but lower than the shoulders.

SIDE   FRONT

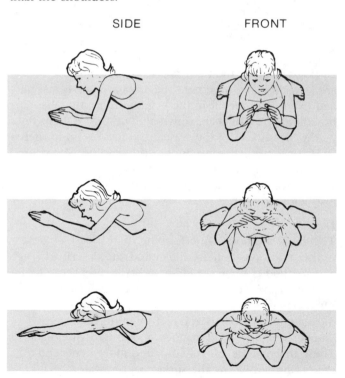

At the end of the pulling action, the arms immediately begin to recover by drawing (sculling) the hands and forearms toward each other while keeping the elbows away from the body, ending with the hands almost touching and the palms angled toward each other. Without pausing, the arms fully extend to their glide position below the surface. During this action, the wrists rotate to bring the hands to a palms-down position.

Breathing

The description of the pattern of breathing that follows is for a noncompetitive style of the breaststroke. The differences in the breathing patterns for a recreational style of the breaststroke and a competitive breaststroke, as well as other differences, are discussed later in this section.

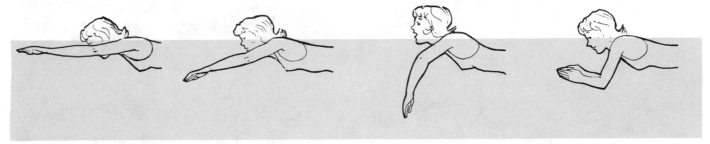

During the outward sweep of the arms, the head begins to lift. It continues to lift, with the lower jaw jutted forward, as the arms and hands begin to pull backward. Near the end of the arm pull, the mouth just clears the water and a breath is taken. As the arms start to recover, the face is lowered into the water. A slow, steady exhalation, primarily through the mouth, begins during the forward extension of the arms and continues until the next inhalation is ready to be taken.

Coordination

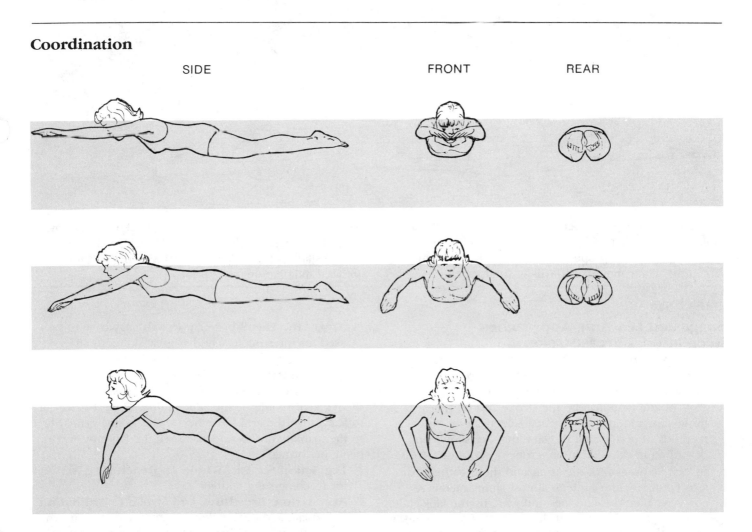

From the glide position, the arms begin their propulsive actions. A breath is taken and the legs begin to recover near the end of the pulling action of the arms.

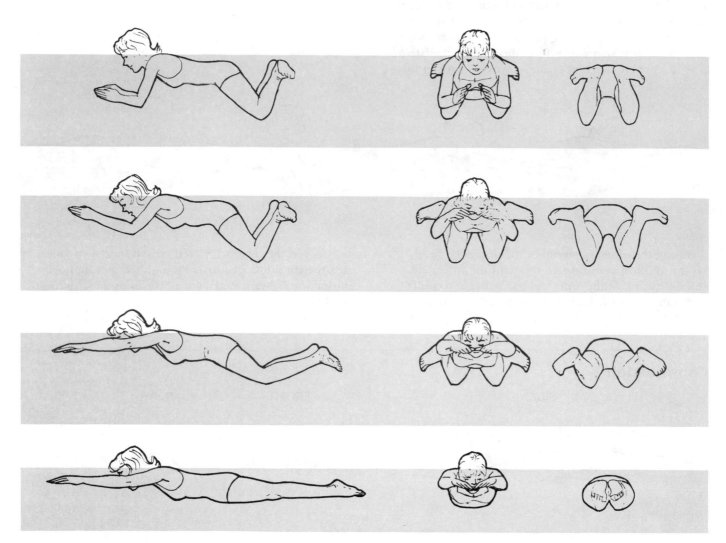

Without pausing, the face enters the water as the arms start to recover, and the recovery of the legs ends with the feet positioned properly for their propulsive action. The arms reach about two-thirds of their extension forward when the feet start to press backward. The arms reach full extension just prior to the completion of the kick. A glide is taken, but not to the point of losing forward momentum.

BREASTSTROKE

Suggested Learning Approaches — Recreational Breaststroke

Whole Approach — The student is nonsupported, or supported by an attachable aid to the upper body or suspended from an improvised flotation device.

1. Explain and demonstrate the stroke several times using slow motion movements. Select one of the methods of performing the kick that are shown and described in the section on stroke description. Stress an easy, short pull of the arms, and the breathing pattern (pull, breathe) and an almost simultaneous recovery of the arms and legs, followed by the kick-glide. Emphasize starting the exhalation during the extension of the arms and continuing to exhale slowly until the next breath is taken.

2. Corrections are made on the parts of the stroke and they are practiced as the student swims the entire stroke. The **Part-Whole Approach** may have to be used for the student who has great difficulty in improving one or more of the parts.

Progressive-Part Approach — The arm action or the leg action may be taught first. Many instructors believe that the leg kick should be introduced first, since it is harder to learn than the arm movements. This is due primarily to the inability of the student to see the leg movements being performed.

1. **Leg Action** See **Part-Whole Approach (Leg Action)** for teaching suggestions.

2. **Arm Action, Breathing, and Stroke Coordination**

   a. Explain and demonstrate the arm actions, the arm actions with the breathing, and the coordination of the stroke. Stress that the arms and legs work in opposition to each other.

   b. The students practice, either nonsupported or supported by an attachable aid or by an improvised flotation device to the upper body. Suggested learning procedures:

(1) The students inhale, place their face in the water, push off into a prone glide, and practice arm movements and stroke coordination for three to four strokes while holding their breath. The students stop, breathe, and repeat the drill until the desired coordination is achieved.

(2) They practice the full stroke with breathing, supported (if necessary) and then without support to the body. Corrections for, and improvements of, the parts of the stroke are made and practiced as the students swim the full stroke.

Part-Whole Approach — Except for the leg action, this approach is used primarily for the students who are having considerable difficulties in learning the other parts of the stroke or the coordination of the stroke through either of the above learning approaches.

Leg Action Following are suggested learning sequences for either one of the two breaststroke kick variations that are shown and described in the stroke description section. After the explanation and demonstration, the students practice the kick while bracketed to the side of the pool or the dock, or they support their bodies in shallow water by placing their hands on the bottom, or they are supported by the instructor, an instructor aide, or a buddy. In special cases, the instructor may have to move a student's feet and legs in the desired patterns of movement. It is recommended that all initial learning be done through commands by the instructor. Select one of the following sequences and have the students repeat each step as often as necessary until the movements are performed correctly.

Sequence 1.

1. The students learn the modified dolphin kick. In the prone position, the students recover the legs by keeping them together as the legs bend and the heels are drawn near the surface to the buttocks. With the feet (toes) pointed (ankles plantar-flexed), the students kick both feet backward simultaneously and easily. Emphasize kicking backward, not downward. Use commands such as "Glide position, Tuck (recover), Kick, Glide position." Add step 2.

2. With the legs fully recovered and the legs and heels together, the students rotate the ankles outward (toes out) and kick both feet **backward** simultaneously and easily. Stress pushing the water backward with the insteps of the feet, and ending the kick with the legs and feet together with the toes pointed to the rear. This step is critical in preventing (or correcting) any tendencies of the students to do a scissors kick. Emphasize turning the feet/toes outward to their correct positions **before** kicking. Check for correct body position. Use commands such as "Glide position, Tuck, Toes out, Kick easily, Glide position." Add step 3.

3. Allow the knees to separate 4 to 6 inches during the recovery. The heels may be kept together or allowed to separate 4 to 6 inches, depending on the style of kick being taught. At the end of the recovery, the feet are set properly in their catch positions (toes out). The feet are slowly pressed backward until the legs and feet are in the glide position. Correct any tendencies to do a scissors kick. Use commands as in step 2, above. Add step 4.

4. Allow the knees to separate as wide as or slightly wider than the hips during the recovery. The heels may be kept together or allowed to separate as wide as or slightly wider than the knees. The feet are then placed in their catch positions. The feet are slowly pressed to the glide position with a slightly outward and backward movement. **The distance between the knees should not increase during the thrusting action of the legs.** Stress keeping the heels near the surface during the recovery, proper body position, the feet turned out at the end of the recovery, and the legs and feet in the glide position at the end of the kick. Use commands such as "Glide position, Recover, Toes out, Kick, Glide." Add step 5.

5. Simplify the commands in step 4, above. Suggest "Up (recover) and (toes out) kick, Glide." Allow the students to kick **backward** with more force. As soon as possible, allow the students to practice on their own with the instructor checking each student and making corrections as necessary. Add step 6.

6. The students practice, nonsupported, using fluid drills. Kick three or four times, stop and breathe, and repeat (or as directed by instructor). NOTE. More continuous practice can be achieved once the students can perform correct breathing for the breaststroke. Minor adjustments in the amount of knee spread can be made (as may be necessary) during this practice. Kicking while wearing **clean** tennis shoes will help develop the feel of pressing the water with the inner sides of the feet.

An acceptable breaststroke kick is achieved when there is a paired action of the legs and feet during the kicking movement, (i.e., they are doing the same thing, in the same manner, at the same time, and in the same plane).

Sequence 2. The following method can be used but it is not a preferred one, since the students learn the basic leg actions while in a body position other than the true swimming position. It has one distinct advantage, however, in that the students can see each movement or position of the legs and feet. This sequence requires the students to be able to hold onto an overflow trough or the edge of a pool or a dock.

1. The students' position in the water should be vertical with their backs to the wall. Many of the static drills and commands for Sequence 1 can be used. To recover, the students draw the heels up the wall toward the buttocks, then turn the ankles (feet) outward, then press the heels and feet outward and down the wall in a circular pattern, ending with the legs in the glide position.

2. As soon as the correct movements are achieved in No. 1, move to steps 4, 5, and 6, from Sequence 1, with the students practicing in the prone position.

Part-Whole Approach — Arm Action/Arm Action With Breathing

1. Explain and demonstrate the arm actions using slow movements. Stress an easy pull and stopping the hands when they are forward of the plane of the head (see stroke description). Point out that the chin begins to lift and jut forward as the hands start to pull backward, and that a breath is taken near the end of the pull of the hands. Emphasize that the tip of the chin is in the water during the inhalation, that the face is placed back into the water during the recovery of the arms, and that the exhalation begins as the arms are extending forward.

2. The students practice nonsupported, except for support for poor floaters, or all the students practice, nonsupported, while using an easy flutter kick.

3. The following drills should be used only for the student who is having great difficulty in learning these skills using the above sequences. The student practices the arm actions and then adds the breathing by —

   a. Standing in waist-deep water and bending forward from the waist until the chest and/or face is in the water. Use commands such as "Pull/Breathe, Extend/Exhale."

   b. Walking slowly across the pool while practicing the arm actions and breathing from position "a." All walking should be in waist-deep water. Use the above commands when practical and as needed.

Part-Whole Approach — Coordination

Poor floaters may learn the coordination faster if supportive aid to the chest area is used first.

1. From the prone glide position, and while holding the breath with the face underwater, the students execute a narrow, short, circular pull, then kick and extend the arms forward to their glide position. Repeat three or four times, raise the head and breathe, and then repeat the sequence.

2. Repeat No. 1, above, but the outward and backward circular pulling actions are increased slightly. The legs recover as the hands begin their inward motion, and the arms extend forward during the kick.

3. Repeat No. 2, above, but increase the outward and backward range of movement of the hands as illustrated and described for the breaststroke.

4. Repeat Nos. 1, 2, and 3, adding the breathing.

THE COMPETITIVE BREASTSTROKE

There are a few albeit significant differences between the style of breaststroke used in present-day competition events and that which has been taught and used for many years for recreational swimming. The reader who desires more detailed information about the competitive-style breaststroke is advised to seek guidance from a knowledgeable swimming coach or from recent publications or articles about competitive swimming.

The differences in the competitive-style breaststroke from the recreational breaststroke are:

• **Arm Action** The hands scull inward to the midline of the body as well as away from the midline. This sculling action provides forward movement of the body. At the completion of the sculling action outward past the shoulders, the wrists rotate the hands from a slight palms-out position to a slight palms-in position. The arms bend as the inward scull begins. The hands are then brought forceably toward each other, ending with the palms almost touching and facing each other, forward of the chin, and 6 to 8 inches below the surface of the water. Without pausing, the hands begin to slide forward. During this action, the elbows continue to squeeze toward each other, which helps keep the arms moving forward. Near the end of the extension of the arms, the wrists rotate inward to position the hands for their outward sculling action.

• **Breathing and Coordination** The exhalation starts gradually during the forward extension of the arms and continues during the outward sculling action of the arms. During these sculling movements, the head begins to lift slowly. The rotation of the wrists to position the hands for their inward scull is accompanied by an explosive exhalation of air that helps create a strong, rapidly accelerating sculling action of the hands to the inside. During this exhalation, the head continues to rise with the lower jaw jutting forward until the mouth is just clear of the water. A breath is taken immediately following the explosive exhalation. The mouth remains clear of the water as the hands finish their inward pressing action and start to move forward. The legs begin to recover as the hands are moving forward. The face slowly returns to a facedown position in the water during the extension of the arms and the completion of the leg recovery. Near the end of the extension of the arms, there is a brief pause as the feet are rotated to their respective catch positions. The arms fully extend and are held together until the legs have almost completed their kicking action. As the ankles and feet complete their extension and come together, the arms begin their sculling movements away from the midline of the body.

• **Leg Action** The kick that is used almost exclusively is shown and described on page 63.

COMPETITIVE BREASTSTROKE
(Swimming Drills)

1. **Head lift and kick** This drill emphasizes the relationship of the timing of the recovery of the legs to the inhalation. The swimmer starts in the prone glide position, arms fully extended, palms down, with the hands kept together by grasping one of the thumbs. It must be continually emphasized that the arms never bend, separate, or press downward during this drill.

During forward momentum from a push-off or previous kick, the swimmer begins to lift the head. The hips and legs begin to bend and start to recover when the face breaks from the surface. The head remains up and a breath is taken as the legs are fully recovered and the feet are positioned for their thrust. The planing action of the thighs as they recover counteracts the tendency of the hips to drop when the head is raised. As the legs start to thrust, the face is lowered into the water and it reaches its maximum facedown position as the legs complete their kick. A glide is taken but not to the point that forward momentum is lost. Repeat the drill as often as necessary.

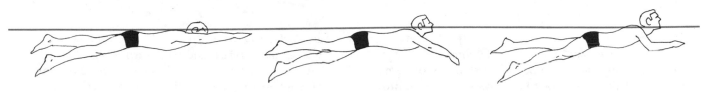

2. **Pull (scull) breast, kick free** This drill establishes a relationship between the actions of the arms and the lifting of the head to breathe. The combination of the arm action and the flutter kick forces a desirable, late breathing pattern. The swimmer starts in the prone glide position and uses a continual flutter kick. The kick provides forward momentum but does not create enough support to allow the swimmer to inhale comfortably at any time other than during the inward sculling movements of the arms. The arm action and breathing pattern are as described for the competitive-style breaststroke.

To start, the swimmer takes a breath, places the face in the water, and kicks six or seven times with the arms extended to the front. Exhalation begins slowly during this action and continues during the outward sculling action of the arms. A strong exhalation occurs as the hands begin the forceful pulling (sculling) action inward. The inhalation occurs immediately after the completion of the strong exhalation and as the hands are continuing their movement inward. As the arms begin to move forward, the face is lowered into the water. The arms are held in their fully extended position for six or seven kicks. Emphasize that this delay is important to the timing of the stroke, since it corresponds to the position that is maintained by the arms during the kicking action in the breaststroke. Repeat the drill as often as necessary.

The coordination of the breaststroke is then practiced. The swimmer has learned the basic coordination through drills 1 and 2. Drill 1 emphasizes the relationship of the head lift to the kick. Drill 2 emphasizes the relationship of the head lift to the arm action. Therefore, the swimmer has virtually learned the relationship of the arm action to the leg action. During the initial practicing of the coordination, a relatively long glide should be used. A longer glide gives the swimmer time to get organized between strokes. The length of the glide is gradually reduced as the swimmer develops proficiency in the stroke coordination.

Other drills of value

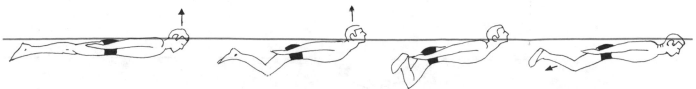

1. **Kick and touch heels** This drill helps the swimmer get the heels closer to the buttocks, which increases the range of motion of the lower legs and the feet. The swimmer is in the prone position with the arms extended to the rear along the sides of the body. The swimmer lifts the head to breathe, then recovers the legs. The swimmer touches the heels during the propulsion when the feet reach a position just outside the hips. The face returns to the water during the balance of the leg kick.

   Two negative side effects may occur if this drill is used extensively. A dropped hip position may result if the swimmer concentrates on drawing the heels forward but forgets to bend at the hips and draw the knees forward. A jerky, stop and start action may occur if the swimmer uses the style of kick that includes recovering the feet directly to the outside of the hips.

2. **One arm breaststroke** In this drill, the swimmer practices the stroke by using the actions of one arm only. The other arm is kept in an extended forward position. This drill helps to emphasize and to improve the outward, slightly downward sculling action and the inward, slightly upward sculling movement. It also helps to correct the tendency of the swimmer who sculls outward and backward too far before starting the inward scull. This drill can be used to practice first one arm and then the other and then alternating each arm.

3. **Short pull breaststroke** This is another drill that helps to correct the tendency to press or to pull too far backward. Using a narrow, circular movement, the hands slide outward and then slightly backward and inward. The elbows bend slightly during the inward action to allow the arms to extend forward at the end of the pull. This drill can be used as a part of the **pull (scull) breast, kick free** drill.

   This drill is also effective for the swimmer who has a tendency to pull and kick at the same time when learning the recreational style of the breaststroke. The range of motion of the hands and arms is grad-ually increased until the desired pattern is attained. Emphasis is continually placed on easy, slow arm movements until correct stroke coordination is developed.

4. **Sculling with flotation to the legs or using the flutter kick** The swimmer practices the arm movements with the legs supported by a swimboard or similar device held between and by the thighs or by a flotation aid (pull-buoy) attached around the thighs. The arm movements can also be practiced while flutter kicking. The face can be clear of the water or in the water during these drills.

Common Faults: Cause(s), Effect(s), Corrective Suggestions

Body Position (During Glide):

1. **Head held too high.** Causes hips and legs to sink. May cause tenseness in neck muscles. Adjust head position. Waterline should be at or just below hairline for most swimmers.

2. **Legs and feet too low.** May be due to excessive arch in back. Correct by relaxing back muscles and tightening abdominal muscles. May also have to lower head. May be caused by holding glide position too long. Shorten glide. May also be caused by piking at the hip joints. Emphasize stretching the body (making the body "long").

3. **Head too low in water.** May cause hips and legs to ride too high in water. Adjust head position as in No. 1.

4. **Body not continuously flat to water.** Rolling to one side can cause scissors kick or vice-versa. (See Common Faults, Leg Action, No. 1.) Rolling may also be caused by gliding too long, especially with very buoyant individuals. Reduce

amount of glide. For twisting of shoulders (one shoulder lower than the other), have student twist to opposite (high shoulder) side (use a fault to correct a fault).

Leg Action:

1. **"Scissoring" during propulsion movement.** Pressure against water is from top of foot. May be caused by body roll or not turning foot out properly. (Example: right foot scissors when body rolls onto right side.) Scissors may also be caused by lack of flexibility (rotation ability) in ankle(s). Individual help by instructor is often necessary in problem cases. With student in shallow water and bracketed to wall, instructor may have to grasp student's feet and move legs and feet through desired pattern of movement, with emphasis on correct position of feet at start of propulsive action. Repeat as much as necessary. For the student who rolls to one side during recovery of legs, use the following corrective techniques: (a) Have student roll to opposite side (use a fault to correct a fault); (b) If (a), above, is unsuccessful, then, in waist-deep water, with student in a prone position, instructor stands at one side of student and places hands (instructor's) on each side of student's hips. Each time student starts to roll to the side, instructor grasps the hips firmly and holds them flat to surface of water. Repeat until student "feels" correct body position.

2. **Tucks legs and draws knees and thighs under hips during recovery or drops knees and feet too far during recovery.** This causes hips to rise and upsets good body position. Both faults cause added frontal resistance from thighs pushing against water. Corrective suggestions: (a) Use a dolphin kick to develop feel of raising and keeping heels near surface during recovery; (b) Movement of student's feet and legs by instructor may be necessary.

3. **Propulsive force is outward, not backward. (Legs then either drift or must be squeezed together).** This causes loss of efficiency. It may be due to improper instruction through use of counting, such as 1 (recover), 2 (extend), 3 (together), 4 (glide). Use words such as recover, kick, glide. Emphasize pressing backward, not outward. Emphasize that breaststroke kick is performed in two basic movements, **recovery** and **propulsion**. Individual help, No. 2(b), above, may be necessary.

4. **Legs moving in different planes (no scissors kick).** Change one leg to match the other to achieve a paired movement. Individual help may be necessary. See No. 1, above, for body position problem. Also see No. 2(b), above.

5. **"Weak kick."** Correct mechanics are used, but little effective forward progress is made. This is often due to weak muscles in the inside of thigh. Practice will help develop these muscles.

Arm Action:

1. **Pulling/pressing backward past shoulders.** This upsets coordination of stroke. It causes added resistance during recovery of arms and may be result of a weak kick. To make forward progress, swimmer compensates by over-pulling. Pulling too far may result from trying to raise head too high to inhale. To correct this, start with a very short pull. Gradually lengthen pull to correct distance. Emphasize easy pull of arms. If necessary, have student practice arm movements with body encased in inflated innertube around upper area of back. Innertube will block upper arms during pull. Practice until student "feels" correct, shorter pattern of arm movements.

2. **Presses almost directly downward to catch position.** This causes upper part of body to rise, (which will "fall" during start of recovery of arms). It may be caused by poor breathing habits and a need to raise head (and shoulders) too high to inhale. Emphasize pressing outward and slightly downward to catch position. Use fluid drills, with or without body being supported. Have student watch hand and arm movements.

3. **Dropping elbows during pull.** This causes loss of efficiency through loss of leverage from lack of constant pressure of water against palms of hands and lower arms. Practice in shallow water, with student standing and bent forward from waist, chest in water. Use fluid drills, with or without body support. Student watches arms to establish correct arm position.

4. **Recovery too slow.** This can upset timing of stroke. Emphasize continuous motion from end of pull to recovery. Emphasize a quick squeeze of hands and forearms toward midline of body at end of pull. Use stationary and fluid drills as in Nos. 2 and 3, above.

5. **Little or no acceleration of arms during pressing movements to outside and/or inward.** This negates an effective forward movement of body. Lack of acceleration of inward sculling action may inhibit ability to lift chin and clear mouth from water to permit a good inhalation (competitive breaststroke). Emphasize acceleration to outside and back to inside. Use supportive aid to body during practice, if necessary.

Breathing:

1. **Lifting face too far out of water for inhalation.** Causes arching of back. Hips and legs may sink. Emphasize lifting (extending) chin just high enough for mouth to clear water. Fluid drills, body supported, will help.

2. **Breathes too early.** Negates effectiveness of early stages of arm pull. Delay clearing mouth to breathe until arms are near end of their inward pull/press. Fluid drills, body supported, will help.

3. **Holds breath or doesn't breathe every stroke.** Inexperienced swimmer may tire quickly. Emphasize breathing every stroke. Emphasize smooth, continuous

exhalation starting with forward extension of arms and continuing through pull. Use shallow water (stationary) drill and/or fluid drills with body supported. Kick may have to be eliminated to allow swimmer to concentrate on arms and breathing.

4. **Excessive inhalation.** Caused by fear of not getting enough air. Difficult for student to completely exhale before next inhalation is ready to be taken. Student may exhale and then inhale almost simultaneously, which can upset good stroke coordination. Use of drills in No. 3, above, will help. Have student inhale same amount as when walking on land.

Coordination:

1. **Pulls and kicks at same time.** Causes incorrect coordination. Student glides with arms at sides. Often caused by weak kick and need to overpull arms to make good forward progress. Corrective suggestions: (Step 1.) Student in prone glide position, legs and arms fully extended, hands holding onto near end of swimboard. Legs recover, board is drawn to head, face is lifted, and a breath is taken — all done simultaneously. Face is lowered, arms are extended forward as kick is performed and breath is exhaled slowly — also done simultaneously. Repeat until swimmer understands that arms and legs work in opposition to each other. (Step 2.) At end of exten-

sion of arms (Step 1), gently push and release board. Repeat Step 1 (without board). At end of extension of arms, glide until hands grasp board, then gently push and release board. Repeat full cycle of releasing and grasping board until swimmer performs this drill satisfactorily. (Step 3.) After releasing board, keep legs straight and together as hands scull outward approximately 9 to 12 inches and then pull/scull back easily toward head. During this pulling action, a breath is taken and legs recover. Then kick and extend arms, grasp board, pause, and push and release board. Repeat as often as necessary. (Step 4.) Repeat Step 3 without using swimboard. Gradually increase range of movement of arms until desired pattern is achieved. Emphasize that recovery of legs occurs as arms start their recovery.

2. **Over-gliding (forward momentum lost before start of next stroke).** See "Laws of Inertia." Start next stroke before forward motion stops.

3. **No glide (fatiguing for recreational swimmer).** At end of stroke, with arms fully extended, have student count to 3 before starting arm pull. NOTE. Amount of glide will vary with individuals, but should not be held until forward momentum is lost.

SIDESTROKE

This style of swimming on the side of the body evolved from the breaststroke and came into being around 1840.* It is used primarily for recreational swimming, since it allows easy, steady progress through the water. It can be used also for exercise in the water and for survival swimming. With adaptations, it can be used for swimming underwater and for some lifesaving skills.

Glide Position

SIDE   FRONT   TOP

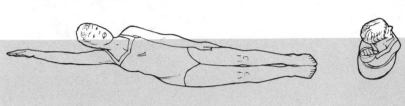 

During the glide or resting portion of the stroke, the body lies on the side, nearly horizontal to the surface of the water. The head, back, and legs are in straight alignment. The legs are together, fully extended, with the toes pointed. The lower arm is extended forward of the head, parallel to the surface, with the palm of the hand down and in line with the body, 6 to 8 inches below the surface of the water. The top arm is fully extended toward the feet, with the palm of the hand resting on top of the thigh. The lower ear rests in the water close to the shoulder. The head is rotated far enough to clear the mouth and nose from the water to permit easy breathing. Generally, the swimmer looks to the side, but occasional glances to the front may be necessary for safety purposes. The head and back should be kept in straight alignment throughout all movements of the arms and legs.

Leg Action

The sidestroke employs the scissors kick, which, when properly performed, provides effective forward progress. All leg movements should be continuous and smooth, and should be performed in a plane nearly parallel to the surface of the water. In contrast to the flutter kick, when the legs are constantly in motion, this kick provides some rest to the leg muscles during the glide portion of the stroke. This kick, or its alternate, the inverted scissors kick, which is discussed in Chapter 12, "Swimmer Course," can be used effectively for lifesaving carries, treading water, underwater swimming, the survival stroke, and the trudgen stroke.

SIDE   TOP

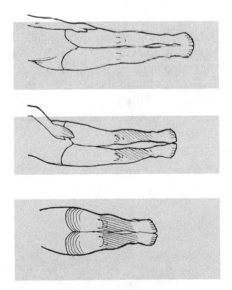 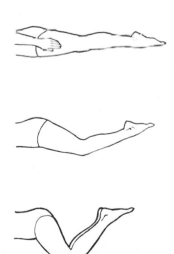

From the glide position, the recovery of the legs starts by flexing the hips and knees and by drawing the heels slowly toward the trunk until the thighs have reached about a 45-degree angle to the trunk. The knees will separate from 3 to 6 inches during the recovery movement.

---

*American National Red Cross, *Swimming and Diving*, pp. 117-119.

SIDE   TOP

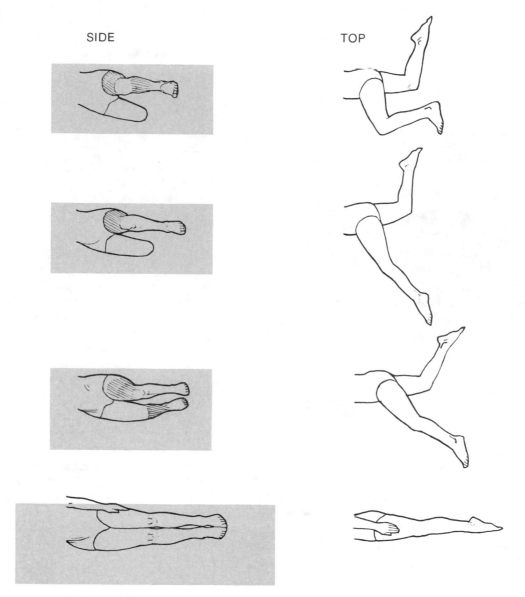

At the end of the recovery and prior to the start of the extension of the legs, the top ankle is bent (dorsi-flexed) and the lower ankle is bent (plantar-flexed). The legs then move simultaneously to their respective extended (catch) positions.

At the end of its extension, the top leg is almost straight and is at about a 45-degee angle to the trunk. At the end of the extension of the lower leg, the thigh is extended slightly to the rear of the trunk, and the lower leg is at about a 90-degree angle to the thigh. Without pausing, both legs press backward and inward simultaneously and vigorously, ending with the legs fully extended and together with the toes pointed to minimize resistance during the glide. During the propulsion backward of the top foot, the ankle bends (plantar-flexes) to allow the sole of the foot to exert maximum pressure against the water.

Arm Action

SIDE   FRONT

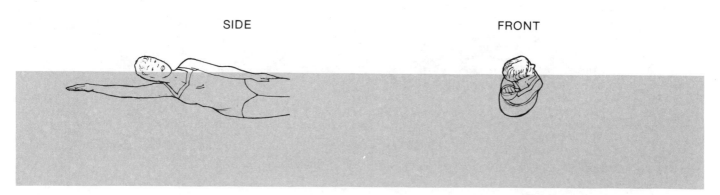

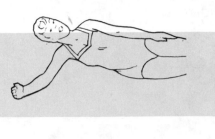

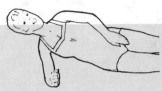

At the end of the glide, the propulsive action of the lower arm starts by rotating the arm slightly to place the palm of the hand in a downward, slightly outward position. From the catch position, the elbow bends as the

hand presses outward and downward slightly and then backward toward the feet, stopping almost in line with the upper chest. The palm of the hand faces toward the feet during most of the propulsive action.

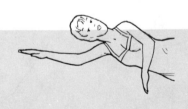

Without pausing at the end of its pressing action, the lower arm recovers by drawing the elbow close to and slightly behind the body. The shoulder (arm) then rotates to allow the forearm to point forward of the body. The arm continues to rotate inward to place the palm of the hand downward during the extension of the lower arm to its glide position.

Near the end of the pressing action of the lower arm, the top arm begins to recover. It continues to recover,

during the recovery of the lower arm, by drawing the forearm along the body until the hand is about in front of the lower shoulder. The hand presses downward slightly and then backward along the body to its glide position with the wrist flexed and the palm facing the feet. The lower arm extends forward as the top arm presses backward. Inhalation through the mouth occurs during the recovery of the top arm. Exhalation occurs during the pressing action of the top arm.

Coordination

SIDE FRONT TOP

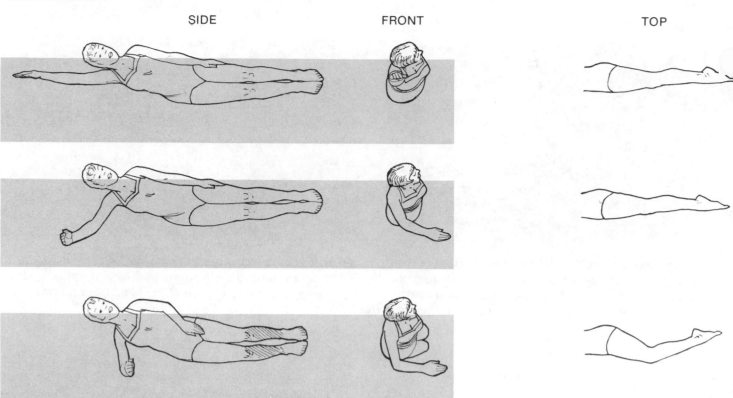

From the glide position, the stroke starts by pressing the lower arm backward. Near the end of this pressing action, the top arm and the legs begin to recover.

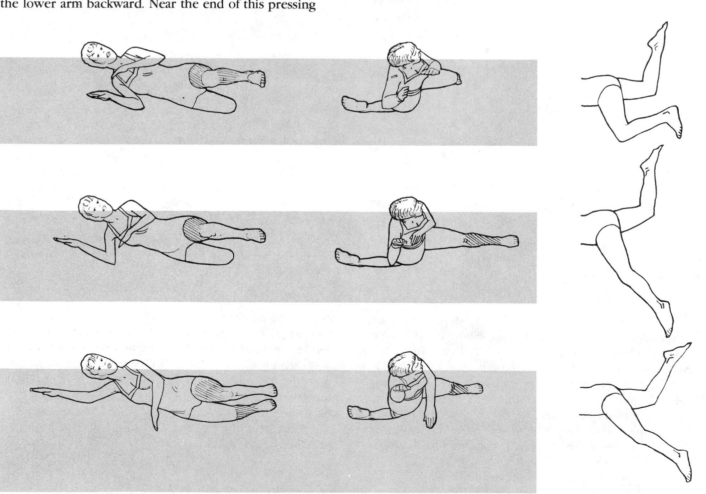

76

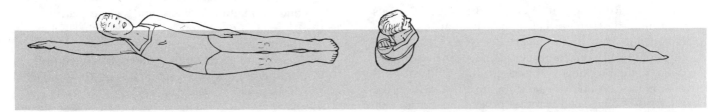

The top arm and the legs complete their recovery actions during the recovery of the lower arm. The legs extend away from the body as the top arm begins its pressing action and as the lower arm begins to extend forward. The lower arm reaches full extension at the completion of the propulsive actions of the top arm and the legs. A glide is taken and the next stroke starts while there is still some forward momentum of the body from the previous stroke.

Suggested Learning Approaches

Whole Approach —
1. Demonstrate the stroke in the water.
2. The students practice, first with the body supported and then without support.

Progressive-Part Approach (Sequence 1) — This sequence involves the learning of sculling and treading water, skills that are also contained in the Intermediate course.
1. The student learns the scissors kick on the side, either through the **Whole Approach** or through the **Part-Whole Approach.** (See this section for teaching suggestions.)
2. The student learns sculling on the back. (See Chapter 10, pages 109-111.)
3. The student learns treading water, combining the scissors kick and sculling with the arm movements. (See Chapter 10, pages 111-112.)
4. The student learns the coordination of the sidestroke, followed by the correct patterns of movement of the arms, using the following sequences:
   (a) The student's position is vertical, in deep water, with one side of the body to the wall, holding onto the side of the pool with the near hand. The student treads water with the free hand, sculling toward the wall during the recovery of the legs, and away from the wall during the thrust of the legs.
   (b) The student pushes away from the wall to scull with both hands while treading water. The hands scull away from the midline of the body during the leg thrust and toward the midline of the body during the recovery of the legs. Repeat until the student can tread water easily using this coordination and then add step (c).
   (c) While continuing to tread water, the student tips slightly onto one side, practices treading using the above coordination, then straightens up and tips onto the other side, continuing to tread. Lean more onto the side, continue to tread, but widen the distance of the sculling action. Practice on both sides. Then lean completely onto one side, treading water, sculling with each hand reaching its respective sidestroke glide position. Continue treading water on the side. Ignore the common faults of the arms at this time.
   (d) Repeat (c) until the student can comfortably "tread water" on both sides, using the standard scissors kick on at least one side, and using the coordination in (b), above.
   (e) Teach the correct arm movements and breathing. (See this section under the **Part-Whole Approach.**)
   (f) The student practices the sidestroke, using correct arm movements and the standard scissors kick.

Progressive-Part Approach (Sequence II) —
1. The student learns the scissors kick through the **Whole Approach** or through the **Part-Whole Approach.** (See the section for teaching this skill.)
2. The student adds the action of the top arm to the scissors kick. The student practices first with and then without support. The support can be to the body, or the student can hold onto the near end of a swim-board with the lower hand.
3. Repeat No. 2, above, practicing the lower arm action with the scissors kick, the body supported by a flotation aid or by the top hand holding a free-floating support over the hip.
4. The student practices the complete stroke, first with and then without supportive aid to the body.

Part-Whole Approach —
1. **Scissors kick** Explain and demonstrate the leg action while lying on one side, and while bracketed to the side of the pool or the dock. NOTE. The instructor should demonstrate the proper method of bracketing to achieve correct body position, and how to shift the position of the lower hand to prevent the body from swaying away from a position perpendicular to the side of the pool. Move the lower hand in the same direction the body tends to sway and exert pressure with this hand against the wall to prevent swaying or to return the body to its proper position.

2. **Stationary drilling in the water** Have all students lying on the same side, 4 to 5 feet apart, bracketed to the side of the pool or the dock, or supported by a buddy in waist-deep water with all the students' heads pointing in the same direction. If a student has a tendency to execute the inverted scissors kick, he or she should roll onto the other side. (Most individuals have a natural tendency to perform the standard scissors kick on one side, and the inverted kick on the other side.) Suggested learning procedures are as follows:
   (a) Have the students recover the legs and stop.
   (b) Each foot should then be properly positioned for the extension.
   (c) Extend the legs (step out/back) and stop.
   (d) Position the feet properly for the thrust.
   (e) Execute the thrust and stop.
   (f) Recover the legs, pause, "set" the feet, pause, extend the legs, pause, "set" the feet, thrust.
   (g) Recover, and extend and thrust. Emphasize that the extension and thrust are one continuous movement.
3. **Land drill** Have all students lying on the same side, heads pointing in the same direction, 4 to 5 feet apart, in a single line or in ranks. During the initial learning attempts, all students should perform the various movements only on command of the instructor, which allows the instructor to spot and prevent or quickly correct errors. The students then practice on their own, with instructor help as needed. Suggested drilling/learning procedures are as above. A major problem in drilling on land is the difficulty of moving the bottom leg. Consequently, the leg movements will be slower than when performed in the water.
4. **Fluid drills** Student with or without support.

Arm Movements and Breathing

Whole Approach — The student is supported by a flotation device attached over the area of the waist or a free-floating aid (pull buoy) held between the legs. The student practices arm movements and breathing after an explanation/demonstration by the instructor or a qualified aide.

Part-Whole Approach — The student stands in chest-deep water, the body bent sideways, the lower shoulder in the water, with the arms in their respective glide positions, horizontal to the surface of the water. Following the explanation/demonstration, either arm may be practiced first, followed by the other arm, and then followed by practicing the arms working as a complete unit.

1. **Lower Arm**
   (a) **From the glide position,** flex the wrist slightly, rotate the little finger side of the hand downward, the palm facing to the side.
   (b) **For propulsion,** the elbow bends as the hand pulls slightly outward and backward to a point in front of the lower shoulder.
   (c) **To recover,** draw the hand toward the lower shoulder and the elbow toward the body.
   (d) **To extend,** rotate the wrist, palm down, with the fingers pointing forward, and slide the arm forward to full extension, 6 to 8 inches below the surface.
   (e) Repeat the above steps as necessary, then drill without pauses between each step. Hold the glide position momentarily.
2. **Top Arm**
   (a) **To recover,** bend the elbow and draw the hand to the lower shoulder. Keep the hand and forearm close to the body during recovery. Inhale during recovery.
   (b) **For propulsion,** press the hand toward the feet until the arm is fully extended, with the palm of the hand resting on the thigh. Keep the hand close to the body during the thrust. Exhale during the thrust.
   (c) Repeat the above steps, as necessary. Repeat without pauses between the recovery and the thrust. Hold the glide position momentarily.
3. **Both Arms**
   (a) Pull the lower arm. Begin to recover the top arm near the finish of the pull of the lower arm.
   (b) Recover the lower arm and finish the recovery of the top arm. Inhale during the recovery of the top arm.
   (c) Exhale as the top arm presses backward and the lower arm extends forward. Repeat, pausing briefly with the arms in their glide positions.
4. **Both Arms — Fluid Drills** The student practices, supported by a flotation device attached to the midsection of the body.

Coordination

1. The student, nonsupported or supported by a flotation aid to the body if necessary —
   (a) Practices the fully coordinated stroke.
   (b) Practices coordination of each arm with the leg action, if necessary, followed by the fully coordinated stroke.
   (c) Practices the full stroke without support.
2. The student, supported by a swimboard or similar aid —
   (a) Practices coordination of the top arm and leg action, holding onto the supportive aid with the lower hand, the arm either fully extended to the front or cradling the aid near the head.
   (b) Practices coordination of the lower arm and leg action, while holding the supportive device over the hip with the top hand.
   (c) Practices the full stroke with and then without support to the body.

Common Faults: Cause(s), Effect(s), Teaching Suggestions

Body Position:

1. **Bent at hips (flexed) or severe arch in back.** Head and shoulder too far forward or backward. Tense back muscles. Adjust head position. Imagine stretching

and relaxing body as if lying on a bed. Practice with free floating support.

2. **Head held high.** Causes tense neck muscles. May cause lowering of legs and added resistance to forward motion. Relax neck muscles and lay cheek and ear in water.

3. **Body is almost turned onto stomach or back.** Top shoulder and head too far forward or backward. Correct as for fault No. 1. Each student will find best balance position on side through experimenting.

4. **Foot of lower leg breaks water, end of extension.** Body has rolled onto stomach. Correct body position.

5. **Foot of top leg breaks surface, end of extension.** Body has rolled onto back. Correct body position.

6. **Body rolls onto back, end of thrust of top arm.** Caused by wide, sweeping pull past thigh. Correction: See Top Arm (faults).

7. **Excessive rolling.** Causes: Loss of forward momentum, glide too long, very buoyant person. Upsets timing/coordination. Shorten glide.

8. **Body bobs up and down.** See Lower Arm (faults).

9. **Lower arm not extended in line with the body during glide.** See Lower Arm (fault No. 7).

Leg Action (Scissors Kick — Recovery):

1. **Draws top and/or lower knee too far forward toward chest.** Upsets body position; causes rounded back and too much hip flexion. Correct by emphasizing relaxation and ease of recovery movement, and keeping back straight. Land drill and buddy-supported drills will help.

2. **Draws lower leg and knee too far forward past imaginary longitudinal axis line of body.** Difficult to extend foot/leg to rear. Keep heels in line with spine during recovery. Land drill and buddy-supported drill will help. Oral and manual assistance may be necessary.

3. **Drops lower leg too far, especially the knee.** Upsets good body position. Reduces effectiveness of kick. Emphasize keeping knees almost together during recovery. Use buddy-supported drill. Oral and manual assistance may be necessary. Land drill, legs extended over the water, or bracket drill also useful.

Leg Action (Scissors Kick — Extension):

1. **Kicking top leg and foot out to extended position from glide position.** Or same movement following too short a recovery. Causes added resistance. Practice correct movement through land, bracket, or buddy-supported drills.

2. **Fails to properly flex top ankle or extend lower ankle prior to extension.** Student should think of stepping out and over an obstacle. Corrective techniques are same as No. 1, above.

3. **Not getting enough leg spread.** Decreased range of movement for thrust. Have student pretend to try and touch the wall, dock, or shore, almost directly in front of and/or behind body.

4. **Reaching too far forward with top leg or too far backward with lower leg.** Upsets body balance.

Emphasize easy, comfortable reach. Stationary and free floating drills helpful.

5. **Top leg going to rear, bottom leg going forward (inverted scissors kick).** Try swimming on opposite side. If fault persists, correct through practice in shallow water using stationary drill.

6. **Forceful extension, very little thrusting action.** Emphasize continuous movement of extension and thrust (propulsion comes from the thrust, not the extension). Use stationary drills with oral instruction.

Leg Action (Scissors Kick — Propulsion):

1. **Failure to bring feet together at end of thrust.** Reduces effective propulsion. Usually because of forceful extension and then letting legs drift together. May be so because of swimmer having learned the kick through a count method (1—up, 2—out, 3—together, 4—glide). Use words such as up/out and together/glide. Use stationary and free-floating drills with oral commands. Emphasize accelerating thrust of legs to end of kick.

2. **Legs and feet cross each other at end of thrust.** Correct by having bottom of top foot "hook" top of lower foot at end of thrust. Practice until student can "feel" when feet should stop at proper time, then practice without "hooking." Repeat drill as necessary.

Arm Action (Lower Arm):

1. **Pressing downward.** Lifts shoulder and head, which may sink during lower arm recovery. May be caused by trying to swim "up" to surface, instead of swimming through water. May be caused by need to raise head for better inhalation. Emphasize outward and backward press. Correct through stationary and free-floating drills. Over-correction with horizontal pull may be necessary.

2. **Pulls too far past lower shoulder.** Upsets timing. Emphasize easy pull. Have student look at hand during pull. Stop pull short of shoulder.

3. **Pulls too wide of imaginary centerline through long axis of body.** Emphasize easy, lateral, backward press, keeping elbow under and in line with body. Stationary drills on land and in shallow water helpful.

4. **Letting arm drop during glide.** Tends to pull swimmer down. Practice reaching ahead and slightly upward toward surface on extension. Keep arm 6 to 8 inches under surface during glide. In chest- to shoulder-depth water, knees bent, feet on bottom, leaning to side, both arms in respective glide positions, push from bottom or side of pool, arms and body assuming glide position. Student looks at lower arm during glide. Repeat drill as often as necessary. In floating support drill, using arms only, student looks at lower arm for proper position during extension and glide.

5. **Hand comes out of water during extension.** Use same drills as in No. 4, above, to correct.

6. **Pushes water during extension.** Causes added resistance. Swimmer fails to recover hand to shoulder and draw elbow into body. Swimmer fails to rotate

wrist before extension. Practice correct recovery and wrist rotation. Emphasize having fingers lead arm during extension. Stationary, shallow water drills may be necessary.

7. **Arm is extended left or right of imaginary centerline through long axis of body during glide.** Causes swimmer to veer off intended line of direction. Correct by looking directly ahead or behind at a stationary object. Keep body in line with this object while stroking and gliding.

Arm Action (Top Arm):

1. **Recovers too far from body.** Causes added resistance by pushing water with lower part of arm. Correct by touching suit and body with thumb during recovery.

2. **Reaching beyond lower shoulder.** May cause body to roll onto stomach. Correct through stationary and fluid drills (top arm only). Have student look at hand. Stop recovery just short of shoulder.

3. **Wide, sweeping pull.** Lateral forces can push body off line. Emphasize bent arm, backward press with forearm and hand. Drag thumb along body and suit during press.

4. **Presses arm past thigh.** Usually caused by wide, sweeping pull. Upsets body position (rolls onto back). Correct as for fault No. 3, above.

5. **Finishes arm thrust, glides with elbow bent.** Emphasize straight, fully extended arm. Imagine throwing a ball as far as possible past feet.

Coordination:

1. **Propulsion of both arms and legs is simultaneous.** Repeat coordination drills using oral instruction as much as necessary.

2. **Jerky, uneven rhythm.** Swim to music of slow to medium tempo, or with a good swimmer to set the pace and rhythm. Swim to oral instructions from instructor.

3. **Little or no glide.** Count 3 to 4 seconds after completion of each stroke. Do not hold glide until forward momentum is lost or until sinking or rolling of body occurs.

Breathing:

1. **Holding the breath, breathing intermittantly, or inhaling on thrust of top arm.** For all of these breathing faults, correction may be given by land or water drills with commands from instructor. Loss of momentum is greatest during recovery of top arm and legs. Inhalation during these movements will create added buoyancy that will help overcome tendency of body to sink.

2. **Lifts head, or rotates head and shoulder of top arm too far away from water on breathing side, to achieve effective inhalation.** Practice rhythmic breathing drills for crawl stroke to improve breathing habits. Head lift may be caused by pressing downward with lower arm. Correction can be made using drills listed in No. 1 of Arm Action (Lower Arm).

3. **Lifting and rotating face forward with each stroke.** Usually owing to swimmer trying to see where he or she is going or from fear of bumping into someone. Student should look before starting to swim and should look ahead occasionally if swimming area is crowded.

BACK CRAWL

The back crawl is the fastest stroke performed on the back and is one of the four strokes used in competitive swimming. Since the face is clear of the water, free breathing is easy; however, a regular cycle of inhalation through the mouth and exhalation through the mouth and the nose should be maintained on every complete cycle of the arms. When the arms and the legs are properly coordinated, this style of swimming can be used to swim almost any distance.

Body Position

SIDE   FRONT

The swimmer is on the back with the body almost horizontal to the surface of the water. During the stroke, the body will rotate on its longitudinal axis. It is important that the head be kept in alignment with the spine. Generally, the ears are covered by the water with the waterline running from the middle of the head to the tip of the chin. This head position will vary with the proficiency of the swimmer, the rate of movement through the water, the various body types, and the amount of buoyancy of the swimmer. The back is kept as straight as possible, with the hips flexed slightly to allow the kick to be performed just under the surface of the water.

Leg Action

The leg action is similar to the kick for the crawl stroke. It is a continuous, alternating up and down movement of the legs, with these actions originating at the hips. The feet are in a slightly pigeon-toed position, and the legs are separated slightly to allow the big toes to just miss each other. The majority of the propulsive force backward to the line of travel comes from the upward kick. This action is similar to punting a football with the top of the foot. Some propulsive force backward is provided during the downward movement of the sole of the foot pressing against the water. In addition to providing propulsion, the kick also serves to balance and stabilize the effects of the motions of the arms and the rolling of the body.

At the beginning of the upward kick, there is greater flexion of the knee, which will allow the upper surface of the lower leg and the foot to apply maximum force backward to the line of travel. The upward movement of the thigh and the knee stops just below the surface, while the foot continues its upward whipping action until the leg is straight and the toes reach the surface.

The leg remains nearly straight during the downward kick. At the end of the downward movement, the knee bends and the upward kick begins. The depth of the kick will vary depending on the length of the legs, the amount of flexibility in the hips and ankles, the pace of the stroke, and the amount of rotation of the body on its longitudinal axis.

Breathing

A regular breathing pattern is established during each complete stroke. Inhalation occurs during the recovery of one arm and exhalation during the recovery of the other arm. If water enters the mouth, the swimmer blows it out and resumes a regular breathing cycle. If the swimmer is bothered by water dropping onto the eyes and the mouth during the arm recovery, the swimmer recovers the arm slightly outside the shoulder rather than directly overhead and down the longitudinal axis of the body.

Arm Action and Stroke Coordination

In this stroke, it is vital that the arms are in constant opposition to each other. The action of the arms resembles that of a propeller. As one end of the propeller is moving, the opposite end is moving at the same rate of speed. This stroke usually employs a six-beat kick to one full cycle of the arms; however, a six-beat kick is not imperative.

SIDE   FRONT

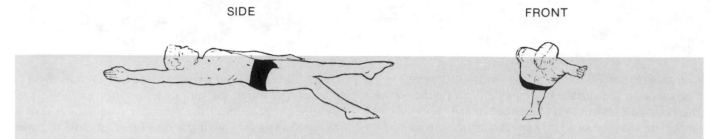

The hand enters the water, little finger first, palm to the outside and slightly down, with the arm straight and in line with the shoulder. The body begins to roll onto the side of the entry arm just prior to the hand entering the water, and the opposite arm begins to lift toward the surface to start its recovery.

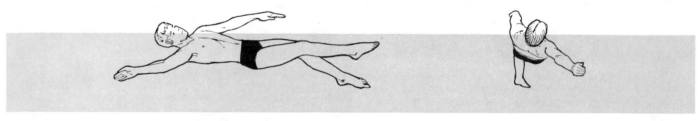

The entry hand reaches forward and downward 8 to 12 inches to its catch position. From this position, the propulsive action begins with the swimmer pressing the hand slightly outward, downward, and backward toward the feet. About one quarter through this pressing action, the arm begins to bend. It continues to bend as the hand presses upward and backward to about the midpoint of its pushing action.

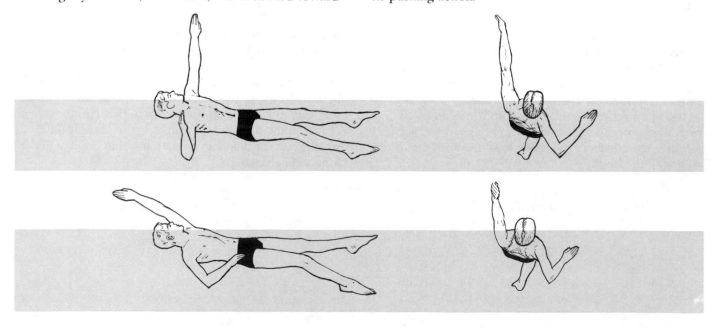

Maximum arm bend, about 90°, is reached at the midpoint of the pressing action. The hand then accelerates its pressing action backward and downward, ending with the arm straight and the hand just below the buttocks. This pressing action provides propulsion as well

as overcoming the tendency of the body to sink because of the weight of the recovering arm pressing the body downward. The hand leads the elbow during this phase of the propulsive action.

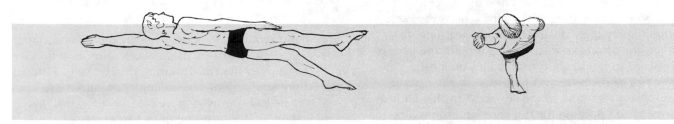

The swimmer begins to roll onto the side of the entry arm as the forward hand is preparing to enter the water. The body continues to roll as the entry hand reaches forward and downward to its catch position, and the opposite arm is lifting toward the surface to begin its recovery.

The propulsive action of one arm and the recovery action of the other arm begin simultaneously. The

recovery is initiated by lifting the arm from the water with either the little finger side or thumb side of the hand leading, or leading with the back of the hand. Some swimming coaches prefer leading with the thumb side up, since this allows greater relaxation of the large muscles on the back of the upper arm. During the recovery, the arm follows an almost perpendicular path to the water back to the point of entry.

Suggested Learning Approaches

Whole Approach — Demonstrate the stroke in slow motion. The instructor should introduce the straight arm pull first, followed by the bent arm pull. Improvement of the stroke parts or the coordination can be achieved through the various drills discussed in the **Progressive-Part Approach.**

Progressive-Part Approach — The back crawl requires a flutter kick, which provides effective propulsion and helps to establish and maintain good body position. All students should be able to perform the kick and maintain a good body position as described in 1(d), below. The following drills can be used by students who need to improve their kick and body position.

1. **Suggested kicking drills**
   (a) The instructor explains and demonstrates the kick and good body position, if necessary.
   (b) The student practices the kick with the arms at the sides. Advance the student to drill 1(c) as soon as a proficient kick is performed.
   (c) The student practices the kick with one arm at the side and the other extended beyond the head, in line with the body, and kept just under the surface, with the body rolled slightly onto the side of the forward extended arm.

The student practices on one side and then reverses arm positions to practice on the other side. Add drill 1(d) when the student demonstrates a good kick and the ability to sustain good body position on both sides.

   (d) The student, on the back, practices the kick with both arms extended directly beyond the head. The kick should be deeper, not above the body line, in order to support good hip position. The arms should be kept straight and, if possible, the thumbs should be touching or even interlocked, which will help stabilize the position of the arms. The arms should be underwater with the palms of the hands near to and almost parallel to the surface. If the arms are too deep, and the wrists are extended with the palms of the hands and fingers angled downward from the surface, the face may be pulled under the surface from the planing action of the arms. NOTE. Because of a lack of flexibility in the shoulder joints or because of bulky upper back muscles, some persons will be unable to bring the arms or hands together. Have them practice with the arms held as closely together as possible without upsetting good body position.

(e) A variation of 1(d) can be performed by having the student hold onto the trailing edge of a swimboard with both hands, with the arms fully extended behind the head.

2. **Suggested drills for arm actions and kicking and stroking coordination** There are many drills that can be used to develop an efficient and rhythmic back crawl. The following drills are effective and are sequenced to force correct patterns of movement that lead to an efficient stroke. Drill sequences 2(a) through 2(e), below, can be used. A more elaborate sequencing of drills would be: Double Under, Double Over, One Arm Backstroke, and Kick 7-5-3 or a variation [(2(a), below), followed by 2(d)].

Explain and demonstrate the actions of the arms, emphasizing that they are in constant opposition to each other. The timing of the arm actions resemble a spinning propeller. During the initial learning, the propulsion arm is kept straight as it pulls and presses backward to the thigh, 6 to 8 inches under the surface. The opposite arm recovers over the water, almost perpendicular to the surface. **Emphasize** the correct hand position for the entry and the rolling of the body onto the side of the entry arm.

Emphasize that the recovery (and pull) should be done quite rapidly. A slow arm recovery may cause the body to sink because of the weight of the arm out of the water pushing the body downward. It is possible to swim slowly and maintain good body position if the actions of the underwater arm are very efficient. A good kick will help to stabilize the body and prevent it from sinking during the arm recovery. To test the effectiveness of the kick to stabilize the body position, have the students swim using slow propulsive and recovery movements. Those students who show a tendency to sink need more practice to develop a stronger kick.

Explain and demonstrate the 7-5-3 drill and its variations (10-8-6-4-3 or 8-6-4-3). The numbering sequence (explained below) indicates on which kick the student pulls and recovers the arms simultaneously. The following drill uses the 7-5-3 kicking sequence. Any similar sequence can be used successfully to prevent or overcome the three common problems that may occur in learning or performing the back crawl. These three problems are improper timing of the arm movements, maintaining a good body position, and lack of smoothness or good rhythm in the total stroke.

(a) The student starts kicking with one arm extended behind the head and the opposite arm alongside the body, with the body rolled partially onto the side of the forward extended arm. On the seventh kick, pull the forward extended arm and recover the other arm simultaneously. Roll partially onto the side of the recovering arm as it is completing its recovery. Kick seven times and pull and recover simultaneously. Emphasize that during the first six kicks, the student must concentrate on being ready to pull and recover simultaneously on the seventh kick. Breathing can occur at any time

during this drill. Repeat until the student performs this drill smoothly and effectively. Emphasize the correct head position. Most students should look almost straight up while practicing.

(b) Repeat the above drill, but have the student pull and recover simultaneously on every fifth kick. Move on to 2(c), below, as soon as the student performs this drill effectively.

(c) Have the student pull and recover simultaneously on every third kick. Repeat until the student performs the stroke effectively, smoothly, and with good rhythm. The student should also develop a regular breathing cycle by inhaling on the recovery of one arm and exhaling during the recovery of the other arm.

(d) **Bent arm pull/press** Explain and demonstrate. Emphasize that the hand accelerates its action and leads the elbow during the last half of the pressing action. The pulling/pressing actions are similar to throwing a baseball or a football. Use the 7-5-3 drill or one of its variations.

(e) **Straight arm pull, using "S" motion patterns with the hand and arm** This drill is effective as a lead up to the bent arm press. From the catch position, the student presses outward and slightly downward and backward and then upward slightly to the midpoint of the backward pressing action, and then backward and downward to the completion of the propulsive phase. Use the 7-5-3 drill or one of its variations.

(f) **Double arm under** Upon establishing a sound supporting flutter kick on the back, the next step is to introduce an arm stroke that incorporates the fundamentals of the arm patterns as simply as possible without interfering with the leg kick. The emphasis should be on a simultaneous pulling of both arms moving no faster than the flow of the moving water. The emphasis is still on the kick with the arms going through and establishing patterns of movement only, and not trying to contribute noticeably to forward momentum. The recovery of the arms is simultaneous and is along the body line, underwater and very slow.

The arm stroke is a straight arm action moving away from the midline of the body and deeper in the beginning, getting shallower in the middle, and deeper in the end. The arms are then recovered along the body line under the water and extended into the stretch position underwater. The arms should remain stretched for four or five kicks or until the body has assumed a horizontal position again. This stretch position is important to emphasize. The emphasis of the arms moving downward on the end of the stroke is for support. As the arms begin to separate during the pull and move farther into the stroke,

84

the center of gravity begins to shift down into the hip region. The pressing action of the hands downward at the end of the stroke counters the potential dropping of the hips.

(g) **Double arm over** Once the arm patterns have been established, a "double arm over" recovery can be incorporated. This drill will help establish a vertical recovery and will put pressure on maintaining a strong supporting kick. There can be more emphasis on the arm pull but not to the point of overpowering the kick. If the swimmer finds it impossible to maintain a good body position, then return to the "double arm under" drill until the body position becomes well-established. As in the "double arm under," the swimmer must delay at the end of the "double arm over" to allow for a recovery of good body position.

(h) **One arm backstroke** The one arm backstroke begins to bring the kicking action and the arm action together. The drill seems to force a coordination between the arms and the legs and continues to force an emphasis on the kick as a supporting device.

The swimmer keeps one arm extended forward of the shoulder and moves the other arm through a straight arm pull and recovery. The arm that is extended underwater must not be used during the drill. An alternate method is to keep one arm alongside the body while practicing the movements of the other arm.

As in the other drills, the swimmer must strive to maintain a horizontal body position, vertical eye sight, and a deep supportive kicking action. This will be the first time in the learning process where some rolling action might be encountered by the swimmer.

This drill is then followed by the 7-5-3 drill, or one of its variations, which is then followed by drill 2(d), above.

Common Faults: Cause(s), Effect(s), Corrective Suggestions

Body Position:

1. **Extreme arch in back; head too far back.** Head may go under; tops of thighs may come out of water. Correct by relaxing the back, tucking chin slightly.

2. **Excessive bending at hips.** Causes frontal resistance. Chin may be tucked too much. Check head position. Flutter kicking practice, with arms extended behind head, will help. Swimmer concentrates on stretching the body and keeping kick lower than body line.

3. **Excessive rolling.** May be due to excessive rolling of head. Keep head relatively still as body rotates on its longitudinal axis. NOTE. Amount of roll will vary between swimmers. Allowances must be made for individual differences.

4. **Head held too high.** Upsets body position. Body may go into sitting position. Legs and feet will sink. Lay head back in water. Adjust chin position to achieve desired body position.

5. **Yawing, side-to-side twisting movement of shoulders.** Usually caused by over-reaching on entry (entering behind head or across midline of body). Can cause hips to sway from side to side, upsetting effective kicking action of legs, and can also cause a jerky stroke and uneven rhythm. Correct by having hands enter water at "11:00" and "1:00." May also be caused by moving head laterally from side to side. Keep head aligned with spine.

Leg Action:

1. **Legs too far below surface.** Check head position. May be too high. Hips may be too low. May also be caused by excessive arch in the back. Stress that toes should reach or almost reach surface at end of each upward beat. Water should "boil" at surface. Downward beat may be too deep. Narrow range of movement.

2. **Kicking upward with ankle flexed (dorsi), toes pointed upward.** Loss of efficiency. Ankles must be flexed (plantar) with toes pointed away from ankles. Practice kicking while lying on one side of body. Student adjusts head position to watch legs and feet. "Kick a football" on forward movement or swing of leg. Use of swim fins will help some students.

3. **Pulls knees toward chin.** Uses bicycle kick or pumping action of each leg. Corrective practice as in No. 2, above.

4. **Wriggly hips, quivering legs.** Ineffective kick. Doesn't use thighs to initiate up and down movements. Practice kicking while lying on one side of body. Start with wide, swinging back and forth kick. Gradually narrow range of movement. Then gradually roll onto back while kicking steadily.

Arm Action (Recovery):

1. **Low, lateral sideways motion.** Can cause shoulders, hips, and legs to sway out of line. Emphasize vertical recovery.

2. **Hand enters water behind head or crosses over imaginary long axis centerline of body.** Can upset body position and cause an overly long lateral sweep of hand prior to start of effective arm propulsion. Entry of the left hand at "1:00" and the right hand at "11:00" will help correct this problem.

3. **Hand and arm cross over imaginary long axis centerline of body during initial phase of recovery.** May cause shoulders to twist out of line. Correct by having student watch the arm recover, keeping it vertical and outside of the centerline of body.

4. **Upper arm, or part thereof, is underwater.** Causes resistance. Caused by swimming too flat or using low, sweeping recovery to the side. Emphasize body roll with vertical arm recovery and high shoulder position for lifting arm.

5. **Recovery too slow.** May upset timing of arms or cause body to sink partially. Emphasize "propeller" action of arms, keeping them in constant opposition to

each other. Use 7-5-3 drill, emphasizing acceleration of propulsion arm and corresponding rapid recovery of opposite arm. NOTE. Ability to swim this stroke slowly and effectively indicates good overall technique.

6. **Enters water with back of hand first.** Hand cannot effectively and quickly reach to catch position. Emphasize rotating the arm prior to entry to permit little finger to enter first, with palm turned outward. Have student turn head to watch hand entry. CAUTION. Use this technique sparingly, since turning the head will upset good body position.

7. **Arms too tense.** Causes fatigue. Have student gently shake arm and fingers during recovery.

8. **"Splash" entry.** Caused by bent arm recovery or when elbow enters water first and forearm and hand are thrown or "smashed" into water. This creates air bubbles under surface and makes it difficult to grasp water with palm at catch position. Emphasize straight arm recovery and **placing** of little finger side of hand in water first. Use 7-5-3 drill. Also see No. 6, above.

Arm Action (Propulsion):

1. **Pulling horizontally with straight arm.** Loss of efficiency, lack of use of good leverage. Correct by using bent arm pull/push to get effective propulsion.

2. **Body bobs up and down.** May be caused by pulling too deep initially with straight arm and then pressing upward to complete propulsive action. Correct by using bent arm propulsive movements. May be caused by weak kick and allowing body to sink partially during arm recovery. Improve kick. May be caused when recovering arm slows or stops momentarily as it is descending for its entry. Weight of arm and loss of forward momentum are transferred downward

to head and shoulders. Correct by swinging recovery arm upward and behind its shoulder with a rapid, continuous movement.

3. **Dropping elbow or leading push with elbow.** Causes loss of effective leverage, constant pressure of hand against water. Use 7-5-3 drills. Have student watch each arm during propulsive action. Use flotation device, if necessary, to allow slow motion drilling.

Breathing

1. **Holds breath.** Causes fatigue. Practice breathing every stroke. Inhale during recovery of right arm, exhale during recovery of other arm; or, inhale as right arm reaches top of its recovery, then exhale immediately, then inhale as left arm reaches top of its recovery and exhale immediately.

Coordination

1. **Arms not in continuous opposition.** Causes jerky stroke, loss of continuous smooth propulsion through water. **Corrective suggestions:** (a) Repeat 7-5-3 drill, (b) have student swim to music or hum a tune that has rhythm slow enough to swim to, or (c) instructor can set good rhythm by facing student while standing near edge of pool or dock, and rotating body from side to side using steady rhythm slow enough to swim to. Student, eyes on instructor, swims away from and in line with instructor. Student pulls/recovers each time instructor rotates sides.

A similar drill can be used in which student swims to rhythm set by instructor who uses arm movements while "swimming" stroke on deck. Practice until student can "feel" and maintain good rhythm.

SEDLACK-1981

CHAPTER 9

ANALYZING AND TEACHING OTHER STYLES OF SWIMMING

*Don't Envy A Good Swimmer
Be One!"*

The Commodore

The strokes that appear in this chapter are variations of modern day swimming strokes. Even though these hybrid strokes are seldom used, they are included for two major reasons:

- To preserve some of the history of swimming.
- To offer additional challenges for swimmers to learn new skills, either through advanced Red Cross swimming courses or through self-learning.

The inverted breaststroke, the overarm sidestroke, and the trudgen stroke are included in the Red Cross Advanced Swimmer course. Consequently, the instructor is provided with comprehensive information about these strokes.

The trudgen crawl, the double trudgen, and the double-trudgen crawl are all strokes using combinations of the arm movements of the crawl stroke and the scissors kick or a combination of the scissors kick and the flutter kick.

The double trudgen stroke is essentially the trudgen stroke performed on one side, followed by the trudgen stroke on the other side. Breathing occurs on one side only. To change from the trudgen stroke to the double trudgen stroke, the pelvis must rotate beyond the prone glide position to the opposite side to permit the top leg to reach forward in a scissors kick.

The trudgen crawl stroke employs a narrowed scissors kick in conjunction with flutter kicks. The trudgen crawl is essentially the trudgen stroke on one side, with the scissors kick followed immediately by three or four flutter kicks. Many swimmers find it easier to coordinate this stroke by using a widened flutter kick on the breathing side instead of a narrowed scissors kick, followed immediately by three or four flutter kicks with the body in the prone glide position. Simply rolling the body more onto the side when breathing will produce a widened flutter kick.

The double trudgen crawl employs a very narrow scissors kick and two flutter kicks on one side. These actions are then repeated on the opposite side. Swimmers who perform the six-beat crawl stroke will find it easier to coordinate the double trudgen crawl by simply rolling the body more to each side, which will produce a widened flutter kick, instead of by trying to develop a narrow scissors kick.

The English backstroke, sometimes called the European backstroke, is being used by competitive swimmers in Masters Senior events that are conducted under the auspices of the Amateur Athletic Union (AAU). This stroke is described very well in the *Book On Swimming*, published in 1915 by the Amateur Swimming Association of Great Britain. The stroke employs the breaststroke kick on the back. The propulsive actions of the arms are as described for the inverted breaststroke. The arms recover over the water simultaneously, in the same manner as the arm recovery for the back crawl. From the inverted breaststroke glide position, the stroke is started by pulling the arms to the thighs. The legs and arms begin to recover simultaneously. The legs complete their propulsive actions as the hands enter the water. A short glide may be taken following the entry of the hands and also at the completion of the pressing actions of the arms. The inhalation is taken during the recovery of the arms and the exhalation during the pressing of the arms.

The butterfly breaststroke was officially recognized and used as a competitive swimming stroke during the 1930s. The techniques of performing this stroke are thoroughly discussed in the book *Competitive Swimming and Diving*, authored by David Armbruster and first published in 1942 by the C. V. Mosby Company, St. Louis, Missouri. Basically, this stroke uses the breaststroke kick in combination with the arm stroke that is used in the butterfly stroke.

OVERARM SIDESTROKE

This variation of the sidestroke enables the swimmer to recover the top arm out of the water, thus increasing the efficiency of the stroke by overcoming the resistance or negative action encountered in the underwater recovery of the top arm in the sidestroke.

The body position, leg kick, breathing, and the action of the lower arm are the same as for the sidestroke. The coordination of both strokes may be the same. However, because of the longer range of movement of the top arm during its recovery in the overarm sidestroke, a slight modification of the coordination should be made to achieve a smoother stroke. Most swimmers develop a smoother stroke by delaying the start of the recovery of the legs until the top hand enters the water.

Arm Action and Coordination

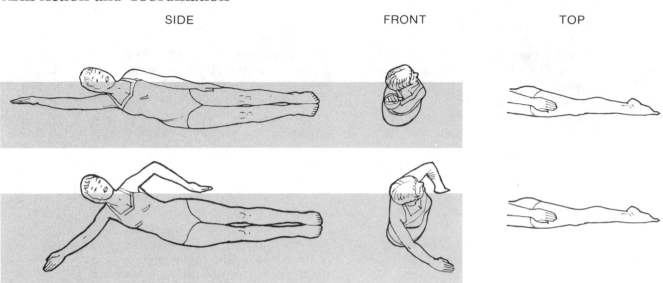

SIDE | FRONT | TOP

From the glide position, the stroke starts with the simultaneous pressing action of the lower arm and the recovery of the top arm. The recovery action of the top arm is the same as for the arms in the crawl stroke.

The forearm, the wrist, and the hand should be relaxed, and they should be kept close to the body during the recovery. The legs remain straight and together during the initial recovery movements of the top arm.

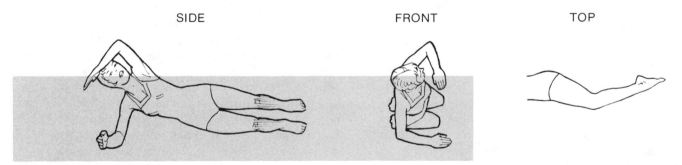

SIDE | FRONT | TOP

The top hand enters the water about in line with the top of the head. During this action, the legs recover as the lower arm is completing its pressing action backward to about the upper chest area.

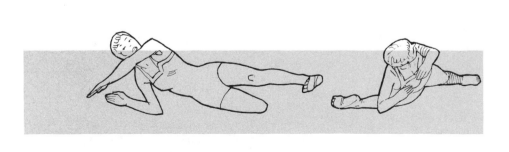 

As the top hand begins to pull, the legs extend and the lower arm recovers. The lower arm extends forward to its glide position during the positive actions of the top arm and the legs. At the completion of the stroke, a glide is taken but not to the point of losing forward momentum.

Suggested Learning Approaches

Whole Approach — The students practice the stroke after observing a skilled demonstration. It may be beneficial for the students to practice the sidestroke first on the side that is most natural for the scissors kick. The students should learn to perform the stroke on both sides, using the standard scissors kick. Emphasize delaying the leg recovery until the top hand enters the water.

Progressive-Part Approach — Use this approach with students having difficulty with the timing in the **Whole Approach.**

1. The student pushes off the bottom or the side of the pool into the sidestroke glide position while the lower hand holds onto the near edge of a swimboard. During forward momentum from the push-off or a previous stroke, the top arm recovers as the lower hand draws the swimboard toward the top of the head. The legs recover as the top hand enters the water. The lower arm extends forward during the propulsive actions of the top arm and the legs. Repeat the exercise until the student performs it with correct coordination.

2. Practice the stroke without support, using the lower arm action as for the sidestroke.

Common Faults: Cause(s), Effect(s), Corrective Suggestions

Body Position, Leg Action, Lower Arm Action, Breathing: See Sidestroke (Faults and Corrections).

Top Arm:

1. **Dragging the hand, wrist, and/or elbow through the water during recovery.** See Crawl Stroke — Arm Action (Recovery).

2. **Over-reaching for entry.** Will cause face to roll into water. Swimmer may roll onto stomach. Stress fingers entering water at a point between hairline and "end" of head. Have student watch fingers enter water.

3. **Pulling wide of body; hand passes by thigh at end of push.** See Sidestroke — Arm Action (Top Arm).

Coordination:

1. **Starting recovery of top arm and legs at same time.** Often causes jerky, uneven stroke. A smoother stroke usually results when legs start their recovery as top hand enters water. If necessary, practice with body supported by flotation device until desired results are achieved.

INVERTED BREASTSTROKE

The inverted breaststroke is an adaptation of the breast-stroke and the elementary backstroke. This stroke, which uses the inverted breaststroke kick, can be an effective and relaxed style of swimming on the back, especially for swimmers who possess good body buoyancy. The coordination is similar to the breaststroke in that it employs an alternating, paired arm and leg action, followed by a glide. All arm and leg movements are performed under the surface.

	SIDE	FRONT	REAR

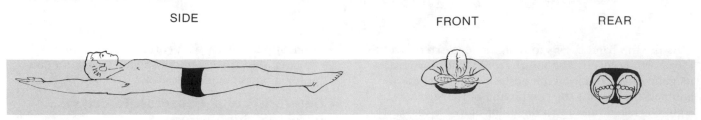

In the starting and the gliding position, the body is in a streamlined horizontal position with the back flat. The head is submerged to about the level of the ears with the chin slightly tucked, thus leaving the face out of the water for free breathing. The arms are fully extended behind the head, with the hands together and the palms up and slightly under the surface. The legs are fully extended, with the hips, the legs, and the feet kept just beneath the surface.

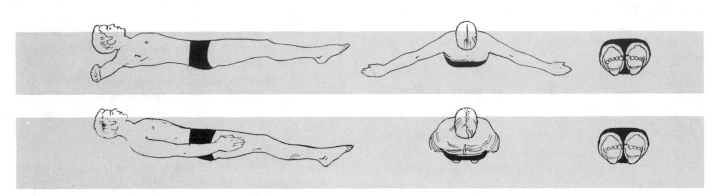

From the starting position, the arms extend laterally and press backward all the way to the sides. The arms may be straight or slightly bent during the propulsive action. Exhalation occurs during this action.

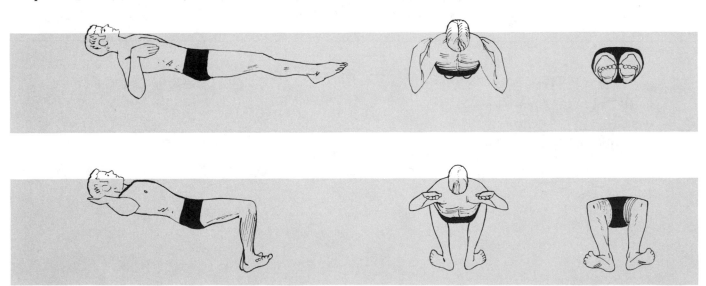

At the end of the arm press, and without pause, the hands recover up the sides as in the elementary back-stroke. Inhalation occurs during the recovery of the arms. When the hands reach a position just below the armpits, the palms are slowly and easily turned up as the hands are drawn over the shoulders. With the fingers leading, the hands slide toward and behind the ears. During the movement of the hands from the armpits to the ears, the legs recover.

90

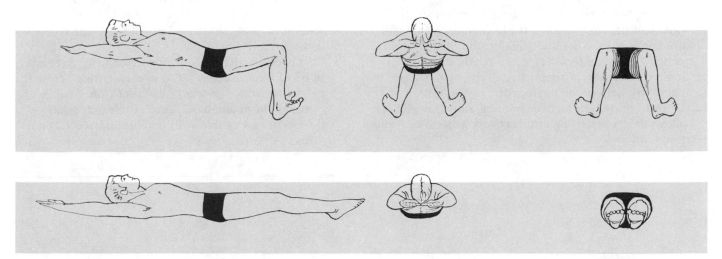

SIDE	FRONT	REAR

The arms begin to extend behind the head as the legs begin their propulsive actions. The arms are about two-thirds extended when the legs start their drive backward. The arms usually reach full extension just prior to the completion of the kick. A glide is taken but not to the point that forward momentum is lost. All recovery movements of the arms and legs should be continuous, easy, and smooth to preserve good body position. Any of the variations of the breaststroke kick on the back, as described in the section entitled "Elementary Backstroke" in Chapter 8, can be used for the inverted breaststroke.

Teaching Suggestions

1. **Whole Approach** — It is recommended that the student practice initially with support to the body, especially poor floaters.
   (a) Demonstrate the stroke. Emphasize a slow recovery of the arms and the transition of the hands from the armpits to alongside the head. Stress keeping the arms underwater and the face out of the water at all times.
   (b) Have the student practice, with and without support.
2. **Part-Whole Approach (if necessary)** —
   (a) The student, with support to the body, practices the full arm movements. Stress the points in 1(a), above. Or, the student, without support to the body, practices the arm movements while using an easy flutter kick.
   (b) The student, with support to the body, practices the fully coordinated stroke.
   (c) The student, without support to the body, practices the full stroke.

Common Faults: Cause(s), Effect(s), Corrective Suggestions
Legs: See Elementary Backstroke (Faults).
Arms and Body Position:

1. **Lifting hands/forearms out of water during movements of hands from armpits to along-side head.** May cause water to be splashed over face. May cause face to submerge if arms are lifted too high. Emphasize slow, easy transition of hands underwater from armpits to sides of head. Emphasize keeping face out of water. Fluid drills, using support to body, helpful.

2. **Submerging face during end of recovery of arms and start of extension of arms.** May be caused by lack of adequate inhalation during arm recovery. May also be caused by lack of forward movement on behalf of poor floater. Negative or poor floaters should speed up recovery and extension of arms. May also be caused by assuming sitting position during recovery of legs. Keep back and hips in good alignment.

3. **Submerging face during extension of arms behind head.** Often due to extending wrists with fingers pointing downward, which planes body downward. Correct by straightening wrists, angling fingers slightly toward surface.

4. **Submerging face during extension of arms behind head.** May be caused by arching the back and throwing head back. Stress keeping body straight and chin slightly tucked.

5. **Pulling too hard with arms.** Usually done to compensate for weak kick. Emphasize easier arm pull as this is a resting-type stroke.

6. **Pulling too deep.** Will cause body to rise and fall. Stress lateral arm pull.

7. **Arms too far apart during glide.** Detracts from "streamlined" look. Glide with arms and hands as close together as possible. Locking thumbs may help. Individuals with "heavy" back muscles will usually not be able to get arms together.

8. **Stopping pull/push short of sides of thighs.** For correct stroke form, hands should push all the way to sides of body.

9. **Recovering hands over chest.** Can lead to splashing water over face. Use correction as in No. 1, above.

Coordination:

1. **Starting leg recovery too soon in relation to position of arms during their recovery.** Emphasize holding legs together and straight until hands reach armpits. Start leg recovery when hands start to move toward head. Use of supportive device to waist or chest will help problem student.

2. **Double glide.** For form swimming, only one glide is allowed. Stress starting arm recovery as soon as hands touch thighs.

3. **No glide.** Have student count up to 3 seconds after arms have reached full extension behind head. Amount of glide, and resultant effective stroke, will vary with individuals.

4. **Completing kick before arms are fully extended behind head.** Causes jerky, uneven stroke. Stress that propulsive action of legs doesn't start until hands are alongside head and have started their extension behind head. Practice with body supported (fluid drills).

TRUDGEN

The trudgen stroke evolved from a similar stroke that was performed by South American Indians, and which was learned by John Trudgen, an Englishman, while visiting Buenos Aires, Argentina, in 1873.

With the deemphasis of the six-beat kick in the crawl stroke, and the recognition that some roll on the long axis of the body is necessary for effective stroking, many skilled swimmers and competitive swimmers are using variations of the crawl stroke that are similar to the trudgen. Its best use is perhaps as a relief stroke for swimmers who wish to continue a hand-over-hand style of swimming, but find that the flutter kick loses its effectiveness because of tiring leg muscles. Briefly, the trudgen employs the arm movements and breathing of the crawl stroke in combination with a narrowed single scissors kick performed on the breathing side only.

Coordination

SIDE   FRONT

For the swimmer who breathes on the left side in the crawl stroke, the trudgen can start with the left arm extended forward of its shoulder and with the opposite arm extended to the rear after completing its backward pressing action. The legs are straight and together.

The initial backward pressing movement of the left arm and the recovery of the right arm occur simultaneously. During these actions, the legs begin to recover. The legs remain together as the heels are drawn slightly upward and toward the hips.

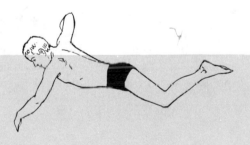

The legs continue to bend and separate slightly in preparation for the scissors kick as the right arm reaches the head during its recovery.

SIDE   FRONT

As the right arm continues to recover, the body rolls about halfway onto its right side as the legs extend sideways. At the end of their extension, the right hand enters the water. Without pausing, the left arm and the legs

complete their propulsive actions as the body slides forward on the extended right arm. A breath is taken near the end of the pressing action of the left hand.

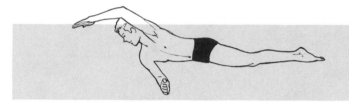

The legs remain straight, together, and streamlined during the recovery of the left arm and the propulsive action of the right arm. Some body roll occurs away from

the breathing side during the last half of the pressing action of the right arm. At the completion of this pressing movement, the next stroke is ready to begin.

Teaching Suggestions

1. **Explain/Demonstrate the Stroke** For correct swimming "form" for the Advanced Swimmer course, the arm on the breathing side must be in its propulsive phase simultaneously with the propulsive action of the legs.
2. **Learning sequence A** Use the **Whole Approach.**
3. **Learning sequence B** Demonstrate the sequence of progressing from the sidestroke to the overarm sidestroke to the trudgen.
   a. Have the students start swimming the sidestroke, lying on the side on which the breath is most comfortably taken in the crawl stroke.
   b. After two or three strokes, progress to the overarm sidestroke (without changing sides).
   c. After two or three strokes, the swimmer rolls onto

the stomach as the top (breathing) arm is recovering. During this action, the opposite arm is pulling/pressing back to the thigh while the legs remain straight and together. This arm then recovers, **underwater,** to its forward, extended position. As this arm is recovering, the body rolls slightly onto the side of the recovering arm, the legs are recovered, and the propulsive actions of the legs and the "breathing" arm are executed simultaneously.
   d. Repeat "c," recovering both arms over the water.
4. **Learning Sequence C** The following learning progressions are recommended for use by students who are having great difficulty in learning the proper coordination through sequence B.

a. Holding onto the near end of a swimboard or similar aid with both hands, the swimmer assumes a position as if practicing the flutter kick in the prone position. For the "left side" breather in the crawl stroke, have the swimmer roll over slightly onto his or her right side, and recover the legs for the scissors kick.

b. Next, the swimmer releases the grasp of the board with the left hand, and simultaneously pulls backward with the left arm and executes a narrow standard scissors kick. An inhalation is taken as in the crawl stroke.

c. Next, recover this arm while rolling onto the stomach, then grasp the board. During this recovery action, the legs remain straight and together.

d. Repeat steps "a," "b," and "c" a few times.

e. Next, add the action of the "nonbreathing" arm. As soon as the hand on the breathing side has grasped the board, the opposite arm executes its full range of movement as in the crawl stroke, ending with the hand grasping the end of the board.

f. The swimmer pauses momentarily to "set" the body as in "a," above. Then repeat steps "b" through "e" until the swimmer can quickly and smoothly switch hands while performing the proper coordination.

g. Practice the stroke without supportive aid. As soon as the student can satisfactorily perform the trudgen stroke with the above coordination without support, have the student practice changing the timing of the arms to that of the crawl stroke.

Common Faults: Cause(s), Effect(s), Corrective Suggestions

For faults and corrections of the body position, the arms, and the breathing, see Chapter 8, "Crawl Stroke." For faults and corrections of the scissors kick, see Chapter 8, "Sidestroke."

Coordination:

1. **Arm on breathing side is recovering/extending forward as propulsive action of legs is performed.** For "form" swimming, arm on breathing side must be pulling as legs deliver their thrust. Corrective suggestion: Refer to learning sequence C, just previously discussed.

2. **Very jerky, uneven rhythm.** Often caused by scissors kick being too wide. Narrow range of lateral extension of legs, or use a widened flutter kick on side. NOTE. This stroke has some stop-and-go action as result of recovery action of legs.

INSTRUCTOR
NOTES

BUTTERFLY STROKE

The butterfly stroke with the dolphin kick was officially introduced into competitive swimming in 1954. Prior to that time, the stroke was performed with the breaststroke kick. Even for modern day, top-level swimmers, it is very tiring to perform, thus making it a stroke that has very little value for recreational or survival swimming. As a recognized modern style of swimming, however, it presents a challenge for swimmers to learn and to be able to perform this stroke effectively.

Body Position

The body is kept nearly horizontal to the surface during all stroking movements. The body is flexible to allow undulating movements of the hips, knees, and feet. Except when breathing, the back of the head is almost submerged. The legs are together with the feet in the pigeon-toed position during the upward kick. The knees and legs separate slightly during the downward kick with the feet in the pigeon-toed position.

Leg Action

The leg action is the dolphin kick, which is performed similarly to the flutter kick in the crawl stroke, except that both legs are together. The kick contributes to the forward progress of the body. An efficient kick requires flexibility in the knees and ankle joints, as well as the natural ability to hyperextend (bend or extend backward beyond a straight line) the knees at the end of the downward kick. The depth of the kick ranges from approximately 12 inches to 18 inches, depending on the length of the swimmer's legs and the amount of flexibility of the ankles.

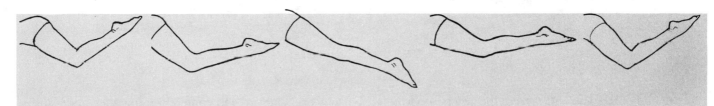

At the start of the downward beat, the knees bend and separate slightly, and the ankles are extended (plantar-flexed) with the toes curled and near the surface. Both legs press backward and downward simultaneously until the knees become hyperextended, allowing the ankles and the feet to follow through with their downward whipping action. At the end of the downward beat, the lift of the legs immediately begins from the hips. The legs are kept straight about half-way up and then the knees begin to bend. As the heels near the surface, the knees continue to bend as the heels are drawn toward the buttocks, ending with the feet positioned to start the downward beat.

Arm Action

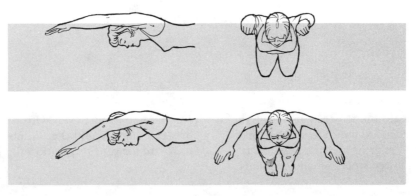

The hands enter the water forward of and slightly outside the shoulders, with the arms almost fully extended and the elbows slightly higher than the hands. At the entry, the wrists, the hands, and the fingers should be kept firm with the wrists rotated slightly so that the thumb side of the hands are down. The palms of the hands then press or scull slightly **downward** and **outward** past the shoulders. This sculling action of the hands provides forward momentum for the body. The hands do not pull backward during this action.

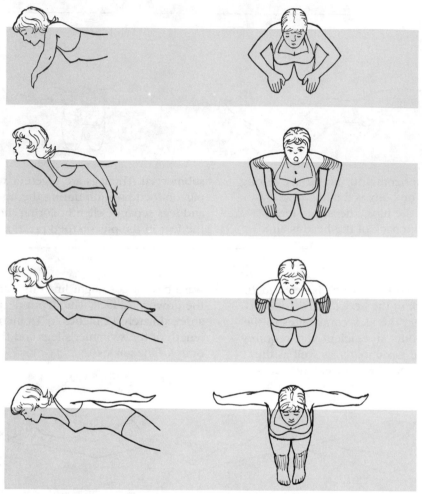

At the end of the outward sweep, the wrists rotate to place the little finger side of the hands slightly downward. The elbows begin to bend as the hands start to pull (scull) toward the midline of the body. The elbows are kept higher than the hands during this propulsive action. The elbows continue to bend as the hands press inward and come close together under the upper area of the chest. From this point, the hands press backward and then outward past the hips until the hands snap out of the water with the little finger sides of the hands leading.

The recovery actions begin immediately by lifting the arms and swinging them forward and laterally just over the surface of the water. The arms are nearly straight through the first half of the recovery. When the hands reach a line almost even with the shoulders, the elbows may rise slightly, and the thumb sides of the hands begin to rotate forward to position the hands for their entry.

Coordination and Breathing

The face is well-down in the water during the entry of the hands. A downward kick is taken that drives the hands forward and downward to their catch position.

The arms are fully extended when the hands reach the catch positions.

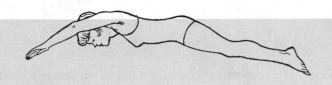 

The legs begin to lift as the arms scull outward. The legs continue to lift as the hands begin to scull toward the midline of the body. During this action, the head

begins to move forward and upward, and the exhalation continues through the mouth and nose.

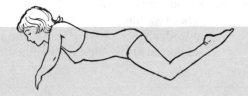 

The legs complete their upward kick, the knees drop, and the legs are ready to start the downward kick when

the hands come close together under the upper part of the chest.

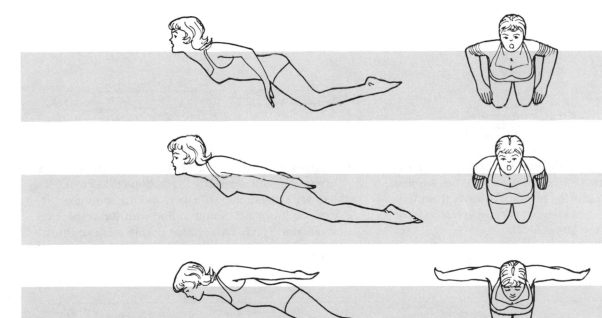

The start of the downward kick and the pressing actions of the hands backward from under the upper chest are almost simultaneous. During these actions, the

chin continues to jut forward and upward. The exhalation is almost completed when the hands pass under the chest. The mouth clears the water and inhalation begins when the hands reach the area of the stomach. The downward kick lifts the hips, allowing the

hands to clear the hips as they complete the press backward and outward.

The face returns to the water as the arms start their recovery and the legs begin their upward beat. The legs finish their upward movement and are ready to start the

downward beat when the hands enter the water. Exhalation begins as the arms pass the head and continues until the next inhalation begins.

Teaching Suggestions

The following sequences for learning the butterfly stroke are suggested for use by nonskilled swimmers. The student learns the basic movements of the arms and the legs, and the coordination, including the breathing. Surprisingly, many students can learn the following

simplified version of the butterfly stroke faster than any other swimming stroke. Negative or poor floaters, or individuals who are leg heavy, should practice first while supported at the hips with a flotation aid.

Learning Sequences

1. **Starting Position** Standing on the deck or in shallow water with the arms extended overhead, the student bends backward (starting position) slowly from the waist, and then bends forward and backward slowly from the waist a few times.

2. **Starting Position — Water** The student repeats No. 1, beginning with the starting position (facedown). The legs are straight and together, and the arms are extended forward of and in line with the respective shoulders. The breath is held during this exercise.

3. **Leg Actions** From the starting position, the legs bend to about a 90 degree angle and the ankles plantar-flex with the toes pointed. The feet kick backward and downward as the hands and the head press downward slightly and the hips rise. Assume and hold the prone

float position momentarily. Resume the starting position and repeat the drill. The student stands, takes a breath when necessary, and repeats the drill. Emphasize slow, deliberate movements.

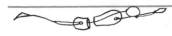  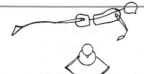 

4. **Arm Actions** From the starting position, with no leg action, press the arms downward and backward easily, ending with the arms fully extended along the sides of the body. The elbows should bend a little as the arms start to pull and press backward toward the feet. At the completion of the press of the arms, they recover slowly **under the water** back to their forward extended positions. Stop, stand, and take a breath whenever necessary. Repeat the drill. Emphasize a slow and easy pull and recovery, and resuming the starting position before starting the next arm pull.

5. **Coordination — Arms and Legs** From the starting position, "set" the legs and the feet for the downward kick and the arms for the start of their pull. Kick and pull the arms back to the sides of the thighs simultaneously. Emphasize an easy kick and arm pull. Recover the arms slowly underwater back to their forward extended positions. Stop, stand, and breathe when necessary. Resume the starting position and repeat the drill. Add step 6 for the breathing.

6. **Coordination With Breathing**
   a. From the starting position, with the legs set to kick downward, start to exhale slowly through the mouth and the nose as the arms and the legs begin their propulsive movements simultaneously. Start lifting the face toward the surface when the hands are almost under the shoulders. Continue to lift the face and jut the lower jaw forward as the hands are pressing backward. The mouth clears the water and a breath is taken during the last part of the push phase of the hands. Relax and place the face in the water at the end of the press of the hands. Recover the arms **underwater.** Hold the breath until the prone float position is reached. Repeat the cycle slowly until the student can perform the single dolphin kick butterfly stroke easily and correctly. Add step "b," below, for the second kick.
   b. As the hands are recovering underwater past the head, position the legs for their downward kick, then kick and glide on the forward extended arms. Repeat steps "a" and "b" in sequence until the student can perform the "double kick" stroke **slowly,** easily, and correctly. Add step "c," for the over-the-water recovery of the arms.
   c. Repeat step "a" with two major changes: Press the hands back faster. Lift the face and inhale when the hands are passing under the stomach. At the end of the arm press, lower the face into the water, and lift and recover the arms quickly and laterally over the water, ending with the hands entering the water forward of and slightly outside of the shoulders. Float, resume the starting position, and repeat the single butterfly stroke until the student is proficient. Add step "d," below.
   d. As the hands are passing the shoulders during the recovery of the arms, the legs lift (kick) upward and are positioned for the downward beat. A downward kick occurs as the hands enter the water. Glide. **Resume the starting position** and repeat the full stroke **slowly** using two kicks. The timing is "PULL-KICK, KICK-GLIDE," or "PULL-KICK-BREATHE, KICK-GLIDE."
   e. Repeat "d," but eliminate the glide and begin to speed up the overall pace of the movements of the arms and legs.

Additional Drills

The following drills will help the student to develop a butterfly stroke that contains effective movements of the arms and the legs, good breathing habits, and relatively good timing of the overall stroke. Students who desire to perfect this stroke and participate in swimming competition will need advanced instruction and training from a competent swimming coach.

Leg Action The following drills will help develop the necessary fishtail action of the hips, the legs, the ankles, and the feet.

1. **Students in the prone position, arms extended to the front.** Practice the double flutter (dolphin) kick. The students concentrate on making some forward movement. The feet are kept nearly together and are in the pigeon-toed position. The thighs can separate slightly.
2. **After forward movement is established,** the students practice the kick while lying on the side (left and right), and on the back. Keep the head and the shoulders steady.
3. **The students practice the kick while lying submerged on one side, and while lying submerged in the prone position.** Kicking underwater puts equal pressure on the legs during the upward and downward (or forward and backward) movements of the legs.

Using any or all of the above drills, have the students practice and develop a range of motion of about 12 to 18 inches in depth depending on the length of the swimmer's legs. The swimmer should concentrate on "bouncing" the feet up and down continuously. There is no pause at the end of the upward or downward movements of the legs.

Arms and Breathing Flotation support to the hips or the legs (pull buoy) may help students to practice the following drills:

1. **Pull and push only with no over-the-water recovery, no breathing, and no leg action.** The students concentrate on moving the hands through an "S"/hourglass/keyhole pattern of movement. Keep the elbows lower than the shoulders and higher than the hands during the pull/press. Use a shallower pull/press than in the crawl stroke. Stress pressing outward with the hands at the end of the push phase, with the little finger sides of the hands leading this action. Start with slow movements. Increase the tempo as patterns of movements are established. Use an underwater recovery. Stop and breathe as often as necessary.

2. **Repeat 1, add breathing.** The chin begins to move upward and forward as the hands begin to move backward. Inhale during the last portion of the pressing action of the hands. The chin should be about at the surface level of the water during inhalation. Drop the head (about face deep) after the end of the arm press. Resume starting position. Start exhaling when the hands start to pull. Complete the exhalation as the chin breaks the water. Repeat until good arm and breathing patterns are established.

3. **Repeat 1, add over-the-water recovery.** The little finger side of the hand leads the recovery action. The arms are nearly parallel to the surface of the water during the recovery. Rotate the thumb side of the hand forward during recovery. The fingertips enter the water first, forward of the respective shoulder. Pause, repeat all arm actions, pause, and repeat all arm actions again until they are satisfactory. Stop and breathe whenever necessary. Then practice without pausing at the front end of the stroke.

4. **Repeat 3, add breathing, first with a pause, then with continuous action.** Breathing every second stroke initially will help the learning process. Stress not raising the head too high to breathe, or dropping the head too deep. Keep the body relatively flat to the surface of the water. The top of the buttocks should rise just above the surface of the water during the entry of the hands to establish the correct position of the legs for the kick that coincides with the hand entry.

5. **Use of the flutterkick (with no support to the body)** will help to develop the above actions and will help to develop the feel of keeping the body relatively flat, or will help to prevent excessive undulation of the body.

Coordination

1. **One arm fly.** The emphasis in this drill is to force the students to time the leg kicks with the arm actions, which overcomes the tendency of most learners to kick faster than the arms can execute their complete arm actions. Two downward kicks occur, the *first* during the entry of the hands, and the *second* during the pulling action of the arms. The second kick helps the arms to finish their pressing actions backward.

Step 1. The students are in the prone position, both arms extended forward of the shoulders, with the head down. Keeping one arm stretched forward, the opposite arm pulls vigorously in time with a downward kick. Continue with the arm recovery over the water and kick downward as the hand enters the water. There is no breathing during the stroking movements. To breathe, stand up, and then repeat the drill. **Swim this drill slowly** to force the kick to be timed with the arms. Practice pulling with the arm for a few strokes and then pull with the opposite arm for a few strokes. Then add alternating arm actions.

Step 2. Add breathing to step 1. In this drill, the breath is taken in the same manner and at the same time as in the crawl stroke. The exhalation begins at the entry of the hand and continues slowly in time with the arm action until the second kick is initiated. At this point, an explosive exhale coincides with the downward kick. The inhalation occurs immediately after the strong exhalation and as the arm finishes its pressing action. Alternate the arms as in step 1 until reasonable coordination is achieved.

Step 3. Introduce the "two arm fly" with breathing to the front. Slow patterns should be emphasized in the initial learning phases.

2. **One arm fly — arm at side.** The one arm fly, No. 1, above, tends to keep the body too flat in the water. This drill helps the students to establish a head drop and hip lift action that helps establish better overall body movements (undulation). The nonpulling arm is held alongside the body. The students practice dropping the head just far enough at the entry of the hand to pop the seat of the swimming suit out of the water. **The majority of the body undulation must occur from the hips through the feet.**

3. **The students in the prone position in shallow water.** The face remains in the water during the following movements. Do a downward kick, leaving the arms extended forward. Next, simultaneously pull the hands and do a second kick and recover the arms to the entry position. Stop the arms in the entry/glide position. Repeat the sequence. Stop, stand, and breathe, as necessary. Repeat the sequence with the students until they begin to feel the rhythm of the stroke. Then add breathing. Emphasize that the head comes up before the arms come out of the water and that the head goes back into the water before the hands enter. Start lowering the head into the water as the arms start their recovery.

4. **The students in standing depth water (variation of 1, above).** The students push off into a prone glide, do a kick glide, and then a kick pull/recovery with both arms simultaneously. Stop, stand, and breathe, and repeat the sequence until a feel for the timing is developed. Then pause/stand after every second stroke. Add breathing. Stress starting to push the chin forward and upward as the arms start to pull, not stopping the arm action at the back end of the stroke, and not starting to pull on the "first" kick (hand entry kick).

5. **The students push off from the side of the pool into a prone glide,** arms extended forward of the shoulders. Do two kicks, then pull the arms, recover, and glide. No breathing. Stop, stand, and breathe. Repeat as necessary. Add starting the arm pull as the legs kick downward on the *second* kick. Repeat as necessary. Then allow the students to do two, three, and four continuous strokes as their abilities progress. Repeat the above sequences, adding breathing.

Common Faults: Cause(s), Effect(s), Corrective Suggestions

The faults that are listed below comprise only a portion of the faults that may occur. The individual who desires to become very knowledgeable about the butterfly stroke is advised to seek information from competent swimming coaches and from current publications on competitive swimming.

Body Position:

1. **Head too low.** Upper body may be angled downward. Causes added resistance. May cause overkicking. Raise head. Except for inhalation, head should be about face deep in water.
2. **Head too high.** Causes hips and legs to sink, creating added frontal resistance. Can slow undulation of legs because of hips being too low. Lower head about face deep. Can interfere with recovery of arms if head is kept up too long following inhalation. Start lowering head at start of arm recovery.

Arm Actions:

1. **Hands enter too flat at entry.** Creates air bubbles. This can cause "slipping," loss of water pressure against palms during propulsive actions. Wrists, hands, or fingers too loose at entry can cause loss of control of hands to properly reach for catch position and to start outward sculling action. Corrective suggestions include use of stationary drills; shallow water drills; fluid drills with or without support to body; practicing arm actions only with emphasis on firm wrists, hands, or fingers at entry; entering with thumb sides of hands rotated downward slightly.
2. **Dropped elbows during propulsion.** Causes loss of effective propulsion. Stress keeping elbows higher than hands, but lower than shoulders. Practice arms alone with body supported. Have student open eyes underwater to observe actions of arms.
3. **Arms too wide, hands too far apart, during backward press under body.** This causes loss of

effective propulsion. Emphasize bending elbows and pressing backward with hands coming close together under body.

4. **Doesn't accelerate arms during last part of stroke.** Causes loss of power, and upsets breathing pattern and effective start of recovery of arms. Stress steady acceleration, backward **and outward,** to completion of push phase. Practice arms alone, body supported.
5. **Recovers arms too slowly.** Upsets timing of stroke. Stress "snapping" hands out of water at end of push phase and immediately recovering arms forward rapidly.
6. **Recovers arms too high.** May cause wasted up-and-down movement of body. Stress starting recovery with little finger sides of hands leading (preferred), and keeping arms low to surface.

Leg Actions:

1. **Lack of continuous up and down motion.** Often caused by over-emphasizing downward beat and pausing before lifting legs. Practice legs alone, arms at sides. Stress "bouncing" toes up and down. Practice fish-tail leg movements while lying on the side or on the back.
2. **Bends knees too soon on upward movement.** Causes loss of pressure of water against bottom of feet, resulting in loss of effective forward movement of body. Practice legs alone, concentrating on lifting upward about halfway with legs straight before starting to bend them.
3. **Kicking down too far.** Can cause hips to rise too far and shoulders and head to drop too low. Practice shallower kick, arms at sides, maintaining steady positions of upper body and head.
4. **Weak upward kick.** Loss of overall effectiveness of kick. Practice kicking, arms at sides or extended forward of head, emphasizing forceful lift upward with legs.

Breathing:

1. **Lifts head too high to breathe.** May be caused by breathing too late. Causes hips and legs to sink too far. Practice arms and breathing alone, using flotation to midsection of body. Concentrate on starting to lift face when hands start to press to the inside. Continue to lift face and jut jaw forward until mouth is just clear of water. Inhale with chin on surface and when hands are under lower area of rib cage.

Coordination:

1. **Putting both kicks on "front end" of stroke.** Use one arm fly drill to develop correct timing. Emphasize keeping arms moving forward and then outside following entry. No "glide" should be taken with arms.
2. **Dropping head before arms start to recover.** Caused by swimmer starting to lift head for a breath as arms begin to pull. Breath is taken and head drops on **second** kick, which makes arm recovery very difficult. Use one arm fly drill to develop correct timing.

CHAPTER 10

ANALYZING AND TEACHING OTHER AQUATICS SKILLS

"If You Want To Get Ashore, Reach For It!"
The Commodore

SURFACE DIVING

Surface diving is a useful skill that enables the swimmer to submerge from the surface of the water to moderate underwater depths. This skill is utilized to rescue submerged victims, to retrieve objects on the bottom, and to participate in underwater activities, such as skin diving.

Water depths for surface diving in the early stages of the learner's development should not exceed 8 to 10 feet. As skills and physical adjustment to water pressure improve, slightly deeper dives can be attempted. It must be remembered that pressure increases rather rapidly as a swimmer descends in the water. A broad guide of 1 pound per square inch for each 2 feet of descent emphasizes the increase of pressure against the body as one dives deeper. Since man lives under a normal atmospheric pressure of 14.7 pounds per square inch, a dive to a depth of 15 to 16 feet would result in a pressure of approximately 22 pounds. This amount of pressure sometimes causes pain in the ears, which can usually be alleviated by pinching the nose, pressing the lips together tightly, and forcing air through the eustachian tubes leading from the mouth to the ears.

Exhaling gently through the nose and mouth during a dive will result in maintaining positive pressure and will prevent water from entering the nasal passages. The diver must reserve enough air to allow time to complete the purpose of the dive and for the ascent to the surface.

Those suffering from ear or nose problems should consult their family physician for advice concerning their participation in surface diving and underwater swimming activities.

Physical discomfort and sinus problems from water being forced up the nasal passages can be prevented by gently placing the face back into the water after inhaling or by exhaling easily and slowly through the nose during the descent.

To avoid injury by striking an object during the descent or ascent, the eyes should be kept open and the arms extended forward of the head.

There are two types of surface dives — feet first or head first. The head-first dives can be performed by any one of three methods: the pike surface dive, the tuck surface dive, or the quick surface dive.

FEET-FIRST SURFACE DIVE

The feet-first surface dive is much safer to use than a head-first surface dive when the diver must submerge in murky water or in water of an unknown depth. Very buoyant individuals may find that the feet-first dive is the only type of surface dive that will enable them to submerge to a depth of 8 to 10 feet without additional swimming.

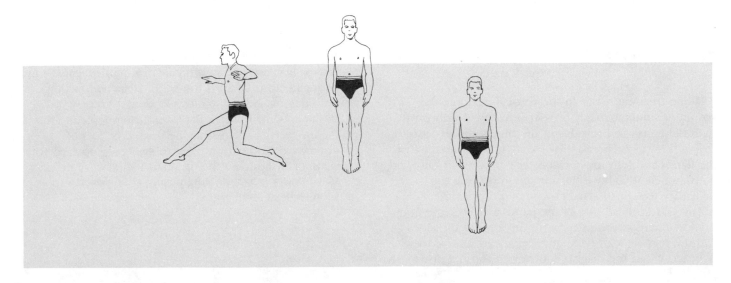

momentum begins to slow down, the wrists rotate to turn the palms outward. The downward momentum of the body continues by pressing vigorously upward with the hands and arms.

As in the other surface dives, exhaling gently throughout the descent is advised. Depending on the reason for the dive, and the condition of the water and the bottom, the swimmer may elect to level off at the end of the downward descent, or may swim to a greater depth by going into a tuck position and rolling forward into a head-down position and then continuing to swim.

Teaching Suggestions

Most swimmers learn this skill easily and rapidly. This skill is based on the students' ability to tread water.

1. Practice on land, if needed. The students extend their arms to the side, palms down, with the elbows bent. The legs are spread fore and aft of the body, ready to execute a scissors kick. Practice jumping straight up into the air by pushing downward with the arms while simultaneously pushing upward with the feet and legs. Push and "kick" vigorously.

2. Repeat No. 1, above, in deep water. Raise as much of the body above the surface as possible. Start the descent with the body vertical and streamlined. Exhale slowly during the descent.

3. The arms remain at the sides until the descent begins to slow down. Sweep the arms upward vigorously, palms up, to continue the descent.

4. Practice swimming underwater after leveling off from tucking and rolling the body forward.

Common Faults: Causes and Corrective Suggestions

1. **Insufficient height achieved to help drive body downward very far.** May be caused by pressing downward with straight arms. Press downward with elbows bent to achieve greater leverage and quicker motion. Keep elbows higher than hands during pressing action. Kick is too narrow or slow. Widen kick. Kick vigorously.

   Poor timing between pressing actions of arms and legs. Use land drills (Teaching Suggestions, No. 1).

2. **Lack of depth achieved during descent.** May be caused because of buoyancy factors. May be caused by sweeping arms upward too soon. Delay arm actions until descent begins to slow. Body not kept streamlined or in vertical plane during descent. "Falling off" vertical plane may be caused by loss of downward momentum prior to sweeping upward with arms, or by body not being vertical at start of descent. May be very buoyant. Start raising hands overhead as soon as head submerges.

While treading water in the vertical position, the swimmer simultaneously presses downward vigorously with the hands to the sides of the thighs and executes a strong scissors or breaststroke kick. It is important that the hands and legs move vigorously in order to raise the body sufficiently above the surface to provide the necessary weight to start a successful downward plunge. At the end of the thrust of the hands and legs, the body is vertical and streamlined, with the arms at the sides, and the legs are extended and together with the toes pointed. When the head is submerged and the downward

PIKE SURFACE DIVE

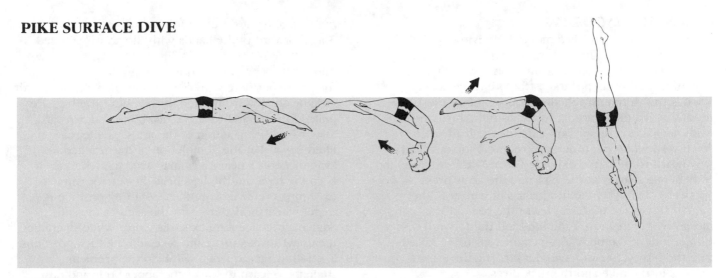

The legs are kept straight and together with the toes pointed throughout the pike surface dive. After taking a breath, the swimmer comes to a fully extended position on the surface. With forward momentum established by a previous swimming stroke, the swimmer lowers the head and flexes at the hips slightly while pressing the arms and the palms of the hands backward to the thighs. These actions bring the hips almost directly over the head. Without pausing, and with the elbows bent, the arms and the palms of the hands circle forward and downward vigorously, ending with the arms stretched and together and facing downward. This action helps to keep the hips near the surface and to stabilize the position of the upper body and the head. The lifting of the legs begins simultaneously with the forward arm press. The head extends forward slightly near the end of the leg lift to prevent the legs from passing beyond the head. The body is now fully extended and streamlined and is almost vertical to the bottom.

When all movements are executed quickly and properly, most of the legs will be above the surface. The weight of the legs will drive most swimmers to a depth of about 8 feet without additional movements of the arms and legs. Exhaling gently during the descent will maintain positive pressure and will prevent water from entering the nasal passages.

Teaching suggestions, and common faults and corrections for this skill are on page 108.

TUCK SURFACE DIVE

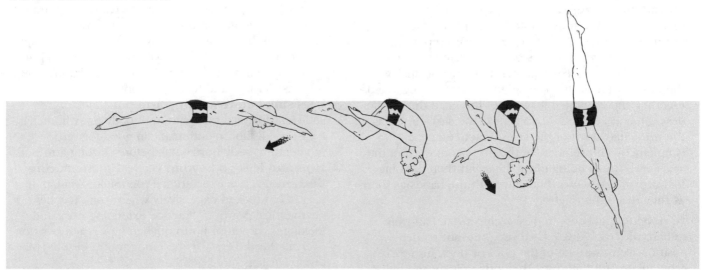

The tuck surface dive is performed in much the same manner as the pike surface dive. During the pressing action of the arms backward to the thighs, the legs are drawn into a tuck position that results in reducing the length of the legs, thereby facilitating rotation of the body into a head downward position. The legs are extended upward quickly during the forward and downward sweep of the arms. The sudden extension of the legs upward will result in a satisfactory descent for most swimmers. Individuals who are very buoyant or cannot flex the hips quickly usually perform the tuck surface dive more effectively than the pike surface dive.

Teaching suggestions, and common faults and corrections for this skill are on page 108.

QUICK SURFACE DIVE

The quick surface dive is a method of diving below the surface of the water from a swimming position when speed is necessary, such as a situation in which a drowning victim disappears just before the rescuer reaches the victim. In this dive, the swimmer must have good forward momentum. To execute the dive, the swimmer takes a breath and extends the lead arm downward while the other arm recovers forward and downward to meet the extended arm. Without pause, the body bends sharply at the hips and the arms press backward slightly as the head starts downward. The sudden resistance of the water to the back of the body, caused by the flexion of the hips and the forward momentum of the body, enables the legs to be raised over the hips very easily without circling the arms forward as in the pike and the tuck dives.

Teaching Suggestions — Head-First Surface Dives In Deep Water

1. The students push off from the wall into a prone glide with the face in the water and the arms extended forward of the head.

2. The students pull the arms back to the thighs with a wide sweeping motion (a modified arm action for the breaststroke).

3. The students bend the arms and swing them vigorously to full extension forward of the head. The palms apply constant pressure against the water.

4. Repeat Nos. 1, 2, and 3, and add lowering the head and flexing at the hips during the forward press of the arms. The students pull the hips over the head. No leg lift.

5. Repeat No. 4. During the forward press of the arms, and when the hips are over the head, add lifting the legs (pike dive) or extending the legs upward (tuck dive). **Emphasize:** keeping the legs straight and together with the toes pointed (feet plantar-flexed) during the lift and descent (pike dive); keeping the legs together with the toes pointed during the upward extension and the legs together and straight during the descent (tuck dive); keeping the arms straight and together and extended forward of the head during the descent; and keeping the hips near the surface during the press backward of the arms. Practice quick, simultaneous movements of the press backward of the arms with the bending of the hips and then pressing forward and downward quickly with the hands as soon as they reach the thighs.

6. To develop quickness in performing a one-half front somersault (tuck dive), have very buoyant students push off from the side of the pool or dock into a prone glide and then tuck the body quickly and pull the arms vigorously, executing a full somersault. Repeat as necessary. Then practice half somersaults. Add step 5.

7. Have the students practice both types of dives while swimming the breaststroke. Start the dive(s) from a glide position. Before starting a dive, the students pick out a target spot on the bottom to dive to (about 3 feet forward of the hands with the arms extended to the front).

8. The students practice and learn both dives starting in the prone position, with the arms at the sides, and with little or no forward motion of the body. The hips are pulled forward and over the head by the downward, forward scooping action of the arms. The legs are lifted upward at the completion of the arm action. Swimmers with heavy legs may need to kick easily to keep the hips and the legs near the surface prior to executing the dive. A stationary starting position is useful when snorkeling with the arms at the sides.

9. Students practice a quick surface dive while swimming the crawl stroke, using the pike and the tuck positions.

10. The following sequence will help the problem students to learn to lower the upper body and raise the legs quickly. In waist-deep water, the student pushes off vigorously from the bottom or the side of the pool into a prone glide. A porpoise dive is executed quickly and the legs are raised out of the water to a vertical position as soon as the hands are placed on the bottom. Repeat these "porpoise dive handstands" as necessary until the students can execute them quickly.

Common Faults: Causes, Effects, and Corrective Suggestions (For All Head-First Surface Dives)

1. **Fails to submerge.** Head and upper body are not lowered enough or are lowered too slowly. Hips do not flex sufficiently during forward and downward press of arms during pike dive, or arms (palms) do not press forward and downward vigorously. Repeat steps 3 and 4 under "Teaching Suggestions."

2. **Fails to submerge to satisfactory depth.** May be "lifting" head and arms too soon. Stress aiming arms and head to target on bottom until downward momentum begins to slow down. May not be raising legs to maximum height above water. Repeat step 4, "Teaching Suggestions," emphasizing quick movements of arms and legs and flexion of hips.

3. **Legs sink before starting arm pull.** Lack of sufficient forward momentum of body or swimmer is leg heavy. Establish and maintain good forward momentum, body horizontal, before starting arm pull.

4. **Hips and legs go beyond vertical plane during descent.** Back may be arched too much. Straighten back. Chin tucked excessively when trunk reaches near-vertical position. Practice extending neck and looking at target on bottom when hips reach position over the head. Legs may be lifting too forceably (pike dive). Lift legs more gently.

5. **Legs not together and streamlined during lift (pike) or extension upwards (tuck), or during descent.** Stress stretching and locking legs together. "Paste" ankles together and point toes (plantar-flex). (Practice forceful prone glides from side of pool, or bottom of pool, followed by porpoise diving into handstands in waist-deep water.)

SWIMMING UNDERWATER

The skill of underwater swimming enables swimmers to recover lost objects, to avoid surface hazards, and to enjoy underwater activities. Many drownings have been prevented through the ability of rescuers to surface dive and to search the bottom by swimming underwater.

Safety Factors

Swimmers with average skills rarely swim at depths greater than 10 to 15 feet. They should not go deeper except to perform an emergency rescue or, following appropriate instruction and practice, to engage in skin diving or other underwater activities. Underwater swimming for any great distance should be discouraged, and the dangers of hyperventilating the lungs before swimming underwater should be thoroughly understood.

Hyperventilation, or deep breathing, increases breath-holding time by blowing off carbon dioxide, thus lowering the amount of carbon dioxide in the blood. If, following hyperventilation, the swimmer attempts to swim underwater for a great distance, a considerable length of time may elapse before the carbon dioxide level, reduced by overbreathing, will provide a strong stimulus to breathe. The danger is that the oxygen level may drop to a point where the swimmer "blacks out" before the carbon dioxide level increases to the point where the swimmer feels the urge to take a breath. Unless help is at hand to get the victim to the surface, drowning will result. All swimmers engaged in underwater swimming should be paired with a buddy and be closely supervised during instruction and practice.

Modifications of the breaststroke and the sidestroke are usually used for swimming underwater. A modification of the breaststroke is generally the most efficient to use. The primary glide position for either stroke is with the arms at the sides when swimming in water with good visibility. In murky water, the glide should be taken with the arms extended forward of the head.

The timing of the modified breaststroke can vary. The arms may pull backward to the thighs, followed by recovering the arms alongside the body to about the head, then kicking and gliding with the arms in the forward extended position. The arms and the legs may deliver the propulsive actions simultaneously with the glide taken with the arms at the sides, or a double glide can be taken by pulling the arms and gliding, followed by a kick glide as in the breaststroke. Complete forward momentum should not be lost before starting the next stroke for any of the variations of stroking.

Swimmers may prefer to use a scissors kick in combination with the same full breaststroke arm action. When a scissors kick is used, the lower part of the body may be rotated slightly to enable the kick to be performed closer to a horizontal plane. Another variation could be the breaststroke arm action combined with the crawl kick.

Direction and the level of the body can be changed by raising or lowering the head and by an arm action of pressing upward at the end of the stroke or downward at the start of the arm movement. Flexing or extending at the hips will also result in some control in moving in a desired direction up or down. Swimmers should keep the eyes open in underwater swimming in order to see any possible obstructions.

The modification of the sidestroke can be effectively used in underwater swimming. Where there is good visibility, a stroke on the side that employs a broad, sweeping, backward action of both arms simultaneously may be used. In this stroke, the scissors kick is used and coincides with the arm action followed by a moderate glide.

Teaching Suggestions

Stress that the students keep their eyes open underwater, and that they not hold their breath too long.

1. The students submerge by porpoise diving, or by pushing off from the side into a prone glide and by angling the body toward the bottom, or by submerging the body and then pushing off the side into a prone glide underwater.
2. With the forward momentum from the push-off, the students practice lifting and lowering the head (and the arms) to change the angle of the body during the glide. The students practice slow exhalation to help keep the body underwater. This is especially important for very buoyant learners.
3. Repeat step 2. Add kicking with the arms extended forward of the head. The students kick (any variation) for a short distance while the hands slide along the bottom. The students stop, stand, breathe, porpoise dive, and then repeat the drill.
4. The students practice full stroking movements (all modifications) in chest-deep water. When they become proficient, they can then practice in deep water. **Stress no hyperventilation before submerging, and surfacing when a breath is needed. Do not hold the breath too long underwater.**

SCULLING

Sculling is a method of using the hands and the arms in paired movements to propel or to support a swimmer in the water in a prone, supine, or vertical position. When applied skillfully, it can be used effectively to maintain or to change the body position in the water, to propel the swimmer in a desired position, and is especially useful in synchronized or stunt swimming.

The palms of the hands exert equal and constant pressure against the water during their continuous movements away from the long axis midline of the body and back to the midline. The continuous pressing actions of the hands provide constant positive force against the water. When sculling, the hands are flat (not cupped), the fingers are together, and the thumbs are alongside the forefingers. The hands remain underwater during all movements.

Two basic hand positions are used in all sculling. During the press away from the midline of the body, the thumb sides of the hands (trailing edges) are slightly lower than the little finger sides of the hands (leading edges). During the inward pressing actions, the thumb sides of the hands (leading edges) are slightly higher than the little finger sides of the hands (trailing edges).

The forces created by the sculling actions of the hands must be in a direction opposite to the desired path of movement of the body (See Chapter 6, "Physical Laws Applied to Body Movements In The Water," section on Newton's Law of Action and Reaction). To keep the body in a stationary horizontal or vertical position, the hands are kept parallel (flat) to the surface of the water (flat scull). With the body in the supine position and the arms extended along the sides of the body, the body is moved in the direction of the head by elevating (extending) the hands about 45 degrees at the wrists (standard scull). A body in the supine position is moved toward the feet by lowering the arms slightly, flexing the wrists, and lowering the hands about 90 degrees (reverse scull).

Supine Position

In Red Cross courses, all sculling movements on the back start with the arms extended along the sides of the body with the palms of the hands down and parallel to the surface of the water.

To maintain the body in a horizontal, stationary position, the hands rotate slightly to place the thumbs down and the hands press outward 12 to 15 inches. The hands then rotate to place the little fingers slightly lower than the thumbs and the hands press back to the hips. The outward and inward movements are continuous and provide a lifting effect for the body, since most of the forces from the actions of the hands are directed downward (flat scull).

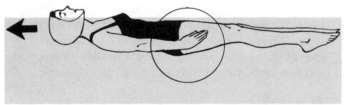

Sculling with the hands elevated (extended) about 45 degrees (standard scull) forces water outward and then inward, and toward the feet, which moves the body in the direction of the head. The thumb sides of the hands (trailing edges) point toward the feet slightly during the outward press. The little finger sides of the hands (trailing edges) point toward the feet slightly during the inward movements. A similar force results from the actions of the feet during their outward and inward propulsive actions during the breaststroke kick.

Sculling in the supine position with the hands flexed at the wrists (reverse or snail scull) moves water outward and then inward, and toward the head, resulting in the body moving in the direction of the feet.

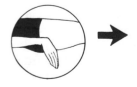

Prone Position

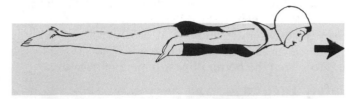

Moving the body in the direction of the head is accomplished by extending the arms along the sides of the body and angling the hands downward about 90 degrees. The thumb sides of the hands (trailing edges) point toward the feet slightly during the outward scull, and the little finger sides of the hands (trailing edges) point toward the feet slightly during the inward scull. Water is forced sideways and toward the feet during these actions (canoe scull).

Sculling with the arms extended forward of the head with the hands elevated will move the body in the direction of the feet. Sculling (flat) with the arms extended away from the sides in a plane between the shoulders and the waist will keep the body in a stationary position.

Vertical Position

Sculling in the vertical position is used when treading water and for recreational purposes. With the body in an upright position, the arms are bent slightly and extended in front of the chest. The flat scull is used to help support the body in the desired position.

Sculling and Swimming

A very efficient method of moving the body through the water when swimming is to employ sophisticated sculling movements of the hands during the propulsive actions of the arms. The best examples are the use of sculling by highly skilled competitive swimmers during the crawl stroke, the butterfly stroke, and the breaststroke. The use of skilled sculling movements enables the swimmer's hands to constantly find still (nonmoving) water that provides continuous traction or resistance to the hand when it is angled properly. Maximum and constant resistance of water to the palms of the hands provides efficient movement of the body in the desired position.

Teaching effective sculling movements for the crawl stroke and the butterfly stroke requires a thorough knowledge of the principles of biomechanics and their application to swimming. Most Red Cross instructors do not have, nor are they expected to have, this level of expertise.

The above information on the use of sculling for selected swimming strokes is to inform instructors of the skills that are developed by many highly skilled competitive swimmers. These sculling movements are rarely, if ever, presented in Red Cross swimming courses because of the inability of students to learn them within the average length of the courses.

Teaching Suggestions

Flat Scull (Vertical Body Position)

A vertical body position is the most advantageous one for learning and refining this skill, since the students can easily observe the actions of their hands. Emphasize:

- Correct hand positions. Keep the hands parallel to the surface, thumb sides down slightly during the outward scull and up slightly during the inward scull.

- That the arms are bent slightly and extended forward of the chest.

- Continuous outward and inward movements, with a range of movement of 12 to 15 inches from the long axis midline of the body.

The instructor can use phrases, such as "out-in," "out-in," or "push out with thumbs, pull in with little fingers," or "smooth sand," to facilitate smoothness and accuracy of movements.

The use of voice cadence with such phrases as suggested above can help increase or decrease the speed of movements of this skill.

1. The students, standing in chest-deep water, practice sculling with the hands kept just below and parallel to the surface. Repeat, standing in neck-deep water.
2. The students scull while in neck-deep water, then they gradually bend their knees and lift their feet from the bottom. They bend forward from the waist slightly and keep their chins on the surface. Repeat until the students can maintain good body position and can breathe comfortably.

3. The students practice in deep water. Mild support by the instructor may be helpful to some students during initial learning attempts. The students practice until they can support themselves comfortably for 20 to 30 seconds.

Standard Scull (Vertical Position)

1. The students, in at least neck-deep water, practice the standard scull.

Standard Scull (Supine Position)

1. The students, in chest-deep water, push off from the bottom or the side of the pool or dock into a back glide and then quickly add the standard scull. Practice until the students can move a distance of from 15 to 20 feet.

Common Faults: Cause(s), Effect(s), Corrective Suggestions

1. **Body bobs up and down in vertical position.** Caused by uneven amounts of pressure against water. Practice "smoothing sand" against side of pool or overflow trough while standing on bottom. Practice sculling (flat) in neck-deep water, feet off bottom, keeping chin level with surface of water.

2. **Lack of effective movement in supine position.** This can be caused by sculling pattern being too wide, insufficient elevation of hands to force water toward feet, or pattern of hand movement being too slow. Make corrections as necessary.

TREADING WATER

Treading water is a skill designed to support the body in an upright position in deep water with the head kept out of the water. This skill is useful for personal safety, for life saving purposes, or for watching or conversing with another swimmer. Treading water with the use of the legs only is often required to support a victim or to handle pieces of equipment.

Treading water is accomplished by using one of several kicks combined with a sculling motion of the hands. These movements are designed to support the head just high enough out of the water to facilitate free breathing. Most of the support for the body is from the actions of the legs. The actions of the arms and the legs are almost continuous. The rate and force of these actions should be only enough to support the body easily in the vertical position.

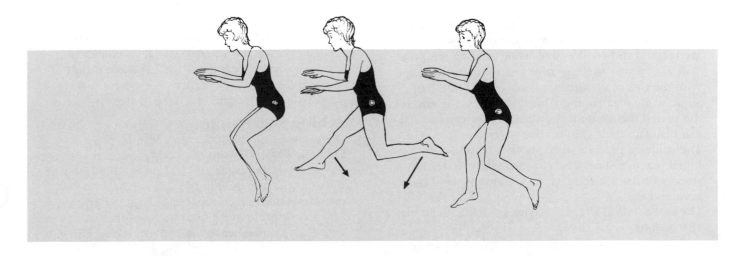

The swimmer is in a nearly vertical position in the water and the upper body is bent forward slightly at the waist with the chin on the surface. The broad, flat sculling motion of the hands is continuous with the hands kept a few inches below the surface of the water and forward of the body. Throughout all movements, the elbows are slightly bent.

The four kicks generally used are modifications of the scissors or breaststroke kicks. All of these kicks are shortened and delivered at a slightly faster rate than in stroke swimming. Just enough thrust is delivered to keep the head above the surface.

The most commonly used kick is the single scissors. This kick, employed when performing the sidestroke, is modified for treading water so that it is slightly wider and finishes the downward thrust without the legs straightening and coming together. This modification provides a wider base of support for the body and tends to eliminate an up-and-down or bobbing action of the body.

The double scissors kick is an alternating scissors action using the same movements as the single scissors kick. This action can be likened to pedaling a bicycle.

There are two ways of utilizing a breaststroke kick while treading water. The first method is as described in the elementary backstroke. The leg action becomes little more than a continuous outward and downward rotation of the lower legs.

A few swimmers may use an alternate breaststroke leg action called a "rotary" or "egg beater" kick. This is essentially a continuous, rhythmical, alternating action of the legs. The development and use of the "rotary" kick is of particular value when playing water polo.

Teaching Suggestions

1. The students practice in neck-deep water, using the scissors kick with sculling. Stress leaning forward slightly from the waist with the chin on the water and using the arms and the legs and gradually reducing the force and the tempo of their actions. Have the students develop the ability to relax and to breathe easily.
2. The students practice in the vertical position in deep water with one side of the body next to the side of the pool, using the scissors kick and sculling with one arm while holding onto the edge of the pool or the overflow trough with the other hand. Practice until the students can maintain a good body position and are relaxed and comfortable while holding onto the wall with a very slight grip or just touching the edge with the tips of the fingers. Practice with the legs alone while maintaining a hand touch on the edge of the pool. Practice until the students are relaxed and can maintain their chin on the waterline.
3. The students practice, using both arms and legs. Initial practice should be close to safety. Have the students strive for relaxed, slow movements of the arms and the legs.
4. The students add alternate styles of kicking with the arm actions.

5. The students practice using the legs alone in deep water and keeping the arms underwater.
6. Games, such as "Circle Ball" and "Volleyball," can be used in deep water to perfect this skill. "Keep the fun in fundamentals."

Common Faults: Cause(s), Effect(s), and Corrective Suggestions

1. **Moving too rapidly.** Unnecessary expenditure of effort and loss of proficiency. Decrease speed of arm and leg movements, bearing in mind that body buoyancy differs with individuals.
2. **Bobbing up and down in water.** Kick is too forceful and/or hands push downward. Repeat "Teaching Suggestions," Numbers 1, 2, and 3, as necessary.
3. **Moving through water.** Improper angle of hands and feet. Unnecessary expenditure of energy. See "correction" under "Bobbing up and down in water," above.
4. **Head carried back too far.** Student does not want face and mouth to be in water. Improper body position. Tense muscles. Stress leaning forward slightly from the waist and keeping chin at surface of water. Practice in neck-deep water to build student's confidence.

BACK FLOAT

Many students learn this skill more quickly with the assistance of the instructor or a partner. Standing in chest-deep water, the learner crouches until the shoulders are just underwater. Standing behind the learner, the instructor or partner places his or her own hands under the learner's shoulder blades. Then the student gently lies back in the water until the ears are submerged with the face parallel to the surface, extends the arms to the sides with the palms of the hands up, raises the hips gently to the surface, and slowly slides the feet away from under the body. Continued practice will enable the learner to perform this skill without the aid of a partner or the instructor. In many cases, the learner's heels will be touching the bottom during the float, but most of the body weight will be supported by the water. The instructor should explain to the students that they will find their respective balanced-floating position after practice in deep water. Persons who cannot float because of negative buoyancy can learn to rest in the back float position by using easy sculling movements of the hands.

Learning to float and relax on the back in deep water is introduced after the students can float comfortably in neck-deep water. Learning to adjust the position of the body is discussed in Chapter 6, "Physical Laws Applied To Body Movements In The Water."

Teaching Suggestions

1. Demonstrate the back float in chest-deep water. Emphasize starting with the body crouched with the shoulders in the water, the feet on the bottom, and the arms outstretched to the sides (palms up) to provide better body balance; inhaling; the gradual laying back of the head until the ears are in the water with the face parallel to the surface; raising the hips to

the surface easily; gradually extending the legs to the rear (**but not pushing off from the bottom or trying to raise the legs**); and a quick exchange of air to retain the float position.

2. Demonstrate the recovery from the back float to a standing position. Emphasize dropping the hips, bending the legs, and drawing the knees toward the chest; bringing the head forward; placing the feet on the bottom; and scooping the arms forward to maintain balance while raising the head and standing. These actions can be described as that of a person reaching behind the body with both arms, grasping an imaginary armchair, and pulling it into position to sit down, followed by standing.

3. Have a student volunteer to demonstrate the float. Assist the student as necessary to achieve a good floating position. A number of students will usually volunteer. Pick one whom you **know** will float. Show proper placement of the hands under the learner's shoulder blades. Emphasize not lifting the learner — let the water do the supporting.

4. Students learn this skill quickly if shallow water (8 to 12 inches) is available. Have the students lie back, ears in the water, and extend their arms to the sides and then gently raise the hips and float. Practice air exchange while floating. Students who are poor floaters should practice rapid exhalation and inhalation (explosive breathing) to prevent the head from sinking.

5. Pair the students off for practice of the float and recovery to a standing position. Emphasize the "supporter" not lifting the "floater," but providing mild support only (students 6-8 years old are usually not good "supporters"), starting with the shoulders in the water and not pushing off from the bottom, removing hand support when the "floater" is in a good position and is relaxed, and the "supporter" being ready to provide assistance if needed.

6. Provide individual help to student(s) having difficulty in keeping the hips up and the head back. Suggested methods include standing behind the student and providing mild support under his or her shoulder blades. Shield the student's face from the sun, if outdoors. Have the students open their eyes to aid relaxation. Correct faults using oral suggestions, or physical help if necessary. Gradually reduce hand contact until the student is ready to float without assistance. Tell the student when you are going to remove your hands and that you are ready to help if necessary.

7. Very buoyant students may not be able to recover from the back float to the standing position. Have them roll over onto their stomach and then recover to the standing position.

8. Have the students practice the back float and recovery in neck-deep water. Emphasize relaxation and breath control. The students (floaters) must learn to float comfortably for 1 minute.

9. Have the students learn to float in deep water.

Suggested procedures are:

a. Have the students face the side of the pool or the dock and hold onto the edge of the overflow trough with the body in a vertical position. With the shoulders in the water, a breath is taken, the head is laid back until the ears are in the water, the hands release their contact, the arms are extended to the sides with the palms of the hands up, and the hips are pushed gently toward the surface. Emphasize explosive breathing, especially for marginal floaters, and not trying to lift the legs.

b. Students take a breath and assume a vertical "standing" position in deep water with the arms, palms of the hands up, extended to the sides and parallel to the surface of the water. As soon as the position of the body stabilizes, the students tilt their heads backward and take a breath as soon as the mouth is clear of the water. Emphasize relaxing and pushing the hips forward and upward easily, exchanging air when needed, or explosive breathing for marginal floaters when needed. Continue practice until the students can float comfortably for 2 minutes.

c. Introduce adjustments of the positions of the arms and the legs to change the position of the body during the float.

SURVIVAL FLOATING

Survival floating is very similar to the "drownproofing" technique that was originated by the late Fred R. Lanoue, former professor of physical education and head swimming coach at the Georgia Institute of Technology. The **primary objective** of survival floating is to allow an individual to remain afloat in deep water with minimum effort.

This survival skill **should not be used in cold water.** Immersion hypothermia studies have shown that loss of heat from several parts of the body in cold water is a contributing factor in many drownings. Submerging the head during survival floating increases heat loss.

To learn and master this skill quickly, learners must first be able to comfortably hold their breath with the face in the water, be able to exhale underwater, get a breath by lifting the head above the water, float fully relaxed in a facedown position, and must have gained confidence in being in deep water.

1. **Resting Position** The swimmer starts with the lungs

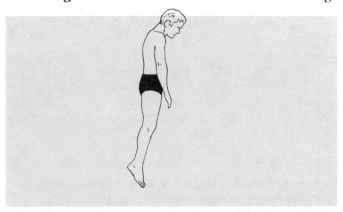

filled with air and holds the breath, letting the arms and the legs dangle. The face is in the water with a part of the head at the surface. The swimmer rests and floats in a nearly vertical position for a few seconds. The breath should not be held to the point that the swimmer becomes uncomfortable.

2. **Preparing To Exhale** While maintaining this body

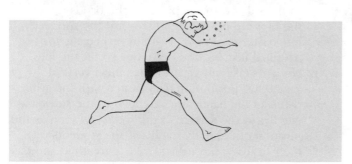

and head position, the swimmer slowly and leisurely recovers or lifts the arms in front of the shoulders to about shoulder height. If leg action is also to be used, the legs slowly separate into position for a modified scissors kick.

3. **Exhalation** The exhalation begins as the chin is

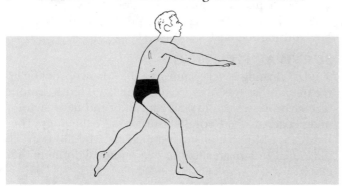

being lifted toward the surface and ends when the mouth clears the water. The exhalation may be through the mouth and nose simultaneously, or through the mouth or the nose. The eyes should be opened to help gauge and judge the level of the chin in relation to the surface of the water.

4. **Inhalation** As soon as the head is vertical and the

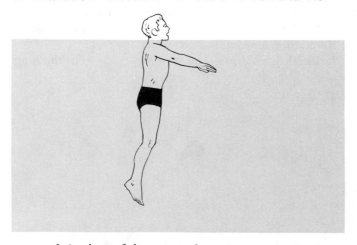

mouth is clear of the water, the swimmer slowly sweeps the hands away from each other and brings

the legs together. The easy pressing actions of the arms and the legs keeps the chin at the surface and allows time for ample air to be breathed in through the mouth. These actions should not be vigorous enough to lift the chin out of the water. Buoyant individuals may need only to use the arms or the legs.

5. **Return to the Resting Position** The swimmer

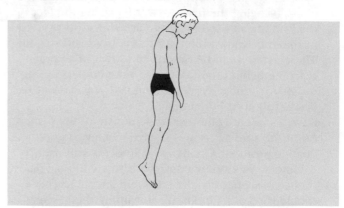

allows the arms and the legs to move back slowly to their free dangling positions, with the face down in the water and the body nearly vertical, and then relaxes. The swimmer rests in this position until ready to exhale and then repeats the cycle. NOTE. If the individual tends to sink too far below the surface when returning to the resting position, a downward press or easy sculling action of the hands will stop the sinking of the body and will help it float back to the surface. A slight scissors kick can also be used to arrest the sinking action.

Teaching Suggestions. (The instructor, or an aide, should first demonstrate each of the following before allowing the students to try.)

1. The students face the side of the pool in neck-deep water. They grasp the overflow trough with both hands and then "hang" in the water with the body in the vertical position. The knees are bent to allow the shoulders to be just under or near the surface of the water. A breath is taken and held as the face is placed in the water.

2. When a breath is desired, the students exhale through the nose or mouth (or both) while lifting the chin **to the surface.** The students inhale, lower their faces into the water, and hold their breath for 3 to 5 seconds. Repeat the breathing cycle. Gradually increase the number of breathing cycles and the amount of time the breath is held between inhalations.

3. The students learn to float in a vertical position in neck-deep water by bending the knees, drawing the feet off the bottom, and letting the arms hang downward.

4. The students do a vertical float close to the wall and facing the side of the pool, combining the float with "bobbing." Emphasize the following to the students:
   - Slowly slide the hands upward and lightly grasp the overflow trough before a breath **is needed.**
   - Exhale through the nose (and the mouth) as the

neck hyperextends, the chin is lifted, and the mouth clears the surface. (Keep the chin in the water.)

- Inhale through the mouth and hold the breath as the head is returned to a facedown position in the water. Slowly slide the hands down the sides of the body and relax and remain motionless in a vertical position until the next breath is ready to be taken. Repeat until the students breathe comfortably, can hold their breath for 3 to 5 seconds, and are fully relaxed in the floating (hanging) position.
- Float vertically with the knees bent in neck-deep water. **Prior to a breath being needed,** the students raise their arms slowly, ending with them extended forward of the head, with the elbows bent, and the palms down and parallel to the surface of the water. The hands scull easily to the outside or they press easily outward and slightly downward when the mouth clears the water and a breath is taken. Emphasize an easy press of the hands to avoid lifting the head too high (a common fault). Have the students resume a floating position. Repeat until the students are proficient in these movements.
- Add leg action to the above procedure. Draw the legs up and extend one leg forward and the other to the rear as the arms are being raised. The legs press downward **easily** (scissors kick) as the hands press outward during the inhalation. Resume the floating (resting) position. Repeat until good coordination of the arms and the legs is achieved. Repeat, increasing the amount of time the float is held (but never to the point where the students become uncomfortable holding their breath).
- Practice in deep water close to some form of safety. Then practice some distance away from some form of safety. Through continued practice, the students should increase their length of time in the floating position, until they average about five breaths a minute.

Some individuals who are poor floaters tend to sink somewhat when resuming the resting position. This is counteracted by pressing the hands downward after the face is placed back in the water. An additional small kick will also help return the body (head) to the surface.

Accomplished deep-water swimmers will quickly learn survival floating using the above procedures or following a demonstration and an explanation of the skill. Through practice and experimentation, many swimmers develop adaptations that best meet their needs. Some will use only the arms. Some may prefer to use an easy breaststroke kick. Some may prefer to press the hands downward easily during the inhalation. **Meeting the objective** of survival floating is **more important** than the techniques used.

SURVIVAL STROKE

This stroke is an adaptation of the "travel stroke," which was also developed by the late Fred R. Lanoue, and is used in conjunction with the survival float. Its greatest value is that it allows floaters and nonfloaters alike to cover a considerable distance in the water with a minimum expenditure of energy. However, swimming long distances to safety should be a last resort. **This stroke is not to be used in cold water.**

1. Following the inhalation in the survival float, the swimmer bends forward at the waist, draws the hands near the head, separates the legs for a scissors kick, and then extends the arms to the front and kicks, driving the head and the body diagonally toward the surface.

2. After little or no glide, the arms sweep easily outward and backward to the thighs and a glide is taken with the body near to and almost horizontal to the surface. When the swimmer feels like breathing, the legs bend and are drawn downward and forward as the hands are drawn near the head.

Nonfloaters may need to pull harder with the arms and then quickly assume the body position just described to prevent the body from sinking.

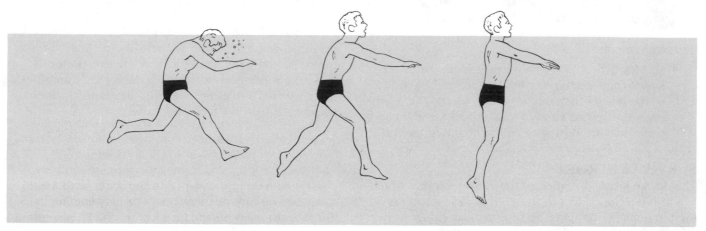

3. The arms extend forward and the legs separate in preparation for a modified scissors kick. The coordination of the arm and the leg actions with the inhalation is the same as for the survival float. The full cycle is then repeated.

Individuals with negative buoyancy can easily remain near the surface by using the survival stroke. These movements must be done more rapidly by nonfloaters to prevent them from sinking prior to the inhalation.

TURNS

The majority of swimming instruction and practice occurs in swimming pools. Since pools are somewhat confined areas for continuing practice, the ability to turn easily at the pool ends is important if such facilities are to be used effectively. Also, since many intermediate swimmers may participate in formal or informal competition, the ability to execute an effective turn involving strokes on the front and the back is desirable. The turns and skills that are described here are treated simply. Information about turns used in modern swimming competition can be obtained from swimming coaches and from books about competitive swimming.

Crawl Stroke Open Turn

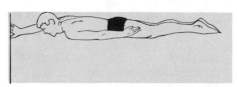
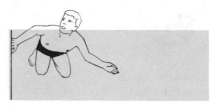
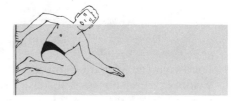

The body rolls slightly onto the side of the leading arm as the hand touches the turning surface. In continuing movements, the lead arm bends as the body tucks, turns, and pivots away from the lead hand, ending with the feet against the wall. During the pivot, the face is lifted and a breath is taken.

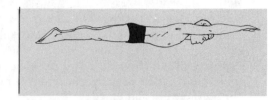

The face returns to the water as the lead hand pushes off and recovers over the surface. The body completes its rotation to the facedown position, ending with the upper body submerged about 10 inches. The arms fully extend as the legs drive the body away from the turning surface. When the momentum of the glide reaches an approximately normal swimming speed, the swimmer angles the head and the arms toward the surface and begins to kick. The leg action drives the swimmer to the surface and stroking resumes.

Teaching Suggestions

1. Demonstrate and discuss the skill.
2. Have the students practice, using the **Whole Approach.** Stress touching, tucking, pivoting/breathing, submerging, and pushing off.
3. **Progressive-Part Approach**
   a. The students, 5 to 6 feet from the turning surface in chest-deep water, extend one arm toward the wall and push off from the bottom into a prone glide with the face down. They roll slightly onto the side of the lead arm. As they place the palm of the hand against the wall (the hand is angled upward slightly and forward of the long axis midline of the body), the elbow bends slightly, allowing the head to come nearer to the wall. The students then stop and stand.
   b. Repeat step "a," adding tucking of the body when the hand touches the wall. Stress tucking the body tightly and quickly.
   c. Repeat step "b," adding turning and pivoting the lower body toward the wall until the feet make contact with the turning surface. Stress pivoting and turning quickly and placing the feet against the wall from 12 to 15 inches below the surface of the water.
   d. Repeat step "c," adding turning and lifting the face from the water as the legs pivot under the hips. Breathe to the side when the mouth is clear of the water. Stress keeping the chin near the surface during the head lift and the turn to the side. **Do not lift the head too high during the turn and pivot of the body.**
   e. Repeat step "d," and add pressing off the wall with the lead hand and recovering the arm over the water as in the crawl stroke. Drive the entry hand forward and downward 12 to 15 inches below the surface. During this action, the upper body drops to a corresponding depth and rotates to a facedown position. The students push off with the arms extended to the front, and the head is positioned between the arms as in the prone glide. Add the kick and angling the head and the arms to the surface when glide momentum begins to slow down.

   f. Practice leading with one arm, then the other, to develop the ability to turn to either side.
   g. Have the students practice turns after swimming up to the wall. Stress swimming up to the wall at normal speed. Slowing down when coming up to the wall causes a loss of forward momentum and makes it more difficult to tuck, turn, and pivot quickly.

Common Faults: Cause(s), Effect(s), Corrective Suggestions

1. **Grasping overflow trough of pool.** May bring swimmers too high out of water, or they may become dependent upon grabbing and pulling themselves around instead of allowing their momentum from stroking to help them. Work on placing hand flat against turning surface about 6 to 10 inches below surface of water.
2. **Keeping lead arm straight after touch.** Does not allow body to get close enough to turning surface. As hand touches wall, elbow should bend enough to allow head to come near wall.
3. **Dropping shoulders or ducking head too low while tucking and turning.** This causes feet to be placed too high on turning surface because of high position of hips. Body may angle toward bottom of pool during push-off.
4. **Lifting head or arching back too soon during push-off and glide.** Swimmers come to surface too quickly, which lessens effectiveness of glide underwater. Body should be stretched and streamlined, just under and nearly parallel to surface of water during initial portion of glide.
5. **Lifting head too high during turn and pivot.** Causes hips and feet to remain too low. Feet are placed too low on turning surface. Angle of body during push-off is toward surface. Stress lifting and rotating head to side only enough to clear mouth from water.
6. **Pushing off and gliding with arms at sides.** This reduces effectiveness of glide because of increased frontal resistance of water to head and shoulders. Pushing off and gliding with arms extended forward

of head reduces this resistance and provides protection to head.

7. **Starting kick too soon.** Not taking advantage of momentum of push-off and glide. Start kick when glide begins to slow down.

8. **Pushing off wall while lying on side.** Fails to complete rotation of body to facedown position during recovery and entry of "lead" arm. Practice "Teaching Suggestions," step 3(e).

Open Turn for Breaststroke and Butterfly Stroke

After the swimmers have learned the turn for the crawl stroke, it is easy to learn the turn for the breaststroke and the butterfly stroke. A slight modification of the crawl stroke turn is made; that is, both hands contact the turning surface simultaneously and at the same level. The body then tucks as the elbows bend, allowing the head to come closer to the wall. The swimmer turns the head in the desired direction and the body turns and pivots in that direction. If turning to the right, the head turns in that direction and the right hand pushes off the wall, which helps the pivoting action of the body. The turn and push-off underwater are completed as in the crawl stroke turn. The swimmer returns to the surface by angling the head and the arms upward more quickly than in the crawl stroke turn. The momentum from the push-off drives the swimmer to the surface.

Sidestroke Turn

For swimmers who wish to continue practicing a sidestroke, the crawl stroke turn can be used with some variation. Contact with the wall can be made with the lead arm and the entire turn can be executed as described for the crawl stroke turn. While the body still has sufficient momentum, after the push-off and during the glide, the swimmer can simply rotate the body to the desired side for continued practice.

Backstroke Turn

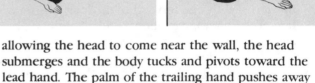

The swimmer gauges the approach to the turning surface so as to be able to contact the wall with one arm fully extended almost directly behind the head. A breath is taken as the leading arm contacts the wall with the palm of the hand, thumbside up. As the elbow bends, allowing the head to come near the wall, the head submerges and the body tucks and pivots toward the lead hand. The palm of the trailing hand pushes away from the hips to accelerate the pivoting action.

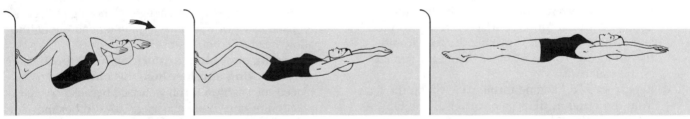

The hands are drawn behind the head as the feet are placed against the wall. The push-off is taken with the top of the head facing the other end of the pool and with the arms fully extended behind the head. Before loss of momentum occurs, the chin tucks, the hands and the arms angle slightly to the surface, and the swimmer returns to the surface by kicking vigorously and pulling with one arm. Air is expelled slowly through the nose during the push-off and the glide to prevent water from entering the nasal passages.

Teaching Suggestions

1. **Whole Approach.** Have the students practice, after a demonstration and a discussion of the skill.
2. **Progressive-Part Approach.**
   a. Have the students stand in waist-deep water, 5 to 6 feet from the turning surface. With their backs to the wall, the students crouch until their shoulders are just under the surface, and they rotate the body at the hips to fully extend one arm behind the head toward the wall. They push off from the bottom, glide up to the wall, touch, tuck, and do a fast spin. Stress the correct position of the lead hand when contacting the wall; bending the elbow, with the head coming close to wall; a tucked body position with the knees near the surface and the head underwater; quickly tucking and spinning with the free hand pushing away from the hips; and placing the feet against the wall. Repeat until the students can execute all the movements smoothly and quickly.

b. Repeat step "a," adding drawing the arms behind the head and pushing off into a streamlined body position underwater with the body angled **slightly** toward the surface. Stress keeping the face, the arms, and the head nearly parallel to the surface during the push-off and the initial part of the glide; keeping the arms, the wrists, and the hands in straight alignment; exhaling through the nose during the push-off and the glide; kicking the body to the surface near the end of the glide; and starting the arm pull when the body is near to or on the surface. NOTE. For students who are having difficulty in getting the correct head and arm positions prior to the push-off, start the drill facing the wall and holding onto the overflow trough with both hands. The body is tucked, the feet are against the wall, and the shoulders are under or near the surface of the water. Have the students drop the upper part of the body back and below the surface, draw the hands behind the head, and then push off almost parallel to the surface. Repeat this exercise until proficiency develops.

c. Repeat steps "a" and "b," if necessary, and practice turning to the opposite side, using the other arm as the lead arm.

d. The students swim up to the wall and execute a turn. Practice on both sides. Stress not slowing down prior to touching the wall and contacting the wall with the lead arm fully extended. If, during normal stroking, the lead arm/hand enters the water within one arm's length (from fingertips) of the wall at the end of the recovery, they should merely speed up the kick to drive the hand to the wall. Taking one more arm pull will bring the swimmer too close to the wall, resulting in either the head or the recovering arm striking the wall. Swimmers can learn to judge their distance from the wall using a variety of methods: observing overhead fixtures in indoors pools, glancing over one shoulder when nearing the wall, or bending the head backward and glancing directly behind the head when nearing the wall (skilled swimmers).

Common Faults: Cause(s), Effect(s), Corrective Suggestions

1. **Slowing down when coming into turn.** Causes loss of momentum to help body pivot. Swim into turn at normal speed.

2. **Grasping overflow trough of pool.** Brings swimmers too high out of water, or they become dependent upon grabbing and pulling themselves around instead of allowing their momentum to help turn them. Practice placing hand, thumbside up, flat against turning surface about 6 to 10 inches below surface of water instead of grasping overflow trough.

3. **Not tucking knees tightly as soon as lead hand touches wall.** Slows down turning or pivoting movement. Practice simultaneously touching wall and drawing knees up quickly.

4. **Not using free arm during turn.** This slows down turn and may allow swimmer to drift away from turning surface. Practice a sculling or backwater action with free hand to help pivot body.

5. **Allowing hips to sink during push-off.** Causes added frontal resistance during initial portion of glide. Have students practice back glides from side of pool with the arms extended forward of the head. Emphasize streamlining body quickly by stretching body from toes to fingertips.

6. **Hyperextending wrists or neck.** Extending wrists or neck backward (downward) during push-off can cause back to arch and body to plane downward in water. Practice keeping hands and arms in straight alignment and forward of head, with top of head pointed toward other end of pool, or face being almost parallel to surface of water. The chin can be tucked slightly to prevent hyperextension of neck/head.

7. **Choking during turn and glide.** Mouth should be closed during turn and glide to prevent water from entering. Exhaling slowly through nose during turn and glide will prevent water from entering nasal passages. Ensure that neck is not hyperextended during push-off, as this position allows water to enter nose more easily.

8. **Starting kick too soon.** Lessens effectiveness of momentum established by push-off. Start kick when glide starts to slow down.

Open Spin Turn on Back

The open spin turn is the easiest turn to learn on the back, since the **face remains clear of the water during the turn and the push-off.** This turn is used primarily when swimming the elementary backstroke or the inverted breaststroke. Swimmers may prefer to use the backstroke turn if they can perform it proficiently.

The procedures for learning the open spin turn are virtually identical to those for the backstroke turn. The hand of the leading arm (selected by the swimmer) contacts the wall, the body tucks and spins toward the wall with the knees drawn toward the surface, and the feet are placed against the turning surface. The free hand is drawn to the wall and the student pushes off **on the surface** into a back glide with the arms at the sides. The push-off into the glide for the inverted breaststroke is done on the surface with the arms at the sides or extended forward of the head. For both strokes, the chin is tucked slightly during the push-off and the glide. NOTE. The face should remain clear of the water during all movements of the open turn.

START ON THE BACK

The start on the back is executed in a similar manner when starting from competitive starting blocks or from a crouched position in the water. Most students will not have starting blocks available during instruction periods.

The following information covers the start from a position in the water when the swimmer's hands can grip an overflow trough or the edge of the pool or a turning board that is close to the surface of the water.

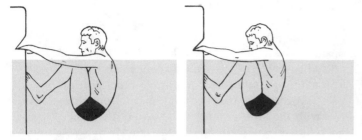
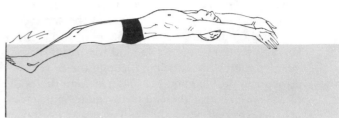

In the starting position, the body is tucked and the hands are about shoulder-width apart. The feet are placed against the wall, just under the surface, about hip-width apart. The feet may be level or one foot may be placed slightly higher than the other. The arms may be straight or bent slightly. The swimmer starts by pulling the body closer to the wall, then pushes strongly with the legs to project the body almost horizontally over and then into the water. The hands push away from the wall and the arms sweep vigorously and horizontally over the water with the palms up as the legs exert their drive from the wall. The fingertips enter the water with the arms fully extended behind the head or the shoulders with the head well-back, the back arched, and the body stretched and streamlined.

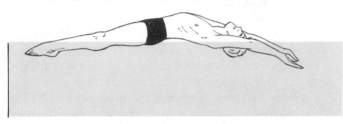
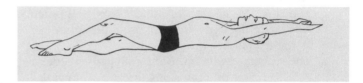

The chin tucks slightly and the arms begin to lift to the horizontal position as soon as the face submerges to prevent the body from going too deep. The body levels off and then angles slightly toward the surface during the glide. When forward momentum begins to decrease, the swimmer returns to the surface by adding the flutter kick and then pulling with one arm.

A breath is taken during the push-off from the wall. Slow exhalation through the nose begins when the head enters the water and continues until the face is clear of the water.

Teaching Suggestions

After a demonstration and a discussion of the skill, have the students use the **Whole Approach** and make corrections as necessary.

Common Faults: Cause(s), Effect(s), Corrective Suggestions

1. **Upper body too high out of water following push-off.** The effect is a loss of thrust in desired direction. Caused by feet being too low in starting position or by head being too high during push-off. Also, arms may be "thrown" vertically rather than horizontally following push-off with hands. Make corrections as needed.
2. **Feet slip downward during push-off.** Feet may be too deep in starting position. Raise feet. Pool wall may be very slippery. Placing one foot slightly higher than the other foot may help prevent slipping. Stress pushing body backward, not upward.
3. **Swimmers hyperextending their wrists during entry and glide.** Causes swimmers to go too deep in water. Practice keeping hands in a straight line with forearms during entry, followed by flexing wrists slightly during glide.
4. **Keeping head back during glide.** Tends to cause swimmer to go too deep. As soon as head and shoulders enter water, head is raised by tucking chin slightly.
5. **Starting leg action prematurely.** Tends to slow down momentum derived from push-off. Start flutter kick as soon as momentum from glide has slowed down to swimming speed. Add pull of one arm when hands near surface.
6. **Getting water in nose and throat.** Caused by keeping head back too long or not exhaling properly through nose. Stress tucking chin slightly and starting to exhale through nose as soon as head and shoulders go underwater.
7. **Poor start and glide.** Caused by feet slipping on wall, weak leg drive from wall, and/or weak throw of arms laterally and behind head. Change position of feet on wall. Practice hard push-off(s) into back glide(s), with arms at sides. Practice "arm throws" while doing "inverted" porpoise dives onto back in waist-deep water.

CHAPTER 11

ANALYZING AND TEACHING ENTRIES INTO THE WATER

*"A Swim A Day Keeps
Old Age Away!"*
The Commodore

The word dive is often used to describe different ways of entering and descending beneath the surface of the water. Entry into the water may be feetfirst or headfirst. Anyone who learns to swim should also develop the ability to jump and to dive safely from a solid surface, a boat, or a springboard, and must also acquire knowledge about the hazards of jumping and diving entries. Developing these skills and knowledge increases the enjoyment and the confidence in one's aquatic abilities and will help to prevent injuries that may result from an improper entry. The information in this chapter deals with safety aspects of diving and jumping, and the progressive steps of learning how to enter the water by jumping and diving.

SAFETY

The number of people who are seriously injured in diving accidents is increasing each year. Especially significant is the number of spinal cord injuries resulting from striking the head against the bottom or the side of a pool, or from striking some other object in the pool. Similar injuries are occurring from striking the bottom of or hidden objects in lakes, streams, or the surf. Injuries to the spinal cord may cause temporary or permanent paralysis to one or more parts of the body, or death. Although there may be less than 200 paralyzing-type diving accidents each year, it is important that aquatic facility owners or managers, home pool owners, and swimming and diving instructors take all reasonable precautions to prevent such accidents.

Of primary importance to diving safety is having ample depth for the individual diver and for the height of the dive, and having a correct entry angle for the dive. Studies have shown that the majority of serious diving injuries occur to males, ages 12 to 31, from diving into a depth of less than 4 feet. More accidents occur from diving from low heights, such as the edge of a pool deck, a dock, or a pier, than from springboards.

Competitive standards call for a minimum depth of 12 feet for a 1-meter board. For outdoor diving areas, the bottom should be cleared of stumps, rocks, and other obstacles. Diving boards should be mounted on a firm foundation and never on an insecure base, such as a float, which can be affected by shifting weight loads and wave action.

Regulation diving boards are 16 feet long by 20 inches wide, with the entire length of the top surface adequately covered with nonskid material. The standard height of the board above the water is 1 meter (39.37 inches). For safety, the front end of the board should project at least 6 feet beyond the end of the pool or the dock. Clearance from the sides of the board should be at least 10 feet and the distance between diving boards should be at least 9 feet. For competitive-type boards, the minimum depth of 12 feet should extend 10 feet on either side of the board and 20 feet forward from a point directly beneath the tip of the board to the point where the bottom begins to slope upward. A diving board should be installed so that it is level, since one that is pitched upward tends to cause the diver to come back down on the board.

If additional boards are planned, they should not be more than 1 meter in height unless expert diving instruction and good supervision is available and board use is restricted to skilled divers. Many diving injuries result from untrained persons diving from a poorly supervised 3-meter board.

In summation, diving boards should be located so that the execution and entry of the dive are not interfered with by the pool sides, the slant of the pool bottom, overhead structures, and other diving structures even if the diver "misses" a dive, resulting from an out-of-line flight and entry.

Diving into shallow water (4 feet or less) by untrained divers, from the side of the pool or the dock, should be prohibited. The untrained diver cannot judge nor control the angle of entry as well as the trained diver who knows the importance of the proper position of the arms and the hands during the entry and the descent. The hands should be kept together and the arms squeezed on either side of the head with the elbows locked. These positions enable the arms and the hands to provide good protection for the head in case the bottom or an object is struck during the entry. An unskilled diver will often enter the water with the arms spread apart and bent. They may even pull the arms back to the sides after the entry. In either case, there is little or no protection to the head.

Rules and regulations concerning diving should be posted, understood, and enforced through proper supervision. Shallow water areas and depths should be clearly marked. Swimming and diving areas should be separated by a lane line or a life line.

Proper supervision should be provided if a slide is used. There must be a safe landing area with a minimum depth of 3½ feet. Head first entries from a slide that exits into shallow water should be prohibited, especially for adults.

Some of the most important safety rules regarding jumping and diving are:

- Never start a dive or a jump until the preceding diver has come to the surface and has moved away from the diving entry area. Compliance with this rule will be much easier if ladders are strategically located to force the diver to swim to a side removed from the diving entry area when getting out of the pool after the dive.
- Dive or jump directly forward from the deck, the dock, the diving board, or the tower.
- Know the depth of the water and know that the landing area is free from obstructions. Don't jump or dive into unfamiliar water offering poor visibility.

- Look before jumping or diving.
- No double or multiple bouncing on the end of the diving board. This can cause the diver to go "off line" during the flight through the air. The diver may strike the side of the pool or another object, or may strike someone else who is in the water.
- A person should learn to dive safely from the side of a pool or a dock before being allowed to use a springboard.

The health and physical condition of the diver should be taken into account. Chill, fatigue, or weakness from a recent illness or injury can adversely affect the diver's performance. Individuals having a history of nasal, ear, or sinus problems should consult a family physician before participating in a diving program.

JUMPING ENTRIES

From a Low Height

Jumping into shallow water can be dangerous. A person jumping from a pool deck or from a dock of similar height into 3½ feet of water may actually drop 4 feet or more before the feet hit the bottom. The force of landing is not slowed by the upward or buoyant force of the water at this depth. This downward force is great enough to break a leg unless the descent is slowed gradually by allowing the knees to bend to absorb the shock of landing. Therefore, the student must learn correct landing procedures before jumping into shallow water.

The beginner swimmer should know how to level off to a horizontal position in deep water and should be able to swim a few feet before learning to jump into deep water. All initial jumps should be performed under the close supervision of the instructor. Students should learn to exhale through their nose during the entry and descent to prevent water from being forced into the nasal passages.

Teaching Suggestions

1. Have the students practice jumping up and down on the deck of the pool or the dock.
2. Have the students, sitting on the edge of the pool or a low dock, push off and land in a vertical position in **chest-deep** water. Emphasize landing on the bottom with the knees bent. Add No. 3, below.
3. As the feet hit the bottom, the students lean forward, extend the arms to the front, and push off into a prone glide.
4. From a standing position, with the toes curled over the edge to prevent slipping when pushing, the students lean forward slightly and jump into **chest-deep** water. The arms are next to the sides of the body (preferred) or extended over the head during the entry. The students then lean forward and push off from the bottom into a prone glide. Leaning forward when starting the jump will prevent the students from falling backward and striking the side of the pool or the dock.

5. Repeat No. 4, with the students jumping into **neck-deep** water. As the feet touch the bottom, the knees bend enough to allow the head to completely submerge with the eyes closed. The students lean forward in a crouched position and push diagonally upward to the surface with the eyes open. Upon surfacing, the students swim a few feet and then stop. Repeat until the students can perform all movements comfortably and confidently.

6. The students jump into **deep water.** During the entry, the body should be straight and nearly vertical, with the eyes closed to prevent possible injury to them. The arms may be along the sides of the body (preferred) or extended over the head. When the downward momentum has stopped, the students lean forward, open the eyes, and either push off from the bottom or begin to kick and to swim diagonally toward the surface using the beginner stroke. Upon reaching the surface, the students level off and swim to safety using the beginner stroke or the crawl

stroke. Some students may prefer to roll over and swim to safety using a stroke on the back. Repeat until the students can perform comfortably and confidently. Gradually increase the distance the students must swim to safety.

Except for medical reasons, all students should perform the final jumps without holding the nose and without wearing nose clips in order to gain confidence in preventing water from entering the nasal passages by exhaling through the nose. Emphasize that the students should exhale slowly during the descent, but should retain enough air to be comfortable until the surface is reached; close supervision of the students, which may include having an instructor or aide in the water to provide assistance if necessary during the initial attempts to perform these skills; and that the students enter with their bodies straight. (Common faults include entering the water with the knees bent or with the body in a crouched position.)

Compact Jump

The compact jump is one of the safest forms of **deepwater** entry from a height of 10 feet or more above the surface of the water. Except for **emergency situations,** the water should be known to be free of underwater hazards before jumping.

Learning to jump from heights of more than 10 feet in Red Cross courses is **not recommended** for the majority of individuals. **Exceptions** may be made in the Aquatics Survival course for persons who may need to learn to jump from relatively high elevations because of their professions, such as construction workers and military and maritime personnel.

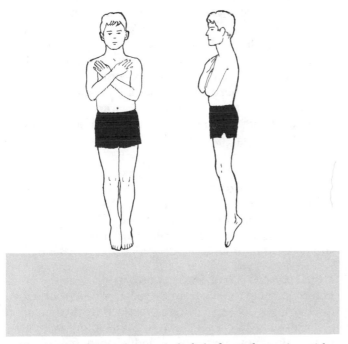

The jumper leans forward slightly from the waist with the head erect and the eyes looking forward during the jump and the descent. As soon as the jumper has leaped clear of the support, the lower arms and the hands are crossed over the chest and are held close to the sides of the body. The legs are brought together (or crossed at the ankles) and are held nearly straight with the toes pointed. During the descent and the entry, the body is kept straight and perpendicular to the surface of the water. The nasal passages may be kept closed by squeezing the nose between the thumb and forefinger of one hand to prevent water being forced up the nasal passages as a result of the increased speed of the body during the entry. If this procedure is not used, the individual should begin exhaling through the nose as soon as the feet hit the surface. Exhaling should continue slowly until the descent stops. Once submerged, the upward force of the water will begin to slow the rate of descent of the person. The rate of descent can be slowed further by spreading the arms and the legs apart or simply by relaxing the rigid body position held during the entry.

Teaching Suggestions

Practice all jumps into a **minimum** depth of 10 feet. From all heights, have the students practice entering the water with the legs uncrossed and with the nose pinched with one hand and then unpinched. When the nose is not pinched, emphasize exhaling through the nose as soon as the feet hit the water.

1. Have the students practice a compact jump from the edge of the pool or the dock. Stress keeping the toes curled over the edge to prevent slipping when initiating the jump.

2. Have the students practice the jump, starting from a standing position at the end of a 1-meter diving board or from a platform of similar height. Emphasize leaning forward slightly as the jump is initiated and keeping the head erect with the eyes looking directly ahead. The body follows the head position during the flight through the air. If the head drops forward, the body will begin to rotate to a prone position. The body will rotate backward if the head is extended backward. This can cause a dangerous fall when starting from a height of 10 feet or more. **Do not allow** the students to jump from a 3-meter board (or higher) until they have full control of their bodies when jumping from a height of about 3 feet.

3. Have the students practice a compact jump from a height of about 10 feet (3-meter board). The jumps can be made by stepping off into space and then bringing the legs together before the entry. To prevent rolling forward, the trunk should be nearly vertical to the water during the takeoff and descent, with the head erect and the eyes looking forward. The knees may be bent slightly at the entry.

Stride Jump

The objective of this method of jumping into the water is to prevent the head from submerging during the entry, which will permit the eyes to maintain visual observation of an individual or an object. The stride jump is discussed in greater detail in the Red Cross publication *Lifesaving: Rescue and Water Safety* (Stock No. 321103).

DIVING ENTRIES

Fundamentals of Diving

Many factors contribute to the development of a skilled diver: body structure, strength and coordination, balance, courage, kinesthetic awareness, determination, motivation, and sound instruction and coaching. Of the various physical factors involved, kinesthetic awareness or sense is one of the most important. Briefly defined, it is the awareness of one's body in space and the ability to perceive the extent, direction, and kinds of movement of the body and body parts. An individual with good kinesthetic awareness is better able to control and to time the intricate body movements required in the execution of a difficult dive. On the other hand, an individual with poor kinesthetic awareness can experience problems in learning to dive. Kinesthetic awareness, and skill performance, can frequently be improved by keeping the eyes open and focused on a fixed, physical reference point while practicing a dive. Any object placed on the bottom that is clearly visible from the surface can be used as a target for the diver.

In diving, the body position must be inverted from the takeoff position to allow the hands and head to enter the water first. Learning to find and to maintain a proper head position during the dive is extremely important because of the effects of head position on overall body position. The body will follow the actions of the head. A beginner lifting the head too quickly while diving from poolside may "belly flop." On the other hand, a novice springboard diver may land on the back because of an "overthrow," caused by dropping the head too quickly during the takeoff or during the flight through the air.

Control of abdominal, back, and leg muscles is also very important in achieving the proper extension and alignment of the body necessary for a safe, effective dive. Failure to tense and to control these muscles at the appropriate time can cause the diver to enter the water in various stages of collapse. Neck, shoulder, or back strain may result. Also, if the arms and the shoulders are not properly tensed on entry, they may be forcefully flung aside owing to the water resistance and serious injury could result.

Listed below are basic guidelines to follow in executing a dive:

1. In performing a headfirst dive, the arms are extended alongside the head in the direction of the line of flight, with the hands together, palms down and thumbs touching, to cut the impact of the water on the top of the head and to protect the diver from injury by striking the pool bottom if the dive is too deep.
2. If a dive is "missed," the diver should assume a tuck position to minimize the amount of body surface that may land flat on the water.

Physical Laws Applied to Diving

Teachers of diving should understand and should be able to explain some of the basic fundamentals of diving. If the body is leaning too far forward at the takeoff, the push of the legs will be backward, which will thrust the body forward rather than upward. If the arms are simply swung forward rather than upward, the arm action will result in a forward thrust of the body. Only if the drive of the legs is downward, and the arms swing upward, and the head remains up, will all the forces be applied in the correct direction for a vertical lift. The body will take off at an angle slightly forward of the vertical because, at the takeoff, the body weight rocks forward to the toes and the arms swing forward and upward. A good leg lift and a drop of the head and arms at the "top" of the dive will then cause the body to rotate as a lever around its center of gravity (pelvic area) and invert for a headfirst entry.

Force applied horizontally does not gain time in the air. To gain time in the air to execute the movements in more complicated dives, the diver's center of gravity must be raised as high as possible above the takeoff point. A springboard, properly used, will enable the diver to achieve a height greater than starting from a solid surface of the same height as the diving board.

When an object spins, the speed of rotation is dependent on the initial force at takeoff and the length of the radius of the spinning object. If the initial force a diver exerts is the same for all types of somersault dives, the diver will spin fastest in the tucked body position, slightly slower in the piked position, and slowest in the layout position. Consequently, it is easier for the novice diver to first learn the tuck somersault with a feetfirst entry. This is a good basic dive for novices, since they learn that by staying tucked they can land on almost any part of the body without getting hurt. In the tucked position, the landing is absorbed by body parts hitting sequentially (rolling) instead of simultaneously (flat). Consequently, the diver should try to assume a tuck position when it is obvious a dive will be "missed."

Divers and diving teachers should understand that the body and the legs will follow the actions of the head. To execute a jumping entry in the vertical position, the head must remain up. To execute **reverse dives,** the head must drop **backward** toward the point of takeoff during the flight of the dive. To execute **forward,** headfirst-entry dives, the head must drop forward and downward toward the water sometime during the flight through the air. Depending on the type of dive, the height of the takeoff point, the amount of force exerted for the takeoff, the height reached at the "top" of the dive, and the vertical angle of the takeoff, divers will learn through practice, instruction, and "feel" (kinesthetic awareness) when the head should be lowered and the body straightened in order to achieve a near vertical entry.

Beginner Diving Progressions

Before learning to dive from the edge of a pool or a low dock, a variety of skills can be practiced by the beginner diver in waist- to chest-deep water, including shallow surface diving or "porpoising," and performing "handstands." Porpoise diving can be practiced by pushing off from the side of the pool into a prone glide and then quickly angling the head and arms toward the bottom, or by jumping forward and upward slightly from a standing position on the bottom and then "diving" toward the bottom, leveling off, and gliding toward the surface. Emphasize keeping the arms extended forward of the head with the thumbs touching or interlocked and opening the eyes during the descent and the ascent. The degree of the angle of the body during the descent and ascent is changed by raising or lowering the head (and arms). These skills allow the beginner to experience and to develop some of the elements of proper body position necessary for effective diving. They build confidence and are enjoyable to perform.

Once the beginner has learned to jump safely into deep water, recover to a horizontal position, and swim comfortably, diving into deep water can be taught. Certain factors must be stressed in each phase of the beginner diving progressions. The eyes should be kept open and focused on the desired entry point until the hands enter the water. The arms, wrists, and fingers are kept in line with the head to help control the angle of entry and to provide protection to the head. Abdominal and leg muscles should be properly tensed to ensure a smooth, streamlined entry and glide underwater with the body fully extended and in good alignment.

Following are some of the precautions that must be taken during diving instruction and practice to prevent the student from striking the bottom or the side of the pool, or another object, which may cause severe injury to the head or spinal column:

- Diving from the sitting position or when kneeling on one knee at the edge of a pool or dock that is no higher than 18 inches above the surface of the water, the minimum depth should be 5 feet for most children who are from 5 to 8 years of age. For older or larger children, and for teenagers and adults, the minimum depth should be closer to 6 feet.
- Standing and running dives, from the same maximum height as above, should be performed in water having a minimum depth of 7 feet under and beyond the entry point when the angle of entry is relatively shallow. Planned entries with the body nearly vertical to the surface should be performed in water having a **minimum depth of 10 feet** under and beyond the entry point.
- The diver's arms, wrists, and fingers should be kept straight and in line with the head until forward momentum has almost stopped.
- The diver should not attempt to lift the arms during the entry when performing a shallow entry dive into a depth of less than 5 feet. Lifting the arms will cause the head to drop. This will cause the upper part of the body to angle downward, resulting in the possibility of the head striking the bottom. All dives must be directly forward of the point of takeoff and at a distance of at least 4 feet from any obstruction to either side of the diver.
- The diving area must be free of any hazards that may cause injury to a diver.

The basic progressions for learning to dive are designed to give the learner a gradual adjustment starting from a position close to the water and graduating to a dive from a standing position. These progressions may have to be varied, depending on the design of the facility. For instance, where there is no overflow trough or similar brace for the feet, it might be necessary and advisable to start from the one-knee kneeling position. The rate at which individual students move through the following progressions will vary greatly. Some will need a great deal of practice and encouragement at each stage. It may sometimes be necessary to go back to a previous step for more practice when the learner experiences difficulty at a particular level. If an individual step proves to be an obstacle, such as the tip-in dive from one leg, it may be advisable to move on to the next step. Students who have very good coordination and kinesthetic awareness may learn to dive very quickly. It may not be necessary for these students to attempt each step in the suggested progressions. Factors such as class size and the students' abilities should determine which diving progressions are taught and in what order.

Step One — Sitting Position

In pools where there is an overflow trough and the pool edge is 6 to 18 inches above the water surface, the sitting dive is usually introduced first.

The learner sits on the edge of the pool, knees spread wide, with the heels resting on the overflow trough (or some other suitable brace) and bends forward at the waist. Both arms are extended forward of the head with the upper arms pressing against the ears. The hands are together, with thumbs touching, and the eyes look under the palms and focus on the desired point of entry (about 3 to 4 feet from the pool edge). When ready, the diver takes a breath and begins to roll in. As the balance is lost, the diver pushes the body forward into a streamlined prone glide position. The body enters the water at a slight angle with the hands entering first, followed by the head with the eyes closed, and then the rest of the body. When entirely in the water, the learner raises the head and the arms, opens the eyes, and angles back to the surface. Repeated efforts will add confidence, allowing the learner to go deeper and hold the glide position longer before surfacing. Emphasize that the eyes close just before the entry for all headfirst entries and that they open when the forward momentum of the body has almost stopped.

If there is no overflow trough present and if the pool edge is nearly at water level, a headfirst "roll-in" can be performed from the sitting position. In this case, the body will be almost completely submerged before the legs are extended by pressing slightly against the pool wall with the feet.

Teaching Suggestions

1. Explain and demonstrate the dive from the sitting position. Emphasize keeping the arms extended throughout the dive until the glide is completed, keeping the chin tucked slightly until the body is fully submerged, pushing with the feet once the balance is lost, and completing the dive with the body fully extended and streamlined.

2. Have the students practice. Make corrections as necessary. The instructor or an aide may want to be in the water to provide individual help when necessary. **Ensure a safe diving area.**

Common Faults and Corrective Suggestions

1. **Raises head; does "belly flop."** Have student tilt head and grip tennis ball or similar-sized soft object between lower jaw and throat. Hold ball in this position until head submerges. Then raise head for

ascent to surface. Or, instructor places own hand on top of student's head, and maintains sufficient pressure to prevent head from being lifted during dive.

2. **Fails to push with feet and to extend body fully.** Practice pushing off hard from side of pool into prone glide and holding this position for several feet. Practice porpoise diving in shallow water. Push off from bottom or bottom step (if one is available). Push hard and hold streamlined prone glide position.

3. **Rolls over or somersaults underwater.** Usually caused by having head too low or arms and head too low. May also be caused by just falling in — not pushing with the feet. Raise head and arms slightly, and have student look and dive to a point 3 to 5 feet forward of side of pool or dock.

4. **Arms bend or collapse at entry, or arms pull backward following entry. Insist** that student maintains correct position of arms throughout dive and glide. Have student practice porpoise diving until correct arm position is achieved. Have student dive, glide, reach, and touch instructor with hands. Instructor stands or treads water 10 to 15 feet from side of pool.

All of the above faults should be corrected before progressing to the next step.

Step Two — Kneeling Position

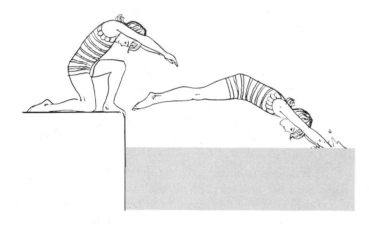

The learner kneels on one knee with the toes of the other foot gripping the pool edge. Again, the arms are extended forward of the head with the upper arms pressing against the ears. With the eyes focused on the desired entry point, the learner leans forward and inside of the "pushing" leg and begins to roll toward the water. When the balance is lost, the student pushes against the poolside with the contact foot. Upon entering the water, the body straightens and both legs fully extend to achieve the prone glide position. Some of the same faults may occur as in the sitting position. Correct these faults through instruction and practice.

> The term **deep water,** which appears in the following sections on diving, is defined as being a **minimum of nine feet.**

Step Three — Tip-In Position

In the **tip-in** dive, the learner assumes the proper head and arm positions while balanced primarily on one leg with the knee bent and the toes curled over the edge of the diving surface. The other leg is lifted to the rear as the body leans forward. It continues to be lifted during the dive. When the balance is lost, the learner pushes off with the contact foot and the leg is then raised to join the other leg. The body is straightened following the entry and a glide is taken underwater before the ascent begins. A correctly performed tip-in dive will result in a more vertical entry. **This dive, if used as a progression, must be practiced and learned in deep water.**

Teaching Suggestions

1. Explain and demonstrate the skill. Emphasize diving to a point 4 to 5 feet forward of the side of the pool or the dock. Point out that the flutter kick may be used, if needed, to help the return to the surface.

2. Have the students practice in **deep water.** Have the students level off and swim a few feet toward safety after surfacing.

Common Faults and Corrective Suggestions

1. **Same faults and corrections as for kneeling dive.**

2. **Fails to lift one or both legs during dive.** In waist-deep water, have students practice porpoise diving into handstand on bottom. Emphasize lifting legs above surface when hands are placed on bottom. Practice bringing legs together, stretching them, and pointing toes.

3. **Fails to straighten and bring legs together during flight through air and entry, or fails to extend ankles and point toes.** Practice jumping into air from standing position on land. Practice porpoise dives or prone glides using hard push-off. Emphasize stretching legs and bringing them together with toes pointed as soon as push (spring) is completed. Maintain long glide with legs in streamlined position.

4. **"Long" dive — legs pass vertical plane during entry.** Caused by chin tucked excessively during takeoff and flight. Student may land on back. Practice looking at and diving to entry point 4 to 5 feet forward of takeoff point.

Step Four — Fall-In Position

In the **fall-in** dive, the student assumes a pike position by keeping the legs straight and by bending forward from the waist. The feet are a few inches apart with the toes of both feet curled over the edge of the pool or the dock. With the head and the arms properly positioned, the student leans forward and falls into the water. The legs press upward following the entry. The advantage of using this progression is that the student learns to dive from a semistanding position. The disadvantage is that the student does not practice pushing off into the dive. **Practice this dive in deep water.**

Step Five — Crouch Position

In this progression, the student stands with both feet on the edge of the pool or the dock. The arms and the head are positioned properly, the knees bend, and the chest is brought down to almost touch the thighs. Reaching for an entry point 3½ to 6 feet from the edge, the student rolls forward. As the balance is lost, the student pushes with both feet and a glide is taken underwater with the body in a streamlined position. Correct any common faults that have been discussed previously. **Practice this skill in deep water.**

Step Six — Standing Dive With Small Spring

From the standing position, the student bends forward slightly from the waist and bends the knees. As the body leans forward and the balance is lost, the feet push off and the legs straighten. The body follows the path of an arc into the water. Following the entry, a glide is taken underwater. **Practice in deep water.** Stress keeping the head down during the flight through the air, keeping the arms extended forward of the head until the glide underwater is completed, pushing off with the feet, straightening the legs, and pointing the toes.

Step Seven — Standing Dive With Vigorous Spring

The student starts the dive with the body nearly erect and the arms extended over the head. The knees bend and, as the body leans forward and the balance is lost, the legs extend vigorously. The body stretches up and over, in an arc, and enters the water in a controlled headfirst position. Stress minimizing the amount of piking of the body during the flight through the air. Use of the pole, as in step eight, will be effective.

Step Eight — Standing Dive With Spring and Arm Action

The amount of spring can be increased by adding an arm action. Standing erect at the edge of the pool or the dock, the student brings the arms down to the sides of the body as the knees bend. As the balance is lost, the knees spring or extend and, simultaneously, the arms are lifted rapidly over the head, ending with the arms and the head positioned as has been previously described.

NOTE. The following steps can be used to help both novices and more advanced students to achieve a more vertical angle of entry and to achieve greater height in the dive. **These steps must be practiced in deep water.** The student dives over an object, such as a light weight pole, which is held by the instructor at a right angle to the line of flight of the diver. The pole is at first positioned at about knee height and a couple of feet in front of the student. Repeat until the diver clears the pole. The pole may be lowered quickly when it is obvious that the student's legs will not clear it. Then, in gradual steps, move the pole closer to the student and raise the pole gradually. Repeat each step until the student achieves a near-vertical entry.

Long Shallow Dive

The long shallow dive is a long, low-projecting dive performed in a streamlined body position that enables the swimmer to enter the water at a controlled, shallow angle with great forward momentum. This dive is used during recreational swimming and in lifesaving situations where speed is urgent. The dive is performed in relatively clear water of known depth that is free of underwater hazards. It can be performed from a standing position or can be preceded by a walk or a run **from a nonslippery surface.**

Shallow Dive — Standing Position

The diver assumes a position on the edge of the pool or the dock with the feet 6 to 8 inches apart and with the toes gripping the edge. The hips and the knees are flexed and the back is nearly parallel to the starting surface. The arms hang loosely with the head erect and with the eyes focused on a point well out in the water. Forward motion is initiated by drawing the arms backward and upward. During this action, the heels rise and the body begins to move forward. The arms begin immediately to swing downward, then forward. When the balance is lost, the hips, knees, ankles, and toes extend forceably to drive the body in a line of flight over and nearly parallel to the surface of the water.

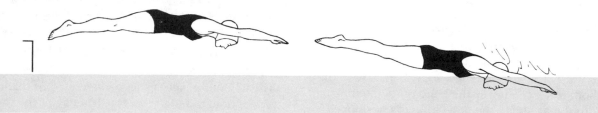

During the flight, the head drops slightly to a position between the outstretched arms, which are angled downward slightly. The entry should be at a slight angle to the surface as opposed to landing too flat on the water and thereby retarding forward movement. The fully extended and streamlined body position is maintained during the glide underwater until the swimmer feels some loss of momentum, at which time the leg kick begins, which will help the diver to regain the surface and start swimming.

The actions of the arms and the head are different when executing a competitive racing dive. From the crouch position, the arms remain in the front hanging position. The hands may actually grasp the front edge of the starting block or the platform (grab start). The arms are swung directly forward from this position as the balance is lost and the dive is initiated. The head position will also vary in a well-executed competitive dive. The chin drops closer to the chest as the body begins to roll forward and the balance is lost. The head lifts quickly to allow sighting down the pool during the thrust of the arms and the legs.

Teaching Suggestions

Demonstrate and discuss the dive and then have the students practice. Emphasize the following:

1. Placing the feet 6 to 10 inches apart. If the feet are too close together, a twisting dive may result because of poor balance during the push-off. Twisting may also result from uneven movements of the arms during their forward thrust.
2. Bending at the knees and the waist. Relax and try to touch the toes with the fingertips.
3. Lifting the heels and starting to roll forward as the arms finish their backward swing and the knees continue to bend.

4. Continuing to roll forward. As the balance is lost, swing the arms forward with the push-off of the legs and lift the head. This body position allows the force of the legs and the feet to be directed backward, not upward. Pushing off too soon may result in too much height and a piked body position.
5. Coordinating the actions of the arms and the legs. This can be helped by keeping the arms bent during the "windup" and the early part of the forward extension. Stress full arms extension during the flight through the air, the entry, and the glide underwater.
6. Raising the head enough during the takeoff to establish a nearly parallel line of flight and to see that the arms are aimed toward the desired entry spot.
7. Dropping the head between the arms and closing the eyes just before the entry. Keeping the head up too long can result in a "belly flop."
8. Diving out and over a pole. Vary the distance and the height of the pole from the starting point of the diver to help establish the correct body position during the flight through the air and the entry. An alternative would be to have the students dive to and through a piece of paper floating on the surface. Remind the diver to drop the head before the entry.
9. Stretching and streamlining the body during the dive, the entry, and the glide underwater. A slight pike position may allow for a clean entry. A severe pike position can cause the hands and feet to enter simultaneously and negate good forward momentum.
10. Practicing a long glide in the streamlined position before starting to kick. Adjust the positions of the head and arms after entry to prevent going too deep or surfacing too quickly.

Shallow Dive — Running Position

This skill requires confidence and good body control, which are developed after considerable practice. This dive is usually introduced at a high skill level, such as in the Red Cross Advanced Lifesaving course. It allows the diver to cover more distance through the air and during the glide than the standing shallow dive. It is **not** to be used in very shallow or unknown waters.

The flight and entry components of this skill are learned in the standing shallow dive. **It is vital that the deck or dock surface be of a nonslip material.** This factor is extremely important for the diver's safety as well as for helping to build confidence while learning the skill. **NOTE. This dive is practiced only in deep water.**

The running shallow dive should be introduced and learned in progressive steps: a one-step takeoff, a slow walk, a slow run, and then a faster run. Following the run, the takeoff into the dive can be from both feet simultaneously, but most divers experience greater success by taking off from one foot. To build confidence and to develop good body control during the dive, all students must be allowed to progress through the above steps at their own pace.

Points of emphasis:
1. The body is more erect at the takeoff than in the standing shallow dive.
2. The foot (feet) pushes off from a position 6 to 12 inches behind the edge of the pool or the dock.
3. During the takeoff, the diver's head is more erect, the eyes do not immediately look for water (landing spot), and the arms extend forward and about parallel to the water.
4. The head and the arms drop sooner during the flight than in the standing shallow dive. Emphasize lifting the legs during the flight through the air.
5. Through practice and instruction, the diver will learn to establish the correct positions of the body, the head, and the arms during the takeoff, the flight, and the entry. This will prevent diving too high or too low or will prevent a "long" dive (tucking the head too soon, thereby causing the body and the legs to rotate over onto the back).

SPRINGBOARD DIVING

Expert diving from a springboard requires a high degree of kinesthetic awareness or knowledge of the actions of the body when it is in space. Also required are good control of all body parts, regular practice with proper supervision, good physical condition, confidence, and courage. A sound progression from basic skills to the more complex movements is also necessary to develop divers of high quality. The information that follows is intended for use in upper level Red Cross swimming courses and from a **one-meter springboard.** Individuals who are interested in diving competitively are encouraged to seek instruction from a competent diving coach.

Standing Front Dive From a Springboard

In progressing from the pool deck to a one-meter springboard, the novice diver must learn to adjust to the height of the board. **The forward fall-in dive, which uses no board action, should be the first skill attempted on the springboard.** The arms are extended over the head, the head is positioned between the upper arms, and the legs are kept straight. The diver bends at the waist, assuming a full pike position. As the diver falls forward, the feet are kept on the board as long as possible. Once the feet leave the board, the diver lifts the hips slightly to align the body properly for the entry. The body is almost fully extended prior to entry and this extended position is maintained as the diver continues underwater.

After the fall-in dive is performed with ease and confidence, the diver does a coordinated standing front dive to gain a feel for the action of the board. The diver stands at the end of the board, the arms extended to the sides or in front of the body, the body and the head erect, with the eyes focused on the desired point of entry. The knees bend and the arms are lowered simultaneously, which forces the board down slightly. Then the arms are brought forward and upward as the legs and the body are extended, driving the diver up and slightly outward from the board. Maintaining proper extension, the body travels through a small arc and enters the water in a nearly vertical position.

Care must be taken to make the takeoff from the board almost completely vertical. Leaning too far forward can cause the diver to push out from the board into a flat, unsatisfactory flight. Dropping the head and the upper body too soon can cause the board impetus to flip the diver over. This standing dive should be practiced until the diver is reasonably comfortable with the spring of the board and has gained good body control during the takeoff, the flight, and the entry. **All diving from a one-meter (or less) board must be performed in water that has a minimum depth of 10 feet.**

Running Front Dive From a Springboard

The basic front dive or running front dive from a springboard consists of three phases — the approach and hurdle, the execution of the dive, and the entry.

The completed running front dive should result in a smooth and effective approach and hurdle, good body position during the flight through the air, and a good entry. The distance from which the diver starts the approach from the takeoff end of the board depends on how many steps the diver will use during the approach. For the minimum three-step approach and hurdle, the diver stands about four walking steps from the takeoff end of the board. This spot should be the approximate starting position, allowing the diver to then take three steps and a hurdle and land on both feet close to the end of the board.

Initially, the diver starts the approach by stepping off with the foot that feels most natural. The choice of feet may change as soon as the learner becomes aware of which foot is the best one to take off from into the hurdle. In the three-step approach, the diver begins with the foot that will be used to initiate the hurdle. For a four-step approach, the alternate foot begins the approach.

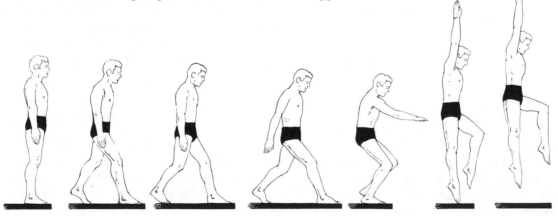

In the starting position, the diver stands erect, feet together, arms at the sides with the fingers extended naturally, and with the eyes focused on the end of the board. The first step is a normal step, the second may be slightly longer, and the third may be slightly longer again and more forceful. The arms can hang naturally at the side during the first two steps. During the third step, the arms are slightly behind the body in preparation for their forward and upward lift during the hurdle. As the diver comes down with the forward foot on the third step, the opposite knee bends and is lifted forcefully and simultaneously with the raising of the arms. When

the arms have reached the extended position over the head, the raised thigh should be at or near a right angle to the body. The push-off leg extends strongly and stays extended until the landing on the board. The coordinated action of the arms and the legs, along with the proper body position, projects the diver into the air and the body remains relatively close to the end of the board.

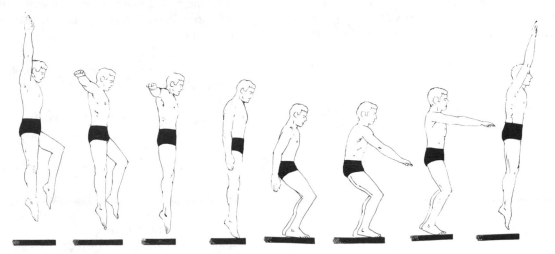

As the diver starts to descend, the knee that is flexed straightens out just before landing on the board. The body is aligned so that the weight is over the extended leg and the head is almost erect with the eyes still focused on the end of the board. Keeping the body vertical and the legs straight, the diver contacts the board first with the balls of the feet. The knees and the hips flex as the heels drop to the board. During the descent, the arms are brought down quickly to the sides. The arms may be straight or slightly flexed. Maximum depression of the board results from both the weight of the body landing on the board and the landing being timed correctly with the downward movement of the arms.

The diver lifts from the board by timing the actions of the leg thrust and the arm lift with the recoil effect of the board. The diver should lean forward slightly dur-

ing the takeoff, diving off the board at an angle of about 80 degrees. The takeoff must be made with the feet pushing simultaneously and with equal force. The legs snap together with the toes pointed as soon as the feet leave the board.

During the flight, the body can be straight or slightly piked. As the diver reaches the top of the arc of the dive, the head is lowered, the body rotates forward, and the eyes are focused on the desired point of entry. During the fall toward the water, the diver stretches and maintains necessary muscle tension to keep the body in proper alignment. The body enters the water a little short of being vertical (an angle of about 80 degrees), since it will continue to rotate forward slightly as it enters the water. The body is kept fully stretched as the dive carries well underwater.

SUGGESTED LEARNING PROCEDURES

Each of the following steps should be demonstrated and discussed before the students attempt the skill. The progress of the students will vary. Aggressive students with good coordination, balance, and kinesthetic awareness will advance quite rapidly. They may not need to practice a one- or two-step approach before progressing to the three-step approach. Many students will need considerable practice, help, and encouragement to master each progression.

Discuss and enforce all rules of safety pertaining to diving. Ensure that the diving equipment is in good condition before allowing the board(s) to be used. Check for the amount of torque (twisting) characteristics of the board. A board that twists can throw the diver off the intended line of flight, which can result in an

accident. The nonskid surface must be in good condition to prevent the diver from slipping. Discuss the use of the moveable fulcrum if the board has one.

Teaching Suggestions

Demonstrate and discuss each of the following progressions, followed by student practice.

1. A forward "fall-in" dive in a pike position from the end of the board.
2. A coordinated standing front dive from the end of the board.
3. A one-step approach and hurdle on the deck. Practice landing with the feet about 12 inches apart. Land with the knees slightly bent. The length of the hurdle should be between 12 and 24 inches. Repeat, adding jumping with both feet into the air with

coordinated arm and leg actions. Stress a slight forward lean during the jump.

4. A one-step approach and hurdle on the board. Keep the eyes on the end of the board. Land easily on the balls of the feet, 4 to 8 inches from the end of the board. Stop. Do not jump or double bounce.

5. Use the one-step approach and do a front jump from the board (vertical entry made feetfirst, the arms at the sides, and the body streamlined).

6. Use the one-step approach and do a front dive from the board. Stress a slight forward lean at the start of the takeoff.

7. Practice a three-step approach and hurdle on the deck until good balance is achieved. Add a takeoff from the deck with a slight body lean.

8. Practice a three-step approach and hurdle on the board (no takeoff).

9. Use the three-step approach and hurdle and do a front jump followed by a vertical entry as in No. 5, above.

10. Use the three-step approach and hurdle and do a front "running" dive from the board.

Common Faults: Cause(s), Effect(s), Corrective Suggestions

1. **Steps too long or too short on approach.** Awkward appearance and poor preparation for hurdle. Stress taking natural strides. Repeat deck practice of approach and hurdle.

2. **Hopping or jumping into hurdle.** Body not properly balanced or aligned to get maximum lift from hurdle. On deck, repeat correct demonstration of hurdle, followed by student practice. Stress natural stride of step leading to hurdle.

3. **Leaning too far forward on hurdle or takeoff.** Flight carries out too far from board. Diver may flip over (long dive). Repeat deck practice. Stress keeping body, head, and shoulders erect during hurdle and descent to board.

4. **Head drops down on hurdle and takeoff, or drops too quickly during flight.** Upper body rotates forward too far. Hips and legs are driven past the vertical plane causing diver to flip over. Stress keeping head erect and eyes on board during hurdle, keeping head erect and eyes looking up and ahead during ascent, dropping head at "top of dive" and start of descent, and looking at and reaching for the desired landing spot.

5. **Failure to lean forward slightly during takeoff. Diver may not carry out far enough to clear board!** Can cause insufficient forward rotation during flight to allow near-vertical entry. Stress slight forward lean. Repeat practice of standing front dive from board or repeat practice on deck.

6. **Failure to lift arms high enough during hurdle or takeoff.** Insufficient height acquired. Repeat deck and board practice of approach into hurdle and into takeoff. Stress arm elevation timed with leg actions.

7. **Hips, arms, or shoulders uneven during hurdle or takeoff.** Weak or unbalanced takeoff. Awkward flight. Low arc during flight. Repeat deck and board drills.

8. **Legs spread, knees bend, hips flex, arms bend.** Sufficient tension not maintained in the muscles of these body parts during takeoff, flight, or entry. Stress extension (rigidity) of these muscle groups and body parts. "Stretch" and streamline body from takeoff until hands touch bottom (10 foot depth) or until downward momentum has stopped if diving in depths of more than 10 feet.

9. **Insufficient height acquired during flight.** Weak leg action during hurdle or takeoff or too much body lean forward at takeoff. Repeat preliminary deck and board drills. Emphasize proper arm actions with leg action in hurdle (knees bending at end of hurdle, and explosive extension of legs during takeoff). Check body position during hurdle and takeoff.

10. **Hips and lower body continue forward rotation beyond vertical position during flight through air and body flips over for awkward, even dangerous, entry.** Caused by diver attempting to make a completely vertical entry, or by lowering head too soon during flight. Stress proper angle of entry (about 80 degrees) and eyes focused on desired entry point during descent. Stress keeping head up sufficient length of time during flight to develop and maintain correct angle of entry. Practice standing front dive from end of board.

Many authoritative books have been written about competitive diving. Students or diving instructors who desire more information on this subject should consult their local libraries or book stores, or competent diving coaches.

CHAPTER 12

SWIMMING AND WATER SAFETY COURSES

This chapter contains the objectives, the skills and knowledge contents, and the tests for the five American Red Cross swimming and water safety courses.

Information about evaluating skills and the use of the *Worksheet for Swimming Courses* (Form 5723) is contained in Chapters 5 and 14. Additional information about evaluating students' performances of skills and combined tests is contained in each of the following course outlines.

Developing correct attitudes and behaviors about safe practices around the water are just as important as teaching skills to students. Instructors must allow time throughout a course to present and to discuss information about how accidents happen and how they can be prevented.

The results of swimming courses are reported to the appropriate Red Cross chapter on the *Course Record for Swimming and Water Safety* (Form 5722), which is available at all Red Cross chapters.

BEGINNER COURSE

Introduction

Teaching nonswimmers to swim is one of the most difficult of all teaching tasks and yet is one of the most enjoyable. To take a group of students at any age level, to introduce them to the water, and then to lead them through successive steps in the mastery of the simple skills involved in getting afloat — observing the joy and exultation that comes with being wholly water-borne and making a little progress — is a most satisfying experience. All of the elements of good teaching — enthusiasm, patience, persuasiveness, encouragement, and teaching skill — must be brought into play. The students' fears and inhibitions must be overcome and the joy and the happiness of achievement substituted for them. Younger students are encouraged to vie with one another as a means of overcoming fear and putting forth extra effort. With children, and frequently with adults, learning how to swim may be played at as an interesting game.

General Information

Course Objective

The objective of the Beginner course is to equip individuals with basic water safety skills and knowledge in order to make them *reasonably safe* while in, on, or about the water.

Course Characteristics

Individuals completing this course must be made aware of the fact that the Beginner course is a basic one. Every effort should be made to encourage them to continue their water safety training by enrolling in the Advanced Beginner course.

Course Eligibility

There are no swimming skill or age requirements for entrance into the course.

Length of Course

The course has no maximum length. A minimum of ten periods of from 30 to 45 minutes in length is recommended.

Safety of Students

Before the students enter the water for the first time, explain the limits of the area within which they will be swimming. Explain the safety rules to be enforced, such as no pushing, running, shoving, or ducking of others, and the reasons for the rules. Before pairing off students, explain the buddy system. Emphasize that this system makes it possible for students to help each other to learn, in addition to providing added safety. During instruction, a lifeguard should be situated in a lookout position to provide extra protection for the students.

Beginner Course Outline

Descriptions of the following skills and the methods to use in teaching them are contained in Chapter 7, *Teaching The Beginner Swimmer*. The order in which they are taught can vary. Instructors may elect to teach all skills in the prone position first, or they may teach them as listed. The manner in which they are taught and learned will also vary according to the teaching approach used.

I. **Physical and Mental Adjustment to the Water**

  A. **Objectives**

    1. To assist individuals in overcoming their fear of the water.

    2. To assist individuals in adjusting their breathing to added pressure.

    3. To give individuals the fundamentals of breath holding beneath the surface, using the mouth for breathing, and opening the eyes beneath the surface.

  B. **Skills to be taught**

    1. Entering the water. Wading and submerging.

2. Underwater breath holding, exhaling, seeing, and hearing. Students must hold their breath, face fully submerged, for at least 10 seconds.
3. Rhythmic breathing. The students, holding onto the side of the pool and kicking, must alternately inhale through the mouth above the surface and exhale through the mouth and the nose with the face submerged at least 10 times.

(NOTE. Use appropriate games and stunts for the above skills.)

II. **Buoyancy and Body Position**
   A. **Objectives**
      1. To give individuals additional practice in breath control and rhythmic breathing.
      2. To give individuals experience in adjusting to the buoyant effect of the water.
      3. To assist individuals in relaxing while in a floating position on the front and in a gliding position on the back.
   B. **Skills to be taught**
      1. Prone float and recovery to a standing position.
      2. Prone glide.
      3. Back glide and recovery to a standing position.
      4. Survival float (see Chapter 10, *Analyzing And Teaching Other Aquatics Skills*). To turn around in the water, have the students use a series of pressing movements to one side with one arm until the desired amount of turn is accomplished. The sweeping movements of the arms are done with the students in the resting position.

III. **Propulsion and Coordinated Stroking**
   A. **Objectives**
      1. To enable individuals to propel themselves in both prone and supine positions.
      2. To assist learners to combine arm and leg movements.
      3. To give learners experience in coordinating breathing with arm and leg movements.
   B. **Skills to be taught**
      1. Prone glide with flutter kick.
      2. Back glide with flutter kick.
     *3. Beginner stroke — arm stroke and breathing.
     *4. Crawl stroke — arm stroke and breathing.
     *5. Beginner stroke — 15 yards. (Must periodically breathe while swimming.)
      6. Combined stroke on the back — 15 yards.
     *7. Crawl stroke — 15 yards. (Must periodically breathe while swimming.)

Some students will be able to perform some form of the crawl stroke prior to enrollment in the Beginner course. It may not be necessary for most of these students to learn the beginner stroke. If some of them do not progress satisfactorily in improving the crawl stroke, they will benefit by learning the beginner stroke well, and then progressing to the crawl stroke.

---

*See Chapter 14, *Evaluating Swimming Strokes*.

IV. **Entries** (See Chapter 11, *Analyzing and Teaching Entries Into the Water*)
   A. **Objective**
      1. To teach the students to enter the water safely and efficiently from the edge of a low deck or a low dock (maximum of 2 feet above the surface of the water).
   B. **Skills to be taught**
      1. Leveling off from a vertical position and swimming.
      2. Jumping into shallow water, pushing off into a prone position, and swimming.
      3. Jumping into deep water, leveling off, and swimming in a prone position.
      4. Jumping into deep water, leveling off into a prone position, turning over, and swimming the combined stroke on the back.
   NOTES.
   • Students **do not** jump from a height of more than 2 feet above the surface.
   • Except for medical reasons, students cannot hold the nose or wear a nose clip for the final examinations.
   • During the final examinations, the students must jump into deep water with the body vertical and straight and with the arms along the sides of the body or extended overhead.

V. **Personal Safety Skills and Basic Rescue Techniques**
   A. **Objectives**
      1. To give individuals the opportunity to learn personal safety skills.
      2. To give individuals the opportunity to learn basic rescue techniques.
   B. **Skills to be taught**
      1. Changing direction.
      2. Turning over — front-to-back and back-to-front.
      3. Release of cramp. Practice from a survival float position in neck-deep water and progress to deep-water practice. (See *Lifesaving: Rescue and Water Safety* textbook, Stock No. 321103.)
      4. Assisting a nonswimmer to his or her feet. Practice with a buddy is started from first session of course.
      5. Reaching and extension rescues. (See Chapter 3, *Lifesaving: Rescue and Water Safety* textbook.) With a buddy in waist-to-shoulder-depth water, rescuer (lying on deck) practices extending arm to buddy. Rescuer, also in shallow water, practices arm and leg extensions. Repeat above in deep-water situations with "victim" who is "safe" in deep water. Progress to extension rescues using pole, towel, or shirt. CAUTION. Younger, smaller rescuers should remain on deck of pool or dock when attempting to rescue a larger person. These rescuers must be firmly braced to avoid being pulled into water.

6. Use of Personal Flotation Device (PFD). (See Chapters 2 and 8, *Lifesaving: Rescue and Water Safety* textbook.) Discuss purposes of PFDs. On land, demonstrate putting on a U.S. Coast Guard approved, wearable device properly. Also demonstrate and discuss use of approved throwable devices. In water, demonstrate staying afloat with the face out of water while in prone, vertical, and supine positions, using a wearable device and a seat cushion or ring buoy.

NOTE. Personal safety skills should be integrated throughout the Beginner course at the discretion of the instructor.)

VI. Artificial Respiration and Safety Information

A. Objectives

1. To give students basic information on resuscitation and the importance of maintaining an open airway.
2. To develop safer behavioral actions of students by discussing causes and prevention of aquatic accidents.

B. Skills and information to be taught

1. An explanation and demonstration of mouth-to-mouth resuscitation (See *Lifesaving: Rescue and Water Safety* textbook.) Instructor demonstrates, followed by students (paired off) practicing correct positioning of their buddy's head and sealing of nose.
2. Safety information. Two or three minutes of each class period should be devoted to a discussion of causes and prevention of aquatic accidents. To make the discussion more meaningful, instructors or students can bring to class articles about aquatic accidents from newspapers or magazines. Using phrases such as "The Red Cross suggests that...," or "According to the Red Cross...," will help to instill in the students the idea that the Red Cross is vitally interested and involved in providing safety education as well as in providing courses that teach people to swim or to swim better.

Combined Skills

Students who take the two combined skills examinations listed below should have demonstrated good competency in deep water prior to the examinations. For reasons of safety, the instructor examines only **one student** at a time. Except for open-water situations (lakes, rivers, etc.), the instructor (and the aide) remains out of the water but constantly ready to provide necessary assis-

tance to the student being tested. Whenever possible, the students perform the following combined skills at least 10 feet from any form of safety. Satisfactorily completing them under these testing conditions provides ample evidence that the student is confident and reasonably safe in deep water.

To satisfactorily pass the combined skills examinations, the student must not touch the bottom or the sides of the pool or the dock, or any other form of safety.

In residential pools of less than 20 yards in length, the student will have to swim about 10 yards, change direction, then swim back to the starting point.

The student must not jump into the water from an elevation of **more than 2 feet above the surface of the water.**

Combined Skills No. 1
The student jumps into deep water, levels off, and swims 20 yards using either the beginner stroke, the crawl stroke, or the combined stroke on the back.

Combined Skills No. 2
The student jumps into deep water, does the survival float for 1 minute, levels off on the front or back, and swims 10 yards to safety.

Adjusted Skills For Beginner Course Taught In Pools With No Deep-Water Area

The purpose of this training in shallow pools is to enable students to complete most of the skills in the Beginner course and to become eligible to receive the Red Cross Beginner certificate in instructional programs where deep-water facilities are unavailable or it is not practical or advisable to use them. The skills that cannot be taught or are not taught are — jumping into deep water, leveling off, and the survival float.

Use of the *Beginner Swimming* Certificate (Cert. 1386)
Chapters issuing *Beginner Swimming* certificates to individuals who have completed the course in a shallow pool using the adjusted skills should stamp or print in ink on the reverse side of the certificate the following notation: *Shallow Pool Program.*

Adjusted Skills and Combined Skills
1. Substitute the jellyfish float for the survival float. As best as possible, the students practice breathing using arm movements for the survival stroke. Very buoyant students should assume a tucked body position, nearly vertical, in order to lift the face from the water to breathe.
2. From a vertical tuck or jellyfish float position, the student levels off and swims 20 yards.
3. From a vertical tuck or jellyfish float position, the student levels off, swims one or two strokes in the prone position, turns over, and swims 15 to 20 yards on the back.

ADVANCED BEGINNER COURSE

Introduction

Since students in the Advanced Beginner course already possess a variety of safety skills and are capable of swimming on both the front and the back, no precise arrangement of course material into lesson contents can be given. Instructors have great flexibility as to sequence and from the following course skills and information should make up their lesson plans in a session-to-session progressive arrangement.

An understanding of Chapter 6, *Physical Laws Applied to Body Movements in the Water,* can be especially helpful to the instructor, since the Advanced Beginner course introduces many skills based upon the principles covered in that chapter.

General Information

Course Objectives

- To increase the aquatics abilities of the individuals by adding to the skills learned in the Beginner course.
- To afford the individuals an opportunity to experience continued success in a reasonable period of time and thus motivate them to continue their water safety training.
- To prepare the students for additional water safety training by introducing them to a series of skills designed to improve their stamina and basic coordination.

Course Characteristics

This course should increase the endurance of the individuals, improve their ability to care for themselves while in the water, and introduce them to additional coordinated movements in a logical and meaningful manner.

Successful completion of this course should equip and motivate the individuals to continue their water safety training by enrolling in the Intermediate course.

Course Eligibility

To be eligible to enroll in the Advanced Beginner course, the individuals must have successfully completed or be able to perform the skills in the Beginner course. To admit students to this course if they cannot successfully perform the skills in the Beginner course is unfair to them, other members of the class, and the instructor teaching the course.

Length of Course

There is no minimum or maximum length.

Advanced Beginner Course Outline

I. **Breath Control** (See Chapter 7, *Teaching the Beginner Swimmer.*)
   A. **Objectives**
      1. To give students additional practice in breath control.
      2. To increase students' ability to resist fatigue.
   B. **Skills to be taught**
      1. Bobbing in deep water
         a. Practicing bobbing in neck-deep water prior to progressing to deep water.
         b. Initial practice in deep water may be started while holding lightly onto side of pool. Definite rhythm should be established with inhalation as mouth clears surface and exhalation as head goes below surface.
      2. Rhythmic breathing to side (rotary breathing).

II. **Survival Float**
   A. **Objective**
      1. Students must perform this skill comfortably in deep water for 2 minutes.

III. **Coordinated Stroking**
   A. **Crawl stroke** (See Chapter 14, *Evaluating Swimming Strokes.*)
      The objective is to enable students to learn or to improve their crawl stroke coordination so that this stroke can be performed effectively for longer distances.
   B. **Elementary backstroke** (See Chapter 14, *Evaluating Swimming Strokes.*)
      The objectives are —
      - To teach students an effective stroke on the back.
      - To introduce students to a stroke requiring a certain degree of coordination.
      - To introduce students to the inverted breaststroke kick with emphasis on the correct pattern of movement.
   C. **Survival stroke** (See Chapter 10, *Analyzing and Teaching Other Aquatics Skills.*)
      The objective is to have students learn a method of moving through water with a minimum expenditure of energy.

IV. **Treading Water and Changing Positions** (See Chapter 10, *Analyzing and Teaching Other Aquatics Skills.*)
   A. **Objective**
      To give the student additional personal safety skills. Treading water is a skill that enables the advanced beginner to keep the face above the surface of the water with the body in a nearly vertical position. The ability to tread water and to go into either a prone or a supine position from the vertical position is an important survival safety skill.
   B. **Skills to be taught**
      1. Treading water—Advanced Beginner level.
         a. Arm action practiced while standing in neck-deep water.
         b. Kick can be a slower and wider crawl (flutter) kick, or breaststroke kick for elementary backstroke can be used.
         c. Students must be able to tread water using arms and legs for 30 to 45 seconds.
         d. Flotation support can be helpful in learning process.
      2. Changing positions
         a. From vertical position to back position. Extend legs forward, lay head back until ears

are in water. Gentle winging or sculling movements can maintain back-glide position.
   b. From back-glide position to vertical position to prone position. Go to vertical position using a method similar to recovering to standing position from back glide, then tread water for a few seconds. Lean forward, extend legs to rear, place face in water, and float in prone position with arms extended forward of head.
   c. Reversal of above procedures. Students should reverse above procedures so that they can comfortably change positions from prone position to vertical position to back position and vice versa. They should make sure that in all positions arms remain below surface. Instructor should stress that head initiates and leads change of body position.
  3. Individual skills performance (changing positions and treading water). Students change from prone position to vertical position and tread water for 30 seconds, then go into supine position. From supine position, students go into vertical position, and in this position tread water for 30 seconds and then return to prone position.

V. **Diving and Underwater Swimming**
  A. **Objectives**
     1. To teach students a head-first entry into water.
     2. To teach students to swim while submerged.
  B. **Diving** (See Chapter 11, *Analyzing and Teaching Entries Into the Water,* "Beginner's dive progressions.") Students dive from edge of pool or dock into deep water for final check off. Height of the takeoff point must be no higher than 2 feet above surface. Dive must be performed in reasonably good form. Falling into water or doing a "belly flop" are not acceptable dives.
  C. **Underwater swimming** (See Chapter 10, *Analyzing and Teaching Other Aquatics Skills.*) Students use flutter (crawl) kick or kick used in survival stroke and arm movements of either beginner stroke or survival stroke. Students learn to swim three or four body lengths underwater. CAUTION. Do not allow students to hyperventilate before swimming underwater.

VI. **Use of Personal Flotation Device (PFD)**
  A. **Objective**
     To give students some experience in using a wearable device to remain afloat.
  B. **Skills to be taught and some teaching hints**
     1. Swimming and floating while wearing PFD
        a. In chest-deep water, practice putting PFD on properly.
        b. Practice staying afloat with face out of water while in prone, vertical, and supine positions.
        c. Practice swimming with PFD. Instructor should stress keeping arms underwater at all times.

  2. Jumping in water while wearing PFD
     a. Prior to jumping in water, students should adjust PFD for a snug fit.
     b. Make initial jumps from a **slight** elevation.
     c. Cross arms in front of PFD, with hands grasping top edges of device to hold it in place on impact with water.
  3. Practice use of seat cushion to support body correctly in water. NOTE. U.S. Coast Guard approved PFDs should be used.

VII. **Artificial Respiration, Basic Rescue Skills, Personal Safety Skills, and Safety Information**
  A. **Objectives**
     1. To give students basic information on resuscitation and to show importance of maintaining an open airway.
     2. To give students additional practice in making simple reaching and extension assists.
     3. To give students additional information concerning causes and prevention of accidents.
  B. **Skills to be taught**
     1. Mouth-to-mouth (mouth-to-nose) artificial respiration
        a. Discuss and demonstrate above techniques.
        b. Have students demonstrate proper head position for keeping an open airway.
        c. Do not demonstrate actual mouth-to-mouth contact or have students practice actual contact.
        d. Have students practice on training manikins, if available.
     2. Reaching and extension rescues. Review and practice rescue skills taught in Beginner course.
     3. Personal safety skills. Review discussion and students' practice of release of cramps in feet and legs. (See Beginner course outline.)
     4. Safety information. Continue discussions from Beginner course on causes and prevention of accidents that can occur in, on, or around water.

Combined Skills
  A. Student dives into deep water, surfaces, and swims crawl stroke for 20 to 25 yards (20 to 25 meters).
  B. Student jumps into deep water, surfaces, and swims elementary backstroke for 20 to 25 yards (20 to 25 meters).
  C. Student dives into deep water, swims at least three but no more than four body lengths underwater, surfaces, and performs survival stroke for 2 minutes in deep water.
     NOTE.
     • All diving and jumping entries are made from pool or dock edge, and from a height of no more than 2 feet above water's surface.
     • See Chapter 14, *Evaluating Swimming Strokes,* to evaluate crawl stroke and elementary backstroke.

INTERMEDIATE COURSE

Introduction

At the intermediate level, instructors will present and teach a wide variety of skills. They must constantly bear in mind that progress in perfecting the skills will be uneven. A high degree of success will only result from well-organized practice sessions and individual correction of errors by the instructors. In order to give the students the opportunity for continued practice of parts of strokes and whole stroking movements, swimboards, flotation supports, and supports attached to the body can be very helpful and desirable.

Even though this course is separated into various segments, there is no precise arrangement of course material into lesson contents. It will be necessary for instructors to set up lesson content on a session-to-session basis, depending upon the students' progress, the facility, the equipment, and the length of each session.

General Information

Course Objective

The objective of the course is to provide the students with the opportunity to learn the elements of good swimming.

Course Characteristics

Students in the course usually experience great unevenness in learning. Some students will make excellent progress in some skills, while other skills may be learned more slowly. Fortunately, the skills are so varied that eventually the majority of the students will reach the end of the course with about the same degree of proficiency. They may, however, vary greatly in freedom of movements, grace, endurance, and speed.

Course Eligibility

To be eligible to enroll in the Intermediate course, the individual must have successfully completed, or must be able to perform, the skills listed in the Advanced Beginner course.

Length of Course

There is no minimum or maximum length.

Intermediate Course Outline

I. **Coordinated Stroking** (See Chapter 8, *Analyzing and Teaching Basic Swimming Strokes.*)

A. **Objectives**
1. To teach students coordination of the side-stroke.
2. To teach students arm and leg movements for the breaststroke, and to provide practice for coordinating the breaststroke. Mastering coordination of this stroke is not expected of students in the Intermediate course.
3. To provide students the opportunity to improve the crawl stroke and elementary backstroke.

II. **Survival Float and Survival Stroke**
Students will improve performance of these skills, which were learned in the Beginner and Advanced Beginner courses. Students will perform the survival float for 3 minutes and the survival stroke for 3 minutes.

III. **Back Float** (See Chapter 10, *Analyzing and Teaching Other Aquatics Skills,* and Chapter 6, *Physical Laws Applied to Body Movements in the Water.*)

A. **Objective**
To teach students to float on the back for 1 minute, either motionless or with minimum sculling movements of hands.

IV. **Sculling on the Back** (See Chapter 10, *Analyzing and Teaching Other Aquatics Skills.*)

A. **Objective**
To teach students a basic style of arm and hand movements on the back that will provide minimum propulsion, add to personal safety skills, and lead to more sophisticated sculling patterns that can be used in some swimming strokes, and that are used in synchronized swimming.

Students must be able to move a minimum of 10 yards in a direction forward (behind) of the head, using only sculling movements of hands.

V. **Turns** (See Chapter 10, *Analyzing and Teaching Other Aquatics Skills.*)

A. **Objective**
To teach students to perform effective turns on front, side, and back that will broaden their overall aquatic abilities.
(NOTE. Turn on side is performed same as turn on front. During glide, swimmer merely rolls onto side upon which sidestroke is to be performed.)

VI. **Treading Water** (See Chapter 10, *Analyzing and Teaching Other Aquatics Skills.*)

A. **Objective**
To improve students' abilities to keep their faces out of water with their bodies in a vertical position.

Students must tread water continuously for 1 minute, using sculling movements of hands, and using either modified scissors kick or breaststroke kick.

VII. **Underwater Swimming**

A. **Objective**
To improve students' abilities to swim underwater. Students must be able to jump into deep water, change body positions, and swim from 15 to 20 feet underwater using modifications of the breaststroke or the sidestroke. Students **must not** be allowed to hyperventilate before entering water. Swimmer must have eyes open and travel in a line of movement that will avoid collision with side of pool or other person(s) in water.

VIII. **Diving From Edge of Pool or Dock** (maximum height of 2 feet above surface of the water). (See Chapter 11, *Analyzing and Teaching Entries Into the Water.*)

A. **Objective**

To improve students' abilities to perform a head first entry into **deep water.**

Students must perform a standing front dive into deep water, using coordinated arm swing with leg spring. Entry should be at about a 45-degree angle to water, with body nearly straight and arms and legs fully extended.

IX. **Handling Neck and Back Injuries in Water** (See *Lifesaving: Rescue and Water Safety* textbook.)

A. **Objectives**

To provide students with information about the causes and prevention of these types of injuries, and to **show** students how to handle them. (NOTE. Demonstrations of rolling victim over onto the back and placing victim on backboard are to be done in waist- to chest-deep water.)

X. **Personal Safety Skill, Basic Rescue Techniques, Artificial Respiration, and Safety Information**

A. **Objective**

To give students additional skills and knowledge related to these subjects.

1. Donning personal flotation devices (PFDs) while in deep water (See Chapter 3, *Safety in Aquatics.*)

Students learn to put on an approved, wearable PFD while treading water and to use a seat cushion to support the body with the head out of water.

a. Suggested Learning Procedures

- Students practice donning and adjusting PFDs on land, using instructions provided by manufacturer of the respective PFD. If no instructions are provided, students determine simplest method(s) by experimenting with assistance of instructor.

- Students learn to put on PFD in deep water using basic techniques learned on land and through continued experimentation.

Types I, II, and III PFDs that have arm holes can be put on quickly in deep water using the following procedures: Students place their PFD in front of them, "outside" portion of PFD flat on surface, with arm holes near students. They slip their arms through arm holes, take a breath and submerge face, reach forward with arms under jacket, and then flip jacket over the head onto the back. While continuing to hold their breath, they reach back with arms, grasp lower front corners of PFD, and pull

jacket around body. Maintaining hold on jacket, they turn their heads to one side and roll over on their backs. In some cases it may be necessary to kick with legs to execute roll over. Once on their backs, they tie straps starting at lower portion of PFD and progressing toward neck. If jacket has a belt, it is then secured in place and adjusted for tightness.

2. Basic Rescue Techniques
   a. Wading rescues using extensions.
   b. Extensions using ring buoy or heaving line.
   c. Rescuer using floating objects, such as swimboard, ring buoy, or inner tube. (NOTE. Above skills should be integrated throughout course at discretion of instructor.)

3. Artificial Respiration

Students should be taught steps for giving mouth-to-mouth resuscitation, but no actual personal contact should be practiced.

4. Safety Information (See **Safety Information,** Beginner and Advanced Beginner course outlines.)

Combined Skills

(See Chapter 14, *Evaluating Swimming Strokes.*)

1. Student swims 50 yards (meters) using elementary backstroke.
2. Student dives into deep water and swims 50 yards (meters) using crawl stroke.
3. Student swims 50 yards (meters) using sidestroke.
4. Student jumps into deep water, rotates body to prone position, swims minimum of three but no more than four body lengths while underwater, surfaces, treads water for 1 minute using arms and legs, then swims survival stroke for 15 yards (meters).
5. Student swims nonstop for 5 minutes using any or all of the swimming strokes in this course (survival stroke excepted). Student cannot touch bottom or hold onto side of pool and rest while making a turn.

SWIMMER COURSE

Introduction

At the swimmer level, the students continue to master the parts of strokes that were learned in previous courses. The emphasis in the Swimmer course is placed on the coordination of whole strokes in order for students to swim them more effectively, and with more ease, relaxation, and smoothness, and for greater distances.

General Information

Lesson Content

For Swimmer courses, the organization and handling of practice sessions definitely change. Mass drill is still given in practicing stroke movements, turns, diving from the deck, and other skills, but a major part of each session is divided between individual instruction and correction and individual lane practice. A typical class session for a Swimmer course could be planned as follows:

- Warm-up drill.
- Mass cross-pool or length-of-pool drills on arm and leg strokes and rhythmic breathing.
- Demonstration and analysis of coordination of specific strokes by the instructor.
- Individual practice of various strokes in lanes, interspersed with instruction to students as needed.

The distances the students swim, using coordinated strokes or practicing arm and leg movements as needed, should be increased gradually each lesson so that the students can easily swim a quarter of a mile continuously at the end of the course.

Course Objectives

- To increase the students' endurance through a considerable amount of swimming.
- To improve the students' abilities to perform coordinated strokes, and the parts of the strokes, which have been learned previously.
- To teach students new skills to increase their overall aquatic abilities.

Course Characteristics

Since stroking movements have not been perfected by Intermediate swimmers, practice on improving the actions of the arms and legs, as well as the coordination of a stroke, should be a part of the regular training in the Swimmer course.

Because of the importance of breath control in coordinated strokes, practice in rhythmic breathing should be given as a part of every lesson.

Course Eligibility

To be eligible, a person must have successfully completed, or must be able to perform, the skills for the Intermediate course.

Length of Course

There is no minimum or maximum length.

Swimmer Course Outline

I. **Coordinated Stroking** (See Chapter 8, *Analyzing and Teaching Basic Swimming Strokes.*)
   A. **Objective**
      1. For the students to learn to effectively perform the parts of, and coordination of, the sidestroke, back crawl, breaststroke, and crawl stroke.

II. **Surface Dives** (See Chapter 10, *Analyzing and Teaching Other Aquatics Skills.*)
   A. **Objective**
      1. To teach students effective methods of going below the surface.
   B. **Skills to be taught**
      1. Pike and tuck surface dives.
         a. Students must learn to perform one of these dives effectively, in good form, and to dive to a depth of at least 8 feet but not more than 10 feet.
         b. Good form is as follows:
            (1) Hips must remain near surface during lift of legs.
            (2) Legs should be raised to about mid-thigh above surface.
            (3) Legs must be extended, together, with toes pointed at start of and during descent.
            (4) Legs must be nearly vertical with no sway to side during descent.
      2. Feet-first surface dive.
         a. Body must be raised about waist high out of water.
         b. During descent, body must be vertical, stretched, and streamlined, with arms along sides of body.

III. **Entries** (See Chapter 11, *Analyzing and Teaching Entries Into the Water.*)
   A. **Objectives**
      1. To improve students' ability to perform a standing dive from edge of pool or dock.
      2. To teach students ways of entering water safely and effectively.
   B. **Skills to be taught**
      1. Long, shallow dive from edge of pool or dock into deep water.
         a. Body can be straight or slightly piked, with arms and legs fully extended and together during entry.
         b. A "belly flop" is not acceptable.
         c. Take-off point must be **no higher** than 2 feet above surface of water.
      2. Jumping entry from standing position at end of diving board.
         a. Entry is made with body in vertical position, legs extended and together, with arms alongside body.
      3. Standing dive from end of board.
         a. Take-off must have good coordination of arm swing and leg spring.
         b. Body can be piked during most of flight through air.
         c. Entry must be made with body straight and streamlined, and at about a 45-degree angle to water.

(NOTE. Entries from the 1-meter board are not required if there is no board available, or if unsafe diving conditions exist.)

    4. Stride jump into deep water from edge of pool or dock (See *Lifesaving: Rescue and Water Safety* textbook and related instructor's manual.)

        a. Face must remain above surface when performing this skill.

        b. Take-off point must be **no higher** than 2 feet above water's surface.

IV. Inverted scissors kick

A. **Objective**

    1. To teach students an adaptation of the scissors kick for use in lifesaving training.

B. **Teaching suggestions**

    1. Use of flotation aids or swimboards can be helpful for students who may be having difficulty during initial learning process.

    2. Emphasize:

        a. Keeping heels in line with spine during recovery of legs.

        b. Plantar-flexing lower ankle before extending lower leg forward of body.

        c. Dorsi-flexing top ankle before extending top leg to rear of body.

        d. Extending and pulling legs together in paired movements.

        e. Keeping legs parallel to surface during all movements.

        f. Not letting legs pass each other at end of kick.

V. Sculling (See Chapter 10, *Analyzing and Teaching Other Aquatics Skills.*)

A. **Objective**

    1. To teach students other ways of moving through water using sculling movements of hands.

B. **Skills to be taught**

    1. Snail scull.

        a. Students in supine position.

        b. Arms extended along sides of body.

        c. Hands angled downward.

    2. Canoe scull.

        a. Students in prone position.

        b. Arms extended along sides of body.

        c. Hands angled downward.

(NOTE. Students must scull 5 yards (meters) using each of above methods, with no use of legs, and with body kept nearly horizontal to surface.)

VI. Skills to review and improve

A. **Turns**

    1. Front.

    2. Back.

    3. Side.

B. **Survival float and survival stroke**

    1. Students must be able to do **survival stroke** for 5 minutes during final tests.

C. **Underwater swimming**

    1. Students must be able to swim underwater for a distance of 20 to 25 feet (7 to 8 meters).

    2. **No hyperventilation** is allowed.

VII. Basic rescue techniques, artificial respiration, and safety information

A. **Objective**

    1. To give students additional knowledge and practice in learning safe rescue techniques.

B. **Skills to be taught or reviewed**

    1. Wading rescues using extensions.

    2. Extensions using ring buoy or heaving line.

    3. Rescues using floating objects, such as swimboard, ring buoy, or inner tube.

    4. Mouth-to-mouth resuscitation.

    5. Causes and prevention of accidents in, on, or around the water.

(NOTE. Above skills and safety information should be integrated throughout course at discretion of instructor. Students should be taught steps for giving mouth-to-mouth resuscitation, but no actual mouth contact should be practiced.)

Combined Skills

(See Chapter 14, *Evaluating Swimming Strokes.*)

1. Student swims breaststroke for 50 yards (meters).
2. Student swims back crawl for 50 yards (meters).
3. Student swims crawl stroke for 100 yards (meters).
4. Student swims sidestroke for 100 yards (meters).
   - Must use standard scissors kick, then the inverted scissors kick, on alternate lengths.
5. Student surface dives, pike or tuck, using good form, to depth of at least 8 feet but no more than 10 feet, swims 20 to 22 feet (7 to 8 meters) underwater, surfaces, and performs survival stroke for 5 minutes in deep water.
6. Student swims 10 minutes nonstop using any or all of basic swimming strokes used above. Student cannot touch bottom of pool or rest while turning.

ADVANCED SWIMMER COURSE

Introduction

The organization and handling of the class instruction and the practice sessions for the Advanced Swimmer course will be similar to those for the Swimmer course. Some mass drills will be helpful, but a great deal of time in each session will be alloted to individual practice and instruction as needed.

General Information

Course Objective

The objective of this course is to provide individuals with the opportunity to learn and perfect new swimming strokes and other skills so that they will become very versatile and skilled performers in the water.

Course Characteristics

The new strokes introduced in this course are variations of three basic swimming strokes previously taught. Skilled swimmers are provided new challenges to learn these stroke variations.

Since this course demands that individuals perform all skills very proficiently, the persons who successfully complete the course will be highly competent performers in the water.

Course Eligibility

To be eligible to enroll in this course, individuals must have successfully completed the Swimmer course or must be able to satisfactorily perform the requirements for this course. They must also show evidence of having completed the Basic Rescue course or the Advanced Lifesaving course, or be a currently authorized water safety or basic swimming instructor.

Length of Course

There is no minimum or maximum length.

Advanced Swimmer Course Outline

I. **Basic Strokes and Variations** (See Chapter 14, *Evaluating Swimming Strokes,* and Chapter 9, *Analyzing and Teaching Other Styles of Swimming.*)

  A. **Objective**

    1. To provide student with ability to perform a wide variety of strokes effectively and with good coordination.

  B. **Skills to be taught and some teaching hints**

    1. Elementary backstroke (review).

    2. Back crawl (review).

      a. Students must learn and use bent-arm pull.

    3. Breaststroke (review).

    4. Sidestroke (review).

      a. Students must learn to coordinate this stroke while swimming on both sides using standard scissors kick and inverted scissors kick.

    5. Crawl stroke (review).

      a. Students must learn to breathe on their "unnatural" side as well as to improve breathing on their "natural" side.

    6. Overarm sidestroke (new).

      a. Students must learn to coordinate this stroke, in good form, while swimming on both sides, using only standard scissors kick.

    7. Inverted breaststroke (new).

    8. Trudgen (new).

      a. Students learn to perform this stroke while breathing to one side only. (Usually to the same side in which a breath is taken during the crawl stroke.)

II. **Other Aquatics Skills (Review)**

  A. **Objective**

    1. To provide students opportunity to improve performance of skills learned in previous Red Cross courses.

  B. **Skills to improve**

    1. Turns.

      a. Front.

      b. Side.

      c. Back.

    2. Surface dives.

      a. Pike.

      b. Tuck.

      c. Feet first.

    3. Survival float and survival stroke while fully clothed (clean clothes, shoes not required).

      a. Students can perform both skills using variations that meet objectives of these skills.

    4. Diving from edge of pool or low dock.

      a. Body must be streamlined, nearly straight, and almost vertical during entry.

      b. Standing dive from 1-meter board into deep water.

      c. Long, shallow dive from edge of pool or low dock.

      (NOTE. Dives from edge of pool or dock must be made into **deep water,** and from a height of no more than 2 feet above surface of water.)

    5. Jumping from 1-meter board.

III. **Entry (New)**

  A. **Objective**

    1. To teach students a "running" dive from a 1-meter springboard, consisting of a minimum three-step approach and hurdle to end of board, followed by take-off and entry into water.

  B. **Skill to be taught**

    1. "Running" front dive. (See Chapter 11, *Analyzing and Teaching Entries Into the Water.*)

    (NOTE. This skill can be waived if no board is available, or if unsafe diving conditions exist.)

Combined Skills

(See Chapter 14, *Evaluating Swimming Strokes.*)

1. Student swims continuously using sidestroke for 50 yards (meters), followed by overarm sidestroke for 50

yards (meters). Each stroke must be performed on each side, using standard scissors kick only, for 25 yards (meters).

(NOTE. With exception of recovery of top arm, overarm sidestroke is evaluated same as sidestroke at Advanced Swimmer level. Recovery of top arm in overarm sidestroke must be made with a high elbow, relaxed lower arm and hand, and with hand entering water about in line with top of head.)

2. Student swims crawl stroke continuously for 100 yards (meters).

3. Student swims back crawl continuously for 100 yards (meters).

4. Student swims breaststroke continuously for 100 yards (meters).

5. Student swims continuously using inverted breaststroke for 50 yards (meters), followed by elementary backstroke for 50 yards (meters).
   NOTE. Use the following criteria to evaluate the inverted breaststroke:

   - Face must remain above water during all movements.

- Arms must pull to sides and immediately begin their recovery.
- Arms and legs must remain underwater during all movements.
- Kick must be technically accurate and effective.
- A glide must be taken with arms extended behind head and with body stretched and streamlined.
- Body must remain flat and nearly horizontal to surface of water.

6. Student swims trudgen stroke continuously for 50 yards (meters).

7. Student performs survival stroke, fully clothed, for 10 minutes.

8. Student swims continuously for 30 minutes using any or all of above strokes. Hanging onto sides (resting) during turns or touching bottom with feet **are not acceptable.**

LEADERSHIP COURSES

CHAPTER 13

WATER SAFETY AIDE COURSE INSTRUCTOR'S OUTLINE

The Water Safety Aide training program is designed to provide training for individuals who wish to assist water safety and basic swimming instructors in conducting American Red Cross swimming and water safety courses. A properly conducted Water Safety Aide training program will accomplish the following:

- Expanding the capabilities of instructors by providing them with qualified, knowledgeable assistants.

- Providing opportunities to individuals for leadership development.

- Providing qualified individuals with opportunities to participate in community service in a leadership role.

Duties of Water Safety Aides

Water safety aides can function in at least four different ways as assistants to instructors:

- **Clerical** Aides often prepare class rolls, call roll at class time, check swimmers in and out of the water or pool area, and prepare course records for instructors.
- **Supervisory** Some of the supervisory duties of aides include helping to maintain order in dressing rooms, in shower rooms, and while waiting for the class to start; supervising check rooms; pairing buddies for class work; assisting with general class control; and acting as safety spotters.
- **Instructional** Because of their swimming ability and water safety training, water safety aides are especially helpful in assisting instructors with the instructional process, demonstrating skills, assisting class members who need individualized instruction on specific skills, and conducting many aspects of class work under the supervision of instructors.
- **Maintenance** The distributing, collecting, and storing of equipment is an especially helpful function of aides. In addition, the aides can assist in removing or minimizing hazards in and around the swimming areas.

Eligibility

Individuals who are 11 years of age or older, who evidence a sincere desire to give volunteer service, and who exhibit a sense of responsibility are eligible to be trained as water safety aides. Prospective aides must also show evidence of completing the Basic Rescue course or must hold current certification in Advanced Lifesaving, and hold a Red Cross Swimmer certificate or be able to perform the skills in this course satisfactorily.

Training

Instructors can train aides in a variety of ways. The group instruction method and the apprenticeship method are most often used.

The group method is used primarily for pretraining a number of aides for an upcoming season or for the initial thrust of a newly inaugurated program. The formal Water Safety Aide training course (group method) is comprised of six units of approximately 3 hours per unit with an additional unit of approximately 1 hour. The course is taught by a currently authorized water safety instructor using the following prescribed course outline. Basic swimming instructors can assist in training the aides to teach the skills in the Beginner, Advanced Beginner, Basic Water Safety, and Basic Rescue courses. Properly trained water safety aides can be of great assistance to instructors in conducting swimming and water safety courses.

The apprenticeship method is used mostly for developing one or two aides at a time, as necessary, by a single instructor.

Water safety aides who have not been trained in Advanced Lifesaving may be used as aides in this course, but they should be used to assist only in teaching lifesaving skills that are in the Basic Water Safety and Basic Rescue courses.

Certification

Students who successfully complete the course will receive a Water Safety Aide certificate and will be eligible to assist water safety instructors and basic swimming instructors in conducting all courses.

Reporting

The instructor responsible for the course will report results, on the *Instructor Aide Examination Record* (Form 5650), to his or her chapter of authorization.

Course Materials

Students in Water Safety Aide courses must possess the American Red Cross publication *Swimming and Aquatics Safety* (Stock No. 321133). Instructors teaching the Water Safety Aide course should utilize the following outline.

Course Outline

Equipment for the first five units includes pencils, whistles, clipboards, sample examination records for each student, the textbooks *Lifesaving: Rescue and Water Safety* (Stock No. 321103) and *Basic Rescue and Water Safety* (Stock No. 321215) for reference, and the text *Swimming and Aquatics Safety* (Stock No. 321133) for each aide. The unit outlines follow.

Unit 1

Objectives To provide a general introduction to the course, to assess the students' skills, and to provide an initial experience of teaching through "buddy coaching."

ACTIVITY	STUDENTS	INSTRUCTOR	INFORMATION FOR INSTRUCTOR

Introduction	Listen	Lecture	1. Stress the following course objectives:
			  a. To provide qualified assistants for water safety instructors and basic swimming instructors.
			  b. To improve personal skills of class members.
			2. Name (give no details at this time) following general duties of water safety aides:
			  a. Clerical.
			  b. Instructional.
			  c. Supervisory.
			  d. Maintenance.
			3. Stress fact that water safety aides are expected to serve in a voluntary capacity.
			                15 minutes

Screening	In water	On deck to observe skill ability of students	1. Have students perform sidestroke, crawl stroke, breast-stroke, elementary backstroke, back crawl, pike or tuck surface dive, approach to submerged victim, and wrist tow for unconscious victim. 2. Either drop students from class who are weak in above skills, or spend extra time in having them improve these skills. **30 minutes**
Demonstration by instructor or someone appointed by him or her	Listen and watch	In water	Demonstrate all skills in beginner and advanced beginner levels. Stress correct movements, done slowly. Point out common errors and methods to correct them. **40 minutes**
Practice by students	In water	On deck	Practice skills in beginner and advanced beginner levels. Stress need for slow, deliberate movements in demonstrating skills. **30 minutes**
Practice teaching by students	Half of class in water; other half on deck. Alternate positions	On deck	Have groups in water work on skills in beginner and advanced beginner levels and have students on deck observe buddies in water and make corrections when necessary. Buddies work together, independent of rest of class. Instructor assists "coaches" to recognize common errors and provides corrective techniques. **70 minutes**
Outside assignment for Unit 2	Listen	Explain assignment	Students read chapters 4, 7, and 8 in *Swimming and Aquatics Safety*. **5 to 10 minutes**

Unit 2

Objectives To increase the students' ability to demonstrate aquatics skills, to develop a positive attitude toward the responsibilities of aides, and to increase the aides' understanding of teaching progressions.

ACTIVITY	STUDENTS	INSTRUCTOR	INFORMATION FOR INSTRUCTOR
Review	On deck and in water	On deck	1. Ask questions about skills contained in Beginner course. 2. Ask various class members to demonstrate certain beginner skills in the water. Allow rest of students to decide whether skills are being done correctly and to make suggestions for improving them. <div align="center">15 minutes</div>
Questions on assignment	On deck	On deck	Ask questions based on assigned reading. <div align="center">10 minutes</div>

Instructional duties defined	Listen on deck	Lecture on deck	This phase should do much to develop proper attitudes in students about teaching.
			1. Discuss following duties of aides:
			  a. To demonstrate skills.
			  b. To serve as group leaders.
			  c. To serve as special instructors for slow learners.
			2. Discuss how to teach swimming. Include:
			  a. Fundamental principles.
			  b. Qualifications of an instructor.
			  c. Approaches to teaching swimming.
			  d. How to teach swimming.
			  e. Safeguarding student.
			3. Discuss teaching ethics, emphasizing relationship of aide to —
			  a. Instructor
			    (1) Aide is an assistant to instructor.
			    (2) Instructor is in charge at all times.
			    (3) Aide and instructor work together as a team.
			
			  b. Fellow aides
			    (1) An aide does not speak in derogatory manner about another aide in presence of students.
			    (2) An aide does not question validity of a statement made by another aide in presence of students.
			  c. Students
			    (1) Aide has feeling of comradeship toward students.
			    (2) Aide is careful not to become overbearing in manner.
			    (3) Aide is friendly but businesslike.
			<div align="center">35 minutes</div>

Progressions for teaching a skill on beginner level	On deck (except two students) In water	On deck	1. Select two students to get into waist-deep water. Put both students through progressions to learn a complex skill, (i.e., beginner stroke). Explain reasons for each step and have class members take notes. 2. Instruct all students to get into water. Repeat progressions with all students going through steps. <div align="center">50 minutes</div>
Assignment	Prepare assignment	Explain assignment carefully	Read Chapter 5 in *Swimming and Aquatics Safety*. <div align="center">10 minutes</div>

Unit 3

Objectives To introduce the aide to the use of teaching aids, to define clerical duties, and to introduce the use of games as a teaching method.

ACTIVITY	STUDENTS	INSTRUCTOR	INFORMATION FOR INSTRUCTOR

Review	On deck	On deck	1. Discuss briefly:
			  a. Teaching ethics.
			  b. How to teach swimming.
			  c. Teaching progressions for beginners.
			       15 minutes

Questions on assignment	On deck	On deck	Ask questions based on assigned reading. 10 minutes

Use of teaching aids	On deck or in water	On deck or in water	1. Introduce and demonstrate (use students if possible) use of —
			  a. Swimboard (kickboard) or other suitable flotation device —
			    (1) Arm practice.
			    (2) Leg practice.
			    (3) Complete stroke practice.
			  b. Face mask.
			  c. Swim fins.
			  d. Nose clips.
			  e. Buddy for support.
			2. Give each student an opportunity to use each piece of equipment. One method is to split into small groups for more efficient use of equipment and to use group leaders.
			       40 minutes

Practice teaching on beginner level	On deck	On deck	Divide class into groups of five. Appoint one in group to act as instructor. Rotate to give all students an opportunity to serve as instructor. 35 minutes

Clerical duties defined	On deck	On deck	1. Discuss following duties:
			  a. Preparation of class rolls.
			  b. Calling roll at class time.
			  c. Use of swimming work sheets. (If possible, have each student complete this form in class; if not, include this work in an assignment.)
			  d. Charting weather conditions, and water and air temperatures.
			  e. Checking students in and out of water.
			       30 minutes

Games on beginner level	In water	On deck	Introduce and play games designed to teach beginners to prone glide, prone kick glide, back glide, and back kick glide. 20 minutes
Assignment	Prepare assignment out of class	Explain assignment carefully	Read Chapters 8 and 9 in textbook *Swimming and Aquatics Safety.* 10 minutes

Unit 4

Objectives To introduce the teaching of advanced beginner and intermediate skills and the use of progressions and formations in teaching, and to clarify the supervisory and maintenance duties of aides.

ACTIVITY	STUDENTS	INSTRUCTOR	INFORMATION FOR INSTRUCTOR

Review	Some in water; others on deck	On deck	1. Ask certain students to demonstrate or explain:
			  a. Use of swimboard.
			  b. Use of flotation devices.
			  c. Beginner progressions.
			  d. Clerical duties.
			  e. Teaching formations for beginners.
			        30 minutes

Questions on assignment	On deck	On deck	Ask questions based on assigned reading. 10 minutes
Progressions and formations for teaching skills on advanced beginner and intermediate level	Half of group in water; other half on deck (groups alternate)	On deck or in water	1. Demonstrate (or have demonstrated) and call attention to various formations (including land drills) and progressions for teaching skills in these two courses. 60 minutes
Practice teaching of selected Intermediate skills	2/3 of group in water; 1/3 on deck. (Alternate)	On deck and in water	Divide class into groups of three and appoint a student instructor for each group. Assign each instructor to an area in pool and have him or her work with group on one of the skills in intermediate level. Have groups move from one instructor to another until they have been to each instructor. Instructor is to correct mistakes and not attempt to teach skill from the beginning. 40 minutes

Supervisory duties defined	On deck	On deck	Discuss the following supervisory duties:
			  a. Maintenance of order in locker rooms.
			  b. Supervision of shower rooms.
			  c. Inspection of bathers for cleanliness.
			  d. Assistance in drying and dressing smaller children.
			  e. The lining up and pairing of class members before they enter water.
			  f. Assistance as auxiliary lifeguards during class periods.
			        10 minutes

Maintenance duties defined	On deck	On deck	1. Discuss distribution and collection of class equipment, such as swimboards, flotation devices, swim fins, face plates, and lifesaving equipment. 2. Stress importance of keeping swimming area clean and orderly, and of cooperating with facility operator. 10 minutes

Assignment	Prepare assignment out of class	Explain assignment carefully	Ask a series of five questions based on the following subjects. (Students may use textbook and should bring answers to next class period.)
			  a. Duties of aide.
			  b. Progressions for teaching beginners.
			  c. Relationships of aide and instructors.
			        10 minutes

Unit 5

Objectives To review skills, class organization, and the use of teaching aids. To give students the opportunity to demonstrate their abilities in conducting courses and teaching.

ACTIVITY	STUDENTS	INSTRUCTOR	INFORMATION FOR INSTRUCTOR
Written test (homework)	On deck	On deck	Collect homework and discuss each question. 20 minutes
Skill review	On deck	On deck	Select class members to demonstrate skills on beginner, advanced beginner, and intermediate levels. Have rest of students observe and check for errors. 40 minutes
Class organization review	On deck or in water	On deck	1. Select various class members and have them arrange class for land, shallow water, and deep water drills. Have rest of class observe and check for errors. 2. Pay particular attention to ability of student-instructors to command respect and to move group efficiently. 30 minutes
Teaching aids review	On deck or in water	On deck	1. Select class members to demonstrate correct use of teaching aids. Ask others to observe and to check for errors. 2. Check carefully on how demonstrators use aids. 30 minutes
Practice test	In water	On deck	1. Test students on skills in beginner and intermediate levels. 2. Stress having students perform skills in slow motion as if they were demonstrating for a class. 3. See Chapter 14, *Evaluating Swimming Strokes,* for criteria to rate basic strokes in beginner through intermediate courses. 30 minutes
Retest	In water or on deck	On deck	1. Discuss mistakes that were made and how they could be corrected. 2. Allow students to practice and take a retest. 3. Let students who have passed test help those who are practicing for a retest. 30 minutes
Assignment			Assign Chapters 3 and 14 in *Swimming and Aquatics Safety.*

Unit 6

Objective Impressing the aides with the importance of their role and their responsibility to students and to the American Red Cross.

ACTIVITY	STUDENTS	INSTRUCTOR	INFORMATION FOR INSTRUCTOR
Test	On deck	On deck	Return test papers and discuss any questions that were difficult for majority of class.

General meeting	On deck	On deck	1. Invite local water safety instructors and the chapter water safety chairman (or other chapter representative) to attend the general meeting to effect a complete understanding of relationship between aides and instructors.
			2. Display water safety aide certificate and water safety aide emblem. Tell students that those who have successfully completed course will receive certificate and that emblem, worn on swim suits, is available through local chapter.
			3. Point out that aides can fulfill their responsibilities to:
			  a. Instructor by —
			    (1) Cooperating at all times.
			    (2) Realizing that they are now part of a team and must all work together.
			  b. Students by —
			    (1) Insuring their safety.
			    (2) Developing in them a desire to learn.
			    (3) Teaching skills thoroughly and correctly.
			  c. Facility operator by —
			    (1) Protecting equipment.
			    (2) Respecting rules and regulations.
			  d. Red Cross by —
			    (1) Upholding standards.
			    (2) Serving others as a volunteer.
			4. Thank aides for participating in course and encourage them to participate in instructor courses when eligible.
			5. Issue course completion certificates to students completing course requirements.

SWIMMER AIDE COURSE INSTRUCTOR'S OUTLINE

The primary purpose of the swimmer aide program is to help chapters better meet the needs of those who want to learn to swim. The swimmer aides who take part in the program will have an opportunity to participate in a meaningful and worthwhile activity, a fact that should be a source of much personal satisfaction.

It is anticipated that many swimmer aides will, as a result of their experience and interest, eventually enroll in Red Cross swimming and water safety courses or participate in other Red Cross activities.

Duties of a Swimmer Aide

The duties of a swimmer aide fall into four categories:

- **Clerical** Preparing class rolls, calling roll at class time, checking swimmers in and out of the water or pool area, and preparing course records for instructors.
- **Supervisory** Helping to maintain reasonable order in dressing rooms and shower rooms, inspecting swimmers for cleanliness, maintaining reasonable order while waiting for class to start, supervising a check-in check-out board, pairing buddies for class work, drying and dressing smaller children when necessary, and keeping students from straying out of the class area.
- **Instructional** Demonstrating skills on the beginner level, conducting land or shallow water drills, assisting individual class members who need special work, and serving as a leader for small groups.
- **Maintenance** Distributing and collecting equipment (such as swimboards and flotation devices), storing or having stored all equipment at the end of the class, and removing or minimizing hazards in and around the swimming area.

Eligibility Requirements

Individuals who are 17 years of age or older, who evidence a sincere desire to give valuable volunteer service, and who exhibit a sense of responsibility are eligible to be trained as swimmer aides. There are no swimming requirements.

Training of Swimmer Aides

Swimmer aide candidates will be enrolled in a 6-hour training course. The course is taught by a currently authorized water safety instructor or basic swimming instructor, preferably selected by the chapter. The course is outlined in the following pages.

Certification

Students who successfully complete the course will receive a swimmer aide certificate and will be eligible to assist water safety instructors and basic swimming instructors.

Reporting

The instructor responsible for the course will report the results of the course on the *Instructor Aide Examination Record* (Form 5650).

Course Outline

The following material is designed to acquaint potential swimmer aides with their responsibilities as aides to water safety instructors or basic swimming instructors.

Since there are no swimming requirements for candidates, it is much more important to stress their total responsibilities as aides rather than to concentrate on their skill development.

There are no tests required or given for this course. All persons participating in the entire course should receive credit for the course. Failure to attend the required sessions, or any conduct that is not in the best interest of the Red Cross, are sufficient reasons for not crediting an individual with successful completion of the course.

The course is designed to be covered in 6 hours. Three sessions of 2 hours each are suggested. However, the scheduling of the class will of necessity have to be determined by the class members and the instructor.

No attempt has been made in the following outline to specify the exact material to be covered. This has been left to the discretion of the instructor. However, in the interest of covering the essential information, a series of activities are listed and a possible approach to the activities is included.

One final suggestion. Students in this class want to help. Don't discourage them by setting up embarrassing situations or by attempting to conduct this course as you would a course where the primary objective is to develop personal skills.

Phase 1

Activity	Opening remarks
Purpose	To give the group an understanding of the purpose of the swimmer aide program and how aides fit into a water safety program.
Time	15 minutes
Required equipment	None

Approach to activity

1. Welcome group to course and thank them for their interest in the Red Cross and the water safety program.
2. Briefly review objective of the Red Cross — people helping people. Follow this with objective of water safety program — helping to make people safe while in, on, or about the water.
3. Point out that objective of making people safe is reached by use of the 3 Es of safety — Engineering, Enforcement, and Education. Red Cross emphasizes educational aspect through textbooks, courses of instruction, posters, motion pictures, demonstrations, and teaching activity of instructors and aides.
4. At this time, introduce, but do not elaborate on, four categories of duties of swimmer aide — clerical, supervisory, instructional, and maintenance. (See Phase 9.) Indicate that these four duties will be discussed as course progresses.

5. Conclude by reviewing content of course, schedule of meetings, and other pertinent business.

Phase 2

Activity Demonstration of skills in Beginner course

Purpose To show students the skills they will be expected to help water safety instructors or basic swimming instructors to teach.

Time 20 minutes

Required equipment None

Approach to activity

1. Arrange class in compact group on deck for demonstrations in water.
2. Stress name of skill being demonstrated, as well as its importance to learner.
3. It may be better if instructor makes comments while someone else demonstrates skills. To do this effectively and efficiently, it will be necessary for instructor and demonstrator to practice before actual demonstration.
4. No effort should be made to demonstrate teaching progressions at this time.
5. Demonstrate skills in a logical sequence in order to make it easier for students to note how skills are related.

Phase 3

Activity Personal skill development — beginner skills

Purpose To give students an opportunity to become familiar with skills in Beginner course as a result of personal experience.

Time 30 minutes

Required equipment None

Approach to activity

1. Have students select a buddy and practice skills.
2. Present skills in a logical sequence.
3. An understanding of skills is more to be desired than perfection of performance.
4. Do not discuss teaching progressions at this time.

Phase 4

Activity Discussion of safety practices in and around swimming area.

Purpose To acquaint class members with accepted safety practices and to alert them to some of the hazards (both environmental and personal) in swimming area.

Time 20 minutes

Required equipment None

Approach to activity

1. Stress fact that safety of students should be No. 1 concern of those in charge of swimming class.
2. Discuss buddy system — how it works and why it should be used in beginner's class.

3. Discuss personal practices that are hazardous, such as running on deck, ducking another swimmer, pushing another person into water, horseplay in and around swimming area, venturing too close to deep water, etc.
4. Discuss danger of sunburn, how to detect too much exposure, and what to do to prevent sunburn.
5. Discuss chilling; how to detect it, and what to do about it.
6. Examine swimming area for hazards and discuss their elimination. If they cannot be eliminated, how can they be minimized?

Phase 5

Activity Demonstration and practice of elementary forms of rescue.

Purpose To teach students simple methods of rescuing a person without endangering their own safety.

Time 15 minutes

Required equipment Towel, shirt, reaching pole, and ring buoy and/or heaving line.

Approach to activity

1. Arrange class in compact group.
2. Demonstrate following skills:
   - How to help a person regain standing position in shallow water.
   - How to release a cramp in leg and foot.
   - Reaching assists from deck (with and without extensions).
3. Practice above skills.

Phase 6

Activity Demonstration and practice of use of stationary and free-floating supports as aids in teaching beginners to swim.

Purpose To acquaint class with knowledge of how equipment can be used to teach beginners to swim.

Time 15 minutes

Required equipment Swimboards, canisters, and other similar supports.

Approach to activity

1. Arrange class in compact group.
2. Demonstrate use and stress importance of the following stationary supports: Deck or ground, overflow trough, a buddy, bottom of shallow area, and other stationary supports unique to area being used.
3. Demonstrate use of free-floating supports, such as swimboard, canister, buddy, and other similar things. Discuss advantages and disadvantages of free-floating supports.
4. Give students opportunity to use equipment demonstrated above.

Phase 7

Activity Demonstrate progressions that can be used to teach a nonswimmer to swim.

Purpose To provide students (aides) with progressions they can use when assisting instructor.

Time 45 minutes

Required equipment None

Approach to activity

1. Arrange class on deck as you would a group of beginners.
2. Introduce each step in water in a logical sequence, teaching from known to related unknown.
3. At conclusion of demonstration, discuss each step and encourage group to ask questions.

Phase 8

Activity Practice teaching and critique.

Purpose To enable students to establish a pattern for teaching on beginner level.

Time 60 minutes

Required equipment None

Approach to activity

1. Work on a one-to-one buddy basis.
2. Each buddy should have opportunity to be both student and instructor.
3. Each buddy should have opportunity to teach at least three skills in Beginner course. Stationary or free-floating supports can be used.
4. Buddy serving as instructor should be encouraged to use notes, if necessary.
5. Class instructor should observe students carefully and make notes of items to be discussed during critique that follows.
6. At conclusion of practice teaching, hold a critique, at which time students as well as class instructor should make comments that they feel are in best interest of class.

Phase 9

Activity Discussion of duties of swimmer aide.

Purpose To pinpoint duties of swimmer aide and to show relationship of aides to water safety instructors, basic swimming instructors, and water safety aides.

Time 30 minutes

Required equipment *Worksheet For Swimming Courses* (Form 5723) and *Course Record For Swimming and Water Safety* (Form 5722).

Approach to activity

1. Duties fall into four categories — clerical, supervisory, instructional, and maintenance.
2. Discuss specific duties of each category:
   - **Clerical** Prepare class rolls, call roll at classtime, check bathers in and out of water or pool area, and prepare course record forms.
   - **Supervisory** Maintain reasonable order in dressing rooms, supervise shower rooms, inspect bathers for cleanliness, maintain reasonable order while waiting for class to start, supervise check-in check-out board if one is used, pair buddies for class work, dry and dress smaller children when necessary, and keep students from straying out of class area.
   - **Instructional** Demonstrate skills on beginner level, conduct drills on land and in shallow water, assist individual class members who need special work, and serve as leaders for small groups.
   - **Maintenance** Distribute and collect equipment (such as swimboards and flotation devices), store or have stored all equipment at end of class, remove or minimize hazards in and around swimming area.
3. Stress fact that swimmer aides and water safety aides assist instructor and must not assume entire responsibility for class.
4. Point out that swimmer aides are only expected to assist instructors with beginner courses while water safety aides, because of their longer training period and more stringent prerequisites for enrolling in that training course, are eligible to assist in other swimming and lifesaving courses as well.
5. If deemed advisable, time should be allowed at this point to enable class to fill out class records used for beginner course.

Phase 10

Activity Demonstration and practice of artificial respiration.

Purpose To equip each student with knowledge required to administer mouth-to-mouth (mouth-to-nose) artificial respiration.

Time 30 minutes

Required equipment None

Approach to activity

1. Comparatively little time should be spent on theory of artificial respiration.
2. Follow plan usually employed in teaching artificial respiration in lifesaving or first aid class.

Phase 11

Activity Critique on entire course.

Purpose To permit students to ask any questions they may desire.

Time 15 minutes

Required equipment None

Approach to activity

(No set approach is suggested.)

1. At conclusion of questions from students, close course by thanking students for their interest and cooperation. Stress their obligation to pass along some of their newly learned knowledge and skills by assisting an instructor.
2. The chairman or a representative of the water safety committee should outline plans involving use of aides and should welcome them into the Red Cross family.
3. Swimmer aide certificates should be presented at this time to candidates successfully meeting course requirements.

CHAPTER 14

EVALUATING SWIMMING STROKES

INTRODUCTION

The information in this chapter is provided for use by Red Cross instructors to evaluate student performances for each of the five basic swimming strokes and for each level of swimming course in which the strokes appear.

Within the context of acceptable performance, instructors must consider the individual differences of students and are reminded that swimming strokes are **adapted to the individual.**

In reference to the charts, a standard of performance for a skill that is acceptable at one level is acceptable for all higher levels unless otherwise stated.

The criteria for evaluation is to be used only for the following purposes. It is not intended to be used during the teaching and learning process.

1. To evaluate the acceptability of performance of the strokes, and their parts, in the course in which the students are enrolled.
2. To screen students for admission into a higher level course in which they plan to enroll.

PERFORMANCE STANDARDS: ELEMENTARY BACKSTROKE

COMPONENT		LEVEL	
	ADVANCED BEGINNER	INTERMEDIATE	SWIMMER/ADVANCED SWIMMER
	Ears must be in water with face kept clear of water.	Ears must be in water; face is parallel to surface or chin may be tucked slightly.	
BODY	Body must approach the horizontal position.	Body must be nearly horizontal.	
	Slight hip pike acceptable during leg recovery and glide.	Slight hip pike acceptable during leg recovery only.	
POSITION	Shoulders and hips may occasionally deviate from level position.	Shoulders and hips must remain level.	
	Deviation from streamlined body position acceptable during glide.	Must be streamlined during glide.	
ARMS	Must pull simultaneously and below the surface.		
	Recovery actions must be nearly simultaneous and beneath the surface.	Must be symmetrical and simultaneous throughout stroke.	
	Must push past waist.	Must push to full arm extension along body.	
	Sculling near thigh permitted.	No sculling permitted.	
	Elbow lead permissible on pull.	Elbow lead not acceptable past midpoint of pull.	
	Straight or bent arm pull permissible.	Straight arm preferred; bent arm pull permissible.	
	Hands recover to about head level.	Hands do not recover beyond head level.	
	Straight arm recovery not acceptable.	Hands must be close to body on first stage of recovery.	
	Fingertips usually lead extension of arms away from body.	Fingertips must lead extension of arms away from body.	

PERFORMANCE STANDARDS: ELEMENTARY BACKSTROKE

COMPONENT	LEVEL		
	ADVANCED BEGINNER	INTERMEDIATE	SWIMMER/ADVANCED SWIMMER
LEGS	Knees may break surface.	Knees may not break surface.	
	Occasional scissors kick permitted.	Scissors kick not acceptable.	
	Deviations in knee or ankle symmetry acceptable.	Occasional deviations in knee or ankle symmetry acceptable.	
	Wide or narrow kick acceptable.		
	Deviations of movements of knees and feet from same plane acceptable.	Occasional deviations of movements of knees and feet from same planes acceptable.	Knees and feet must move in same planes.
	Must make some forward progress with kick.	Kick must be effective.	
	Legs usually recover simultaneously.	Legs must recover simultaneously.	
	Legs are usually together during glide.	Legs must be extended and together during glide.	Legs and feet must be fully extended and together during glide; toes must be pointed.
BREATHING	Must inhale every cycle during recovery of arms, and exhale during glide.		
COORDINATION	Some glide preferred.	Glide required.	
	Arms can recover with or before leg recovery.	Arms must start recovery before legs recover.	
	Start of arm pull and kick nearly together acceptable.	Arm pull must start with kick.	
	Legs must finish kick before arms finish their pull.	Arms must finish pull slightly after, or simultaneously with, finish of kick.	

PERFORMANCE STANDARDS: SIDESTROKE

COMPONENT	LEVEL	
	INTERMEDIATE	SWIMMER/ADVANCED SWIMMER
BODY POSITION	Head can tilt forward or backward occasionally.	Head must remain in line with spine.
	Occasional deviation from horizontal position acceptable.	Body position must approach horizontal.
	Body must be in side layout position, nearly straight.	Hip pike not acceptable.
	Some front/back lean acceptable.	Body must not lean to front or back.
	Some head lift acceptable.	Lower ear must remain in water.
ARMS	Top hand can pass hips occasionally at end of pull.	Top hand cannot pass hips at end of pull.
	Top arm can occasionally recover away from body.	Top arm must recover close to body.
	Top arm must be bent and can occasionally pull outward from body.	Top arm must be bent, with arm pull close to body.
	Lower arm can occasionally deviate from being in direct line with head during glide.	Lower arm must be in line with head during glide.
	Lower arm must be straight, palm down, during glide.	
	Occasional lateral pull with straight arm (lower) acceptable.	Must pull with lower arm bent. Pull is in line with body.
	Top arm must be extended and near body during glide.	Top arm must be fully extended and resting on top of upper leg during glide.
	Lower hand can deviate from being in line with spine at start of arm extension.	Lower hand is near head, in line with spine, at start of arm extension.
	Pull of lower hand can occasionally pass shoulder.	Pull of lower hand cannot pass shoulder.
	Top hand can occasionally break surface at end of pull.	Top hand and lower arm remain underwater at all times.

PERFORMANCE STANDARDS: SIDESTROKE

COMPONENT	LEVEL	
	INTERMEDIATE	SWIMMER/ADVANCED SWIMMER
LEGS	Heels must be drawn toward buttocks during leg recovery.	
	Top ankle may occasionally be plantar-flexed during forward extension of leg.	Top ankle must dorsi-flex during extension of leg.
	Legs must be extended on glide; may occasionally deviate from being together.	Legs must be straight and together during glide.
		Toes must be pointed during glide.
	Legs can occasionally pass each other at end of kick.	Legs cannot pass each other at end of kick.
	Breaststroke kick not acceptable.	
	Lower leg can occasionally drop during recovery or kick.	Both legs must remain parallel to surface during all movements.
	All similar movements must be simultaneous.	
	Heels can occasionally separate laterally during leg recovery.	Heels must be closely aligned with spine during leg recovery.
BREATHING	Must inhale during recovery of top arm.	
COORDI-NATION	Trailing arm and both legs must recover together.	
	Lead arm recovers and extends as legs and trailing arm apply propulsive action.	
	Minimum glide required.	Definite glide on extension of lower arm; glides in streamlined position.

PERFORMANCE STANDARDS: CRAWL STROKE

COMPONENT	LEVEL			
	BEGINNER	ADVANCED BEGINNER	INTERMEDIATE	SWIMMER/ ADVANCED SWIMMER
BODY POSITION	May deviate from near horizontal.	Must be nearly horizontal.		
	Excessive body roll acceptable.	Occasional excessive body roll to breathing side acceptable.	Excessive body roll not acceptable.	
	Some hip or shoulder sway acceptable.	Minimal, occasional hip or shoulder sway acceptable.	Hip or shoulder sway not acceptable.	
ARMS	Occasional underwater recovery acceptable.	Arms must recover over the water.		
	Over-water recovery may be with bent or straight arm.	Bent arm recovery required.	Elbow must be higher than hand during recovery.	Recovery must be a smooth, continuous action with relaxed wrist.
	Hand entry can be outside of shoulder or across midline of body.	Hand entry may occasionally be outside of shoulder or across midline of body.	Entry must be in line with head or shoulder with elbow slightly higher than hand.	
	Hand or forearm may enter water first.	Hand/forearm occasionally entering water first acceptable.		Fingertips must lead on entry.
	Pull must extend at least to the waist.	Pull must extend past waist.	Pull ends with arm almost completely extended.	Pull must start with arm fully extended at "catch" position.
	Bent or straight arm pull acceptable.	Occasional straight arm pull acceptable.	Pull must be with bent arm, hand lower than elbow, and elbow lower than shoulder.	
	Occasional pull outside of width of shoulders acceptable.		Line of pull must be no wider than width of shoulders.	
	Nonrhythmic arm action acceptable.	Arm action must be almost continuous.	Arms must alternate with with near-equal timing.	Arms must alternate with equal timing.
LEGS	Some deviation from a continuous flutter kick acceptable.	Pumping action from knees not acceptable.	Flutter kick must be continuous and effective.	
	Occasional lifting of feet from water acceptable.	Heels occasionally breaking surface acceptable.		
BREATHING	Must periodically breathe while swimming.		Must breathe every stroke.	
	Head may be lifted to front or turned to side to inhale.	Head may be lifted and turned to side.	Head must rotate to side.	
	Must exhale underwater.		Exhalation must be slow and continuous.	Effective explosive breathing acceptable.
COORDINATION	Breathing and arm action not well-coordinated acceptable.	Breathing usually well-coordinated with arm action.	Breathing must be well-coordinated with arm action.	
	May breathe any time.	Must breathe at least every other cycle.	Must breathe every cycle (stroke).	
	Is reasonably confident in deep water.	Is confident in deep water.		
	Poor coordination acceptable.		Stroke must be coordinated and effective.	Must be well-coordinated, balanced, smooth, and effective.
	More or less than 6 kicks per cycle acceptable.			

PERFORMANCE STANDARDS: BREASTSTROKE

COMPONENT	LEVEL	
	INTERMEDIATE	SWIMMER/ADVANCED SWIMMER
BODY POSITION	Occasional body roll during propulsive actions acceptable.	Shoulders and hips must be level to surface during propulsive actions.
	Deviations from streamlined body position acceptable during glide.	Must be streamlined during glide.
ARMS	Arm action must be paired.	
	Arms must move in same planes.	
	Shoulders must be level with surface during pull and recovery.	
	Pull wider than shoulders acceptable.	
	Backward pull past shoulders not acceptable.	
	Some deviation from palm-down glide acceptable.	Must glide with palms down and with arms fully extended.
	Arms must be nearly extended and together during glide.	Arms must be fully extended and together during glide.
LEGS	Hips may occasionally tilt during propulsive actions.	Hips must be level with surface during propulsive actions.
	Occasional scissors kick acceptable.	Scissors kick not acceptable.
	Feet must be higher than knees during recovery.	
	Moving in slightly different planes acceptable.	Legs must move in same planes.
	Legs must be straight and together during glide.	Legs must be straight and together with toes pointed to rear during glide.
	Buttocks occasionally breaking surface during recovery acceptable.	Buttocks cannot break surface during recovery.
	Pushing feet straight back not acceptable.	
	Heels can break surface occasionally.	Heels cannot break surface.
	Must be paired action.	
	Lack of good propulsion acceptable.	Must have good propulsion.
BREATHING	Face must be in water except for inhalation.	
	Chin can be lifted from water during inhalation.	Chin must be on surface during inhalation.
	Must exhale underwater.	
COORDINATION	Kick and pull must be alternate actions.	
	No glide required.	Some glide required.
	Effective stroke not required.	Must be smooth and efficient.

PERFORMANCE STANDARDS: BACK CRAWL

COMPONENT	LEVEL	
	SWIMMER	ADVANCED SWIMMER
BODY POSITION	Roll on long axis of body required.	
	Hip sway not acceptable.	
	Head must be aligned with spine and can rotate slightly to each side.	
	Slight hip flexion acceptable.	
	Must be nearly horizontal to surface.	
ARMS	Arm action must be continuous with arms in constant opposition.	
	Recovery must be almost vertical and in line with, or slightly outside of, shoulder.	
	Bent arm recovery not acceptable.	
	Occasional straight arm pull acceptable.	Straight arm pull not acceptable.
	Occasional elbow lead past midpoint of propulsion acceptable.	Elbow lead past midpoint of pull not acceptable.
	Propulsion can occasionally end with palm of hand along side of thigh.	Propulsion must end with downward press of hand.
	Hand enters water little finger first, approximately in line with shoulder.	
LEGS	Kick must be continuous and effective.	Up-beat emphasis required.
	Toes may break surface occasionally.	
BREATHING	Breathing each cycle required.	
COORDINATION	Must be reasonably well-coordinated and effective.	Must be well-coordinated, smooth, and effective.

CHAPTER 15

ASSEMBLY LINE METHOD OF TEACHING SWIMMING

INTRODUCTION

The assembly line method of teaching swimming is not unlike the assembly line used so successfully by industry. The line is characterized by a series of stations, where parts of a skill or a complete skill are taught by water safety instructors, basic swimming instructors, water safety aides, and swimmer aides.

The assembly line method can be used for any level swimming course. A major advantage is its use in teaching beginners. The majority of students enrolling for instruction in a learn-to-swim program are beginners and there may be a shortage of instructors to adequately handle large numbers of beginners. This potential problem is overcome by training aides to teach a few skills that make up one station. Trained aides, working under the supervision of one or more instructors, can conduct most, if not all, of the instruction in shallow water. Practice by students in deep water, plus the final testing and evaluation of students, is the direct responsibility of instructors. Other advantages of this instructional system are that large groups become comparatively small groups, that students are able to work on their own skill level at their own rate of achievement, and that inexperienced instructors and aides soon become skilled in teaching the skills of their station.

Some of the disadvantages are that there is a loss of personal contact between the instructors or aides and the students, that there is a possibility of the instructional staff becoming bored as a result of teaching the same few skills, and that instructors lose the satisfaction they experience when taking a class of students through the complete course.

HOW THE ASSEMBLY LINE OPERATES

The mechanics of setting up an assembly line are comparatively simple. Decide what is to be taught at each station and train the aides for their specific teaching assignments. Students learn best through the **Whole Approach** or the **Progressive-part Approach.** The skills of each station should be structured so as to contain as much of a **whole** movement when a sufficient number of *instructors* are available. However, if **aides** are used almost exclusively, it may be advantageous to use the **part-whole** teaching approach.

Students are usually moved through the line in one of two methods. In the more formalized method, the students are screened and assigned to a station and

remain there for a predetermined period of time to receive instruction and to practice the skills required at that station. At the end of the instructional period, a signal is sounded by the head instructor for the testing phase. At the end of the predetermined time for this phase, another signal is sounded. Those who have satisfactorily completed the requirements then move on to the next station. Those who need more practice remain at the same station. This procedure continues until the end of the period, at which time the names of the students at various stations are taken and the students are told to report to that station when they return to the next class period.

Another method sometimes employed is to have the students move from station to station as soon as they display sufficient ability in the required skills. This method eliminates the necessity for timing the instructional and the testing phases. However, if this method is used there is a possibility that the inexperienced instructor or aide may encounter some difficulty in organizing the class for work.

The number of instructors and aides required will depend on the number of stations to be established. At the beginning of a series of lessons for beginners, there will be a need to man every station with aides or instructors. As the students' abilities progress, there will be a need to move the instructional staff from lower level stations to increasingly higher level stations. The ability to move staff will depend on the amount of training they have received. The ideal situation is in utilizing only water safety instructors and basic swimming instructors, since they are trained to teach and to test all Beginner course skills.

Suggested Stations and Skills

I. **Whole or Progressive-Part Teaching Approaches**

   A. **Physical and mental adjustment skills** This station may not be needed, since students may learn these skills through learning a whole movement, such as the beginner stroke.

   B. **Beginner stroke** This can include the prone float/glide and recovery, the prone kick glide, bobbing and rhythmic breathing, and artificial respiration.

   C. **Crawl stroke** This includes the same skills as in

GAMES AND STUNTS

CHAPTER 16

FUN IN FUNDAMENTALS

It is an accepted fact that recreational aquatics activities play an important part in the swimming instruction program. This fact was ably demonstrated by Commodore Wilbert E. Longfellow, the founder of the Red Cross Water Safety Program, who constantly applied a favorite motto "Keep the Fun in Fundamentals," and who became an outstandingly successful teacher of swimming for people of all ages. Many activities can be used effectively to overcome the fear of water that inhibits many individuals. These activities tend to relieve tension that can result from concentrated practice and effort. They may be used to create confidence and to teach skills. Many instructors use games as an excellent device for tapering off the formal instruction phase. Regardless of the choice of activity, the safety of the participants must always be a main consideration.

Selection of Activity

The instructor, or leader, must use good judgment and discrimination in the selection of the activity. It should meet the needs of the group at that particular time. The game, contest, or stunt should be simple. Games and stunts for preschool children should revolve around simple play and fantasy. The very young can readily imagine themselves as characters in the children's books and songs with which they are familiar. For example, a prone glide can be a "torpedo," a kicking race using kickboards can be called "outboard motors," finding and retrieving small weights from the bottom can be "finding hidden treasure," and exhaling can be "blowing bubbles." Most simple games can be adapted for use in shallow water for this age group.

Elementary school children have been exposed to class and group discipline and as a result they understand game rules and like to compete. Relays and simple team games that utilize skills they have learned or are learning should be emphasized.

Older children will enjoy games and contests that require a few more rules and strategy. Spelldown games requiring simple props and equipment can be used to good advantage. Familiar land games are easily adapted and, depending on swimming ability, deeper water activity can be utilized. The least skilled swimmers may be placed in a comparatively shallow depth of water or given a game responsibility that enables them to enjoy the activity in a manner commensurate with their ability.

In all recreational activities, the leader should plan the activity in advance. A simple and clear explanation of the activity plus an opportunity for the learner to ask questions will go a long way toward ensuring the success of the fun period. The following games and stunts are included to indicate the kind of activity that is suitable for the various swimming levels. Some are for individuals and some are for groups. Many land games can be adapted by the resourceful leader.

Individual Contests and Stunts at the Beginner and Advanced Beginner Levels

1. With face in water, touch toes as called for.
2. Sitting on bottom, exhale underwater. (Repeat 5 times.)
3. Prone float to the counts of 10, 15, 20, etc.
4. Prone glide for a distance of 10, 20, or 30 feet.
5. Spread-eagle float on the back.
6. Glide for distance on the back. (Give points for each foot over 10 feet.)
7. Winging on the back for a distance of 15 feet.
8. Winging on the back in a 15-foot circle.
9. Race for 20 feet, face up, using a crawl-kick glide.
10. Race for 25 feet, face down, using a crawl-kick glide.
11. Race 30 to 40 feet, face down, using the beginner stroke or the crawl stroke.
12. Race 10 yards on the back, winging with a flutter kick.
13. Swim 10 yards on the front, do a roll-over, and swim 10 yards on the back.
14. Bob 10 times in neck-deep water.
15. Swim 10 strokes and on cry of "shark," turn and swim back.
16. Shark game, varied by swimming to right and left.
17. Do a plain front dive and glide for distance.
18. Push off into a back glide and roll into a prone float.
19. Push off into a prone glide and roll into a back float.

Group Games and Contests at the Beginner Level

1. Catching and passing ball while standing in waist- to chest-deep water.
2. Water dodge ball, in circle (promotes submerging).
3. Tunnel ball (passing ball back under the legs of several players).

4. Cat and mouse. (Cat is outside circle and mouse is inside.)
5. Poison tag.
6. Spoon and Ping-pong ball relay race.
7. Relay race in shallow water (running, gliding on front, gliding on back).
8. Kickboard race for 15 yards.
9. Kickboard relay for width of pool.
10. Circle catch. Players join hands in two or more circles of even numbers. A leader is chosen for each group. At a signal, each leader passes the ball to the left or to the right. The object of the game is to see which side can pass the ball around the circle one or more times and get it back into the leader's hands first. If a contestant misses the ball, he or she must recover it as quickly as possible.

Team Games for all Levels

1. **Cork Game** The teams are lined up on opposite sides of the pool and 100 or more corks or floats are thrown into the water. At a signal, the teams swim toward the center and attempt to get as many of the corks as possible. The team collecting the greatest number in a given time wins.
2. **Challenges** Challenges made between individuals within a group or leaders of different groups are always good fun. The challenger performs the stunt. If the opponent cannot do it, a point is scored for the challenger.
3. **Drop the Puck** This game is played like drop the handkerchief except that a puck or other weighted object is used. The players form a circle around which "it" swims with the puck in his or her hand. He or she drops it behind one of the players, who must recover it and give chase around the circle, trying to catch "it" before he or she can succeed in taking his or her place.
4. **Retrieving** Twenty or more bright tin plates or similar objects are thrown into the water. Teams line up on shore. On a signal, the teams dive in and the team recovering the greatest number of objects wins.
5. **Volleyball** Any number of people may play. Players divide into two groups, one group on either side of a net that is hung so that the bottom is 2 or 3 feet above the water. Have the players rotate from shallow to deep water if possible. A water polo ball is batted back and forth over the net by hitting it with the hands. Float lines can be used to mark the outside play area. The regular rules for volleyball are used.
6. **Punch Ball** A heavy wire is stretched down the middle of the pool about 9 feet above the surface, running the length of the pool. Suspended from the wire on a sliding brass ring is a punch bag attached with a 7-foot rope and a snap buckle. The snap enables the leader to remove the bag when not in use. When attached, the bag hangs 1 foot above the surface. The playing group is divided into two teams, each of which remains on its side of the wire. The team batting the bag to its end of the pool scores a goal. In the melee, the pool looks like a veritable

"punch" bowl. The game is good fun even without definite rules.
7. **Water Baseball** The "diamond" may be all deep water or all shallow water or only the outfield may be deep water. Use a plastic ball and bat.
8. **Water Basketball** Goals are set 60 feet apart, or a shorter distance according to the size of the playing area. All play should be in deep water. The procedure is the same as in land basketball.
9. **Tug of War** Prepare a long strip of heavy rope with stationary loops of heavy canvas to serve as shoulder loops, one for each swimmer. Tie a red cloth to mark the center of the rope. Float a rope for a center line. Players line up at the rope, each adjusts one shoulder loop over his or her shoulder and, at a signal, they try to tug the rope toward their own goal. Each player has to swim hard against resistance. (VARIATION. Two teams line up on shore. Two players hold a floated rope, with the center marked, parallel to the shore. At a signal, the teams rush to the rope and try to tug it to their side by swimming.)

Mass Games

1. **Swimming Spelldown** The leader calls out a stunt. Swimmers performing the stunt remain in the game; others are eliminated as in a spelling match until a champion is left. Start with easy stunts to prevent players being eliminated too fast and then gradually make the stunts more difficult.
Suggested stunts for a spelldown:
   A. Swimming with one arm out of water (side-stroke).
   B. Swimming on back with both arms out of water.
   C. Steamboat. (With body in extended glide position, feet perform crawl kick.)
   D. Duck Dive (surface dive).
   E. Log roll. (Keep legs, body, and arms stretched in straight line; roll.)
   F. Pike surface dive with hands kept at sides.
   G. Corkscrew surface dive.
   H. Marching on water. (On back, move legs in walking motion, pressing lower leg back against water on each "step.")
   I. Sculling feetfirst, hands at side, prone position.
   J. Sculling feetfirst, hands extended overhead, supine position.
   K. Porpoise dive. (Surface dive to bottom, spring up for air, and repeat.)
   L. Crab swimming. (Move backwards by reversing arm action of breaststroke.)
   M. Crab swimming sideways. (On back, scull so as to move sideways.)
   N. Mermaid's prayer. (Scull with body in a kneeling position.)
   O. Waterwheel. (Scull on back so that body rotates in a circle.)
   P. Front somersault.
   Q. Back somersault.
   R. Sculling on back with one foot out of water.
   S. Sculling on back with both feet out of water.

T. Human bobber. (Balancing stunt. Take hand-stand position in deep water and scull so as to move forward with feet out of water.)

U. Swimming with hands clasped and feet together.

V. Treading water waist deep. (It requires strenuous treading to raise body in deep water so that swimmer is treading with shoulders and chest out of water.)

W. Walking home from a boat ride. (Perform chest-deep treading of water and propel one's self forward.)

X. Rotary crawl. (Change alternately to front crawl and back crawl on every arm stroke.)

2. **Neptune's Call** Players are lined up on one side of the pool. The one who is "it" stands or treads water in the center of the pool. When "it" shouts, "Neptune's call, come one and all," the players must swim to the opposite side, and "it" tries to tag as many as possible. All the players tagged must remain in the center and help in tagging the others until all are caught.

3. **Pigeon** Everyone sits on the edge of the pool or low dock with the knees under the chin and the hands clasped around the legs. At the leader's signal, players dive in and swim to the other side of the pool; those who reach there last become "pigeons" and must drop out of the game. (Leader designates the number of players who will be classified as "last.") At camp, the games may be played from the side of a raft and the players can swim around it. This is a fine game to give learners practice in getting into and out of the water and to test their swimming and diving ability.

4. **Leapfrog** The players line up, starting in shallow water, with those in deep water treading water. The end player on each line puts his or her hands on the shoulders of the player in front of him or her, pushing him or her underwater while he or she leaps over with the legs widespread. Procedure is continued until the former first-in-line becomes last. This is a fine game to make swimmers feel at home in the water and can be played as a team game also.

5. **Pom-Pom Pullaway** The players line up on one side of the pool or swimming area. "It" is on the opposite side (called "the line"). When "it" calls out "Pom-Pom Pullaway," players must swim across to the opposite side while "it" tries to catch them before they reach the line. Those who are tagged must join "it" and try to tag the others.

6. **Poison** The players form a ring by joining hands or by grasping an endless rope. "Poison" is some floating object anchored in the center of the group. The aim of the action is to pull others so that they touch poison but keep from touching it themselves. Anyone touching poison is eliminated from the ring until only one person is left. (NOTE. This and other circle games can be played in shallow water by children. They have value in getting beginners adjusted to the water.)

7. **Water Tactics (Grand March, etc.)** The group, in deep water, executes movements at the command of the leader, who orders facings, marching, and salutes for individuals. In rows of two or four, the groups execute marching, wheelings, etc., in parade style.

8. **Stunt Tag** The leader calls out a certain part of the body and a player is safe from being tagged when that part of the body is out of the water. "It" may tag any player not thus immunized and the person tagged becomes "it." (VARIATION. The leader calls out more than one body part, as, for example, "head submerged, hand out," or "both feet out.")

9. **Ball Tag** This game is played in a limited area, in waist-deep water for nonswimmer or in deep water for swimmers. "It" tries to tag someone by tossing the ball. The one who is tagged becomes "it."

10. **Japanese Tag** The leader announces a certain part of the body that must be tagged by "it." Those who are tagged must join "it" and try to tag the remaining players.

11. **Hold Tag** The one who is "it" walks or swims after the players, attempting to tag them. The player tagged must place his or her left hand on the spot where he or she was touched and, holding this position, must attempt to tag someone else.

12. **Will-o'-the'Wisp** This very interesting game is preferably played with six or eight swimmers. All are blind-folded except one person who is "it" and has a bell. "It" submerges and swims underwater. Each time he or she surfaces he or she must ring the bell and those blindfolded must try to tag him or her. The player who tags the bellman becomes "it" and gets the bell. The tagged player joins the blindfolded group and the game continues. A whistle may be substituted for the bell.

13. **Under Cover (Duck Under)** This is a variation tag game. In order to be safe from being tagged, the players must be completely submerged.

Relay Races

1. **Variations** Any of the events described as racing events under "Individual Contests and Stunts at the Beginner Level" may be used as relay races when desired.

2. **Leapfrog Relay** The teams line up in shallow water and a goal is designated in deep water. At a signal, the player in the last position on each team leaps over the players in front of him or her, one at a time, and then swims to the goal. When he or she has reached the goal, the player who is now in the last position starts the same leapfrog process and the relay continues until all the team members have reached the goal.

3. **Obstacle Relay** The teams line up on the shore. At a signal, the first swimmer in each team races to a log anchored in the water, climbs over the log, turns and swims under it, and returns to the start. Then the second swimmer follows suit and the procedure is

repeated in turn by the remaining team members. Other obstacles might be barrels, spars, life buoys, or other flotation devices.

4. **Disrobing Relay** The first swimmer in each team wears an assortment of clothing over his or her bathing suit. Such clothing may be pajamas or a complete street outfit. At a signal, the swimmer dives in, swims to a raft or to the other side of the pool, climbs out, disrobes (down to the bathing suit), and returns to the starting point. On the return, the second swimmer goes to the raft or poolside, climbs out, and dresses in the outfit discarded by the first swimmer.

5. **Touch Relay** The teams line up on opposite sides. The object of the game is to touch whatever the leader calls out and return to the starting place as quickly as possible. The leader may involve any number of skills learned or a combination of skills by calling "touch bottom," "touch toes," "touch float line," etc.

6. **Swim-the-Duck Relay** A wooden decoy duck for each team is the only equipment used. The "duck" is carried in a swimming position on the surface by one hand, requiring each team member to swim with the other hand and the legs. "Ducks" must not be submerged or clutched against the swimmer's body and must be advanced toward the goal at all times.

7. **Flag Relay** This event is designed to develop and to utilize the side-carry position employed in lifesaving. A small flag may be carried in the upper hand and passed to teammates in the water. (VARIATION. The swimmers, in turn, carry a large parade flag [a 6-foot flag on a 8-foot staff] with the base of the staff resting on the swimmer's upper hip. The flag is carried upright and must be kept dry. Red Cross flags, flags with aquatic symbols, or international flags may be used. The shallow arm pull and the scissors kick must be used.)